IEP–2005:
WRITING AND IMPLEMENTING
INDIVIDUALIZED EDUCATION
PROGRAMS (IEPs)

ABOUT THE AUTHOR

Edward Burns received a Ph.D. from the University of Michigan in 1971. His areas of specialty include special education and psychoeducational assessment, assistive technology, and issues concerning the interpretation of and compliance with the individuals with Disabilities Education Acts amendments of 1997. He has written numerous articles in such journals as *Educational Technology, Journal of School Psychology, Journal of Learning Disabilities, Reading Research Quarterly, Journal of Special Education,* and the *American Journal of Mental Deficiency* and is the author of nine books including, *The Special Education Consultant Teacher* (Thomas, 2004), *Development and Implementation of Individualized Education Programs* (Thomas, 2001), *Test Accommodations for Students with Disabilities* (Thomas, 1998), and *The Development, Use, and Abuse of Educational Tests* (Thomas, 1979). He is currently involved in ensuring compliance with IDEA "to enable children with disabilities to be educated with nondisabled children to the maximum extent appropriate."

IEP-2005

Writing and Implementing Individualized Education Programs (IEPs)

By

EDWARD BURNS

State University of New York at Binghamton

CHARLES C THOMAS • PUBLISHER, LTD.
Springfield • Illinois • U.S.A.

Published and Distributed Throughout the World by

CHARLES C THOMAS • PUBLISHER, LTD.
2600 South First Street
Springfield, Illinois 62704

© 2006 by CHARLES C THOMAS • PUBLISHER, LTD.

ISBN 0-398-07624-3 (hard)
ISBN 0-398-07625-1 (paper)

Library of Congress Catalog Card Number: 2005052940

With THOMAS BOOKS *careful attention is given to all details of manufacturing
and design. It is the Publisher's desire to present books that are satisfactory as to their
physical qualities and artistic possibilities and appropriate for their particular use.*
THOMAS BOOKS *will be true to those laws of quality that assure a good name
and good will.*

Printed in the United States of America
MM-R-3

Library of Congress Cataloging-in-Publication Data

Burns, Edward, 1943–
    IEP–2005 : writing and implementing individualized education pro-
grams (IEPs) / by Edward Burns.
        p. cm.
    Includes bibliographical references and index.
    ISBN 0-398-07624-3 (hard) – ISBN 0-398-07625-1 (pbk.)
    1. Children with disabilities–Education–United States. 2. Individualized
education programs–United States. I. Title: Individualized education programs–Two thousand five.

LC4031.B825 2006
371.9073–dc22
                                                              2005052940

PREFACE

The purpose of this book is to provide guidelines to develop appropriate Individualized Education Programs (IEP) for children with disabilities based on the Individuals with Disabilities Education Act amendments of 2004 (IDEA–2004) or Public Law 108–446. These guidelines are intended to result in IEPs that are streamlined, focused, and reasonably calculated to provide educational benefit. The overriding goal is to develop IEPs that provide every child with a free and appropriate public education, rather than to develop IEPs that merely show compliance with IDEA but which confuse rather than address educational needs.

E.B.

PUBLIC LAW 108–446 IEP–2005 HIGHLIGHTS

The various changes to IDEA–2004 relating to IEPs have placed a great deal of emphasis on streamlining the IEP process. The following is an alphabetized listing of IDEA changes and modifications that highlight the 2004 Public Law 108–446 amendments:

- **Academic and developmental needs:** During the development of the IEP the **academic and developmental needs of the child**[1] has been added to the list of items the IEP Team must consider (which also includes the results of the initial or more recent evaluation, the strengths of the child, and the concerns of the parents).

- **Accommodations:** The statement of accommodations in a child's IEP in the administration of State or districtwide assessments requires any **individual appropriate accommodations that are necessary to measure the academic achievement and functional performance** of the child.[2]

- **Amending an IEP:** Changes to the IEP may be made by the entire IEP Team or by amending the IEP rather than by redrafting the entire IEP.[3]

- **Complaints:** Parents can present a complaint relating to IDEA but must do so with a two-year period before the date of the alleged violation or when the alleged violation should have been known.[4]

- **Consent for services:** If the parents of such child refuse consent for the evaluation, the agency may continue to pursue an evaluation by utilizing the mediation and due process procedures under section 615 (no change from IDEA–1997. But consent for services has undergone an extremely important change: **if the parent of a child refused to consent to services, the local educational agency shall not provide**

special education and related services to the child by utilizing due process procedures (e.g., mediation, due process hearing), and the local educational agency is no longer required to provide a free appropriate public education.[5]

• **Consolidation:** To the extent possible, the local educational agency shall encourage the consolidation of reevaluation meetings for the child and other IEP Team meetings for the child.[6]

• **Eligibility:** The **Special Rule for Eligibility Determination** states that a child is not eligible for special education because of "lack of appropriate instruction in reading, including in the essential components of reading instruction (as defined in section 1208(3) of the Elementary and Secondary Education Act of 1965); lack of instruction in math; or limited English proficiency."[7] An IEP is not intended to solve all educational problems; every IEP has the very specific goal of providing services and accommodations related to a child's disability.

• **Elimination of benchmarks:** A major change has been the **elimination of short term objectives and benchmarks** from the statement of measurable annual goals (including academic and functional goals).[8]

• **IEP Team attendance:** An IEP member is not required to a meeting if the parent and local educational agency agree that attendance **is not necessary because no modification to the member's area of the curriculum or related services is not being modified or discussed in the meeting**.[9]

• **Model IEP form:** Not later than the publication of the final regulations for IDEA a model individualized education program form to States, local educational agencies, and parent and community training and information centers.[10]

• **Multi-year IEP:** Parents and local educational agencies may address long-term planning by offering the option (as part of a multi-year IEP demonstration pilot program) of developing a comprehensive multi-year IEP, not to exceed 3 years, that is designed to coincide with the natural transition points for the child.[11]

• **Present Levels of Academic Achievement:** The IEP statement of the child's present levels of educational performance has been changed to

**present levels of academic achievement and functional perform-
ance.**[12]

- **Reevaluation:** A reevaluation of a child's IEP must be conducted if the
  school determines that the educational services needs warrant a reevaluation; or if the child's parents or teacher requests a reevaluation; but a
  reevaluation shall occur not more than once a year, unless the parent
  and the local educational agency agree otherwise; and at least once
  every 3 years, unless the parent and the local educational agency agree
  that a reevaluation is unnecessary.[13]

- **Regular classroom teacher IEP input:** The regular education teacher
  of the child participates in the development of the IEP of the child,
  including the determination of appropriate positive behavioral interventions and supports, and other strategies, and the determination of
  supplementary aids and services, program modifications, and support
  for school personnel.[14]

- **Services:** The statement of special education, related services and
  supplementary services has added the phrase **"is based on peer-
  reviewed research to the extent practicable."**[15]

- **Streamlined IEP:** The IEP process is simplified in that additional
  **information need not be included in a child's IEP beyond what
  is explicitly required**, and information included under one component of a child's IEP need not be included under another component.[16]

- **Time period for evaluation:** The determination as to whether a child
  has a disability is made **within 60 days of receiving parental consent for the evaluation**, or, within the timeframe established by the
  State.[17] For IDEA–1997 the requirement was a "reasonable period of
  time" from consent to initial evaluation, and 30 days from determination of eligibility to an IEP meeting.[18]

- **Transition services:** The statement of transition services has been
  simplified to begin **not later than the first IEP to be in effect when
  the child is 16, and updated annually thereafter** and to include
  **appropriate measurable postsecondary goals based upon appro-
  priate transition assessments.**[19]

CONTENTS

IEP–2005:
WRITING AND IMPLEMENTING
INDIVIDUALIZED EDUCATION
PROGRAMS (IEPs)

Chapter 1

IEP–2005

There is "a presumption that children with
disabilities are to be educated in regular classes."[20]

The Individuals with Disabilities Education Act amendments of 2004 (IDEA–2004) was signed into law as Public Law 108–446 (P.L. 108–446) on Friday, December 3, 2004 by President Bush. Public Law 108–446 provides the basis for providing children with disabilities an appropriate education. The Individualized Education Plan (IEP) is the cornerstone of IDEA–2004 and outlines the accommodations, goals and services a child needs to receive an appropriate education. As stated in *Honig v. Doe* the IEP is "the centerpiece of the statue's educational delivery system for disabled children"[21] so that a free and appropriate public education or FAPE is predicated on the development of a document "that meet the child's needs that result from the child's disability to enable the child to be involved in and make progress in the general curriculum"[22] Although IDEA was signed into law in 2004, the IEP requirements became effective July 1, 2005 and thus IDEA will be referred to as IDEA–2004 and the IEP as IEP–2005.

The "Centerpiece"

Envisioning the IEP as the centerpiece of the statute's education delivery system for disabled children, and aware that schools had all too often denied such children appropriate educations without in any way consulting their parents, Congress repeatedly emphasized throughout the Act the importance and indeed the necessity of parental participation in both the development of the IEP and any subsequent assessments of its effectiveness.

–Honig v. Doe, 484 U.S. 305 (1988)

The motivation for the IEP described in Public Law 94–142 in 1975 was "the movement toward the individualization of instruction, involving the child, the parent and other educational professionals" to construct an individualized program based on the following tenets:[23] (1) each child requires an educational plan that is tailored to achieve his or her maximum potential; (2) all principals in the child's educational environment, including the child, should have the opportunity for input in the development of an individualized program of instruction; (3) individualization means specifics and timetables for those specifics, and the need for periodic review of these specifics—all of which produce greatly enhanced fiscal and educational accountability.[24]

When Congress first considered the need for individualized education programs before the passage of P.L. 94–142 (Education for All Handicapped Children Act or EAHCA) in 1975 there was some debate as to whether individualized programs should be developed by emphasizing the development of an Individualized Education Program document or whether a series (at least three) of individualized instructional planning conferences that would yield a written statement of "appropriate educational services."[25] Congress agreed that the IEP was of primary importance, but this plan must be the result of a collaborative planning effort between school and parent.

The IEP, as described in the regulations for IDEA–1990, centers on the IEP meeting, decision making, and an IEP document which is "a written record of the decisions made at the meeting." The IEP and the IEP process has a number of purposes relating to communication between school and parents, conflict resolution, a commitment of resources, management, compliance and evaluation:

> **Communication:** The IEP meeting serves as a communication vehicle between parents and school personnel, and enables parents, as equal participants, to jointly decide what the child's needs are, what services will be provided to meet those needs, and what the anticipated outcomes may be.

> **Resolution:** The IEP process provides an opportunity for resolving any differences between the parents and the agency concerning a child's special education needs; first, through the IEP meeting, and second, if necessary, through the procedural protections that are available to the parents.

> **Commitment:** The IEP sets forth in writing a commitment of resources necessary to enable a child to receive needed special education and related services.

Management: The IEP is a management tool that is used to ensure that each child is provided special education and related services appropriate to the child's special learning needs.

Compliance: The IEP is a compliance/monitoring document which may be used by authorized monitoring personnel from each governmental level to determine whether a child is actually receiving the free appropriate public education agreed to by the parents and the school.

Resolution: The IEP serves as an evaluation device for use in determining the extent of the child's progress toward meeting the projected outcomes.[26]

Much of the litigation involving IEPs, and disagreements regarding educational placements, is the result of IEPs developed to **show compliance** but IEPs which do not provide an appropriate education. As a result, many IEPs are filled with regulatory guidelines, bureaucratic lists and checkboxes, and IEP content that does not outline a reasonably calculated plan much less provide educational benefit. For example, many IEPs include a checklist for the special factors that the IEP must consider. However, what should be included in the IEP are any services and accommodations that result from this consideration and not a list to show that these factors have been considered. The primary purpose of the IEP is often ignored in lieu of the single-minded quest to produce a *legally* acceptable IEP, an IEP that *ostensible* shows compliance, but an IEP that is not a real plan to provide appropriate goals, services and accommodations.

IEP Criticisms

The criticisms of IEPs have been many and often center about required IEP content and/or the process used to develop IEPs. For every IEP both **content** and **process** are critical factors and the foundation for developing an **appropriate** and **reasonably calculated** IEP. The IEP Team must consider each component of the IEP so that each IEP element is an integral part of the overall planning document. In addition, the IEP Team must be deliberate in developing IEPs that are logically consistent and are based on a collaborate effort between IEP Team members and the parents.[27]

One of the more disturbing criticisms of IEPs is the disconnection between the IEP and every other aspect of the special education process. A child's IEP appears to follow the regulations; the IEP contains all the required components (and a good deal more); and the IEP has been dutifully signed by the parents and a host of IEP members. But the IEP is stored away in a drawer only to surface again when the IEP is reviewed. The IEP is not a real plan; the IEP does not guide service providers; and the IEP is most certainly not a plan to provide an appropriate education. One might conclude that many IEPs are legally calculated to show compliance but not reasonablt calculated to meet individual needs.

Data-based IEP

A major criticism of many IEPs is that they are not data-based, but are often documents intended to show compliance with IDEA or to serve as a license to remove a child from the regular education classroom. Individual need as determined by a careful examination of all available data should be the guiding factor for developing and implementing IEPs.

The task of the IEP Team is not to invent levels of performance and annual goals for the sake of occupying IEP document space and thereby to create a document that appears to provide an appropriate educational plan. The IEP must be data-based; levels of performance must be specific and based on data; measurable annual goals must be based on measured levels of performance; and accommodations must be based on need and data. The role of the IEP Team is not to thoughtlessly construct an IEP from checklists (e.g., creating goals and selecting accommodations) but construct an IEP based on data, based on need, and an IEP that is reasonably calculated to provide an appropriate education.

Goals

Goals are often unrelated to present levels of academic achievement. This can occur when a goal is not provided to meet a necessary need, or when a goal is provided for a nonexistent need. The meaningfulness of goals is also suspect when picayune daily instructional objectives are substituted for measurable **annual** goals. A list of 100 computer-generated goals (e.g., ability to use long vowels) might make for a weighty IEP, but measurable annual goals are intended to be accomplished over the course of one year. Regardless of the quality of the goal if the goal is never measured, the fact that the goal is "measurable" is pointless. If a frivolous goal such as "to improve classroom behavior to 85 percent as determined by teacher observation" is never measured, will never be measured, and was not included in the IEP to actually be measured, the goal is nothing more than a compliance charade. The measure of an IEP is not the number of goals, but whether the goals provide a reasonably calculated plan for meeting a child's academic and other needs.

Goals must be based on need and data; goals must be important; and goals must be measured. The one factor that affects the meaningfulness of goals and the ability to actually measure annual goals is specificity. Standardized reading scores are available but not specific information relating to reading (e.g., percent reading comprehension), or a behavior problem is cited but the number of occurrences or a detailed description of the behavior/event is lacking.

IEP Development

The IEP is often not developed in a logical and coherent fashion. Behavior is cited as a need but goals are not provided to address the specific behavior; accommodations are unrelated to levels of performance or actual classroom needs; services and placements are not based on the IEP. Part of the reason for the haphazard approach to the development of IEPs is an emphasis of **form over substance**. Too much attention is given to completing the IEP form rather than developing an appropriate IEP that provides a logical and integrated plan for best meeting a child's individual needs.

The IEP must be developed by the IEP Team and not one person. A special education teacher is often assigned the task of developing the IEP prior to the IEP meeting. Parents are then disingenuously told that this IEP is just a "proposal." This has become such a common, albeit wrong practice that even the most rule-abiding IEP Team member rarely gives this a second thought. A similar practice occurs when the special education teacher is told to develop goals following the meeting after a child has been placed. The inability of an IEP to provide an appropriate education becomes most obvious when IEP goals never change from one year to the next. If all IEPs for all children never change, something is wrong.

When needs are not understood as reflected by measured beginning levels of performance, the resulting IEP might result in a very low expectation of annual performance, or an unrealistic expectation of performance. The IEP appears to be a plan but a plan that has no bearing on reality. The IEP is more often a bureaucratic processing instrument rather than an educational planning document (e.g., medicaid number, physician name and signature, phone, Medicaid Discharge Plan/Disposition, extensive parent information, codes used for funding, State codes, and a "for official use only" section).

Placement versus Services

The greatest error an IEP Team can commit is misunderstanding the task of determining services and placement. The telltale sign of a misguided IEP Team process is a placement not based on the IEP (which is why the placement should never be on the first page of the IEP). There are three specific problems that the IEP Team must avoid: (1) placements that preclude (or make difficult) participation in the regular classroom, (2) a belief that special education requires a special education placement, and (3) IEPs that never increase regular classroom participation. If a child does need a restrictive placement, the extent that a child can participate in the regular classroom and general curriculum must be determined. Special education is not about placement but about services. The regular education classroom is always the presumed placement and always the preferred placement for all children unless performance cannot be achieved satisfactorily with supplementary aids and services.

The IEP Team must ensure that both services and placements are as least restrictive as possible. Just as a child might warrant more time to participate in the regular classroom, a service in the regular classroom could be overly restrictive if actual regular classroom participation is denied. A child might need less direct services, less resource room services, or less time with a one-to-one aide. In addition, providing accommodations that are not needed also violate the least restrictive environment mandate.

The Cornerstone

The IEP is the cornerstone of special education, and, paradoxically, the IEP can prevent a child from receiving an appropriate public education. The criticisms of IEPs are not only true, but generally understated. Many IEPs are burdened by excessive paperwork, obscure rather than detailed appropriate educational programs, and are often little more than officious compliance documents rather than the "reasonably calculated" plan envisioned by the Supreme Court in *Hudson v. Rowley*.

The IDEA–1997 attempted to reduce redundancy within the IEP by stipulating that the IEP Team need not "include information under one component of a child's IEP that is already contained under another component of such IEP."[28] Public Law 108–446 places an even greater emphasis on reducing the amount of paperwork, increasing parent participation, and providing straightforward guidelines for the development of a streamlined IEP document. Of the various changes made in IDEA–2004, none have greater impact than the *mandate* not to include information in IEPs that is "beyond what is explicitly required" in IDEA.[29] This means that the IEP should not be weighted down by the inclusion of every rule or consideration cited in the Act and the regulations. As stated in the House report for IDEA–2004 "this provision is intended to indicate to States and local educational agencies that these requirements are all that is required for an IEP to comply with this Act. While States and local educational agencies may add their own additional requirements, such requirements should be identified as State- or locally-mandated."[30]

The erosion of the IEP from a real educational plan to legalistic document to show compliance has trivialized the importance and use of the IEP. The Senate report for IDEA–2004 explains that "the committee has examined a number of actual IEPs, and has discovered that many items in those documents are not required by federal IDEA law" and that "the committee wants to ensure that the federal law does not contribute to this problem."[31] Finally, the Committee expressed a "desire for a streamlined, straightforward, expression of only the requirements mandated by this Act."

The IEP Team is encouraged to produce a streamlined IEP, an IEP which is not necessarily "lengthy and complex" (a criticism cited in the Senate report for IDEA–2004), and, of course, an IEP that is appropriate and beneficial. To this end the following basic requirements are intended to provide an appropriate education so that the IEP outlines a meaningful plan rather than a document to show compliance with IDEA.

IEP Basic Requirements

- **Every child with a disability should have an IEP in effect at the beginning of the school year;**

- **The IEP is developed after a child is determined to have a disability under IDEA and needs special education;**

- **The IEP is the result of a team process which very prominently includes the parents;**

- **The IEP should be "reasonably calculated" to provide educational benefit;**

- **The IEP Team must comply with IDEA (and the regulations for IDEA) when developing IEPs;**

- **The IEP should focus on the specific IEP content and processes cited in IDEA;**

- **IEP goals should provide an outline of the**

annual plan for providing an appropriate
education;

- The IEP should focus on meeting educational needs and not educational bureaucracy;

- One purpose of the IEP is to monitor compliance but the IEP document is not intended to show compliance with every requirement and "consideration" listed in IDEA;

- As much as possible the IEP should be streamlined;

- The child's placement is made after the IEP has been developed.

Disentangling Disability and Need

The regulations for IDEA–1997 contained a provision that a child cannot be determined to have a disability because of a lack of instruction or limited English proficiency (see 34 CFR 300.534[b]). The purpose of this provision is to differentiate children with disabilities under IDEA and children who have educational needs but are not disabled. This requirement is designed to ensure that resources for disabilities are used appropriately, and that children are not misidentified and thereby prevented from participating in the regular classroom and general education curriculum. This requirement has been incorporated in IDEA–2004 as a "Special Rule for Eligibility Determination"[32] so that the team of qualified professionals and the parent shall determine that a child is the child with a disability if the determinant factor is lack of appropriate instruction in reading, including in the essential components of reading instruction, lack of instruction in math, or limited English proficiency.[33]

Many of the problems associated with IEPs can be traced to the fact that all children with educational needs do not have disabilities under IDEA or do not need special education. Obviously, providing specially designed instruction for children who should be receiving services through regular classroom resources is disingenuous with respect to developing an individualized education program when such a program is not needed.

Misclassification detracts from services for children who are disabled, and can result in discriminatory practices if a child is prevented from participating in the regular classroom or general curriculum because of a nonexistent disability. If a black child is placed in a separate educational setting because of identified mental retardation when, in fact, the child is not mentally retarded, the very premise of *Brown v. the Board of Education* that segregation is inherently unequal and invidious is contravened. If black children are disproportionately classified as mentally retarded (as they are by almost 3 to 1 in comparison to white children), the magnitude of the disproportionality is egregious and discriminatory because the identification and the classification can restrict access to the regular classroom and curriculum. This is the case for all children who are misclassified, regardless of race, in that misclassification can prevent access to the regular classroom and curriculum and is therefore segregative in the most pejorative sense.

Special Rule for Eligibility Determination

In making a determination of eligibility under paragraph (4)(A), a child shall not be determined to be a child with a disability if the determinant factor for such determination is—

   (A) lack of appropriate instruction in reading, including in the essential components of reading instruction (as defined in section 1208(3) of the Elementary and Secondary Education Act of 1965);

   (B) lack of instruction in math; or

   (C) limited English proficiency.

                                                    –P.L. 108–446, 614(b)(5)

The Congressional findings for IDEA–2004 openly acknowledge the many problems relating to misclassification including the following concerns: (1) overidentifications of minorities as disabled; (2) not providing incentives for whole-school approaches, scientifically-based early programs, positive behavioral interventions and supports, and prereferral interventions to reduce the need to label children as disabled in order to address their learning and behavioral needs; (3) apparent discrepancies in the levels of referral and placement of limited English proficient children in special education; and (4) the need for greater efforts to prevent the intensification of problems connected with mislabeling.[34] For children who are not disabled, especially for minority children, the individual evaluation and IEP can serve as a license for removal from the regular classroom. Although over five million children are currently receiving services, and each child is required to have an IEP, many are not disabled under IDEA.

As strongly worded in the House report for IDEA–2004 special education is not intended to compensate for general educational and instructional deficiencies, or to serve as a dumping ground for children who "need extra support or intensified instruction:"

> **The Committee is discouraged by the practice of overidentifying children as having disabilities, especially minority students, largely because the children do not have appropriate reading skills. Special education is not intended to serve as an alternative place to serve children if the local educational agency has failed to teach these children how to read. The bill updates language within the Act to contain a specific requirement that a child cannot be determined to be a child with a disability solely because the child did not receive scientifically based instruction in reading.**

> *And*

> **too often students are referred to special education because they are not succeeding in the general education setting and they need extra support or intensified instruction. While they do not need special education, they are referred there anyway. Frankly, too many general educators are not skilled in meeting a diverse range of student learning needs, so they are eager to *dump* students out of their classes and off of their rosters so they are not responsible for them.[35]**

Needed IEP Changes

Many of the problems associated with IEPs and the IEP process could be resolved by refocusing attention to the fundamental task of providing an *appropriate education* in the *least restrictive environment* with the *least restrictive modifications.* The IDEA–2004 has attempted to accomplish this task by simplifying the IEP process and requirements, and empowering parents to play a more active role in the determination and provision of services. As listed below, there are a variety of factors that must be considered in order to invigorate, if not validate, the task of designing individualized education programs that actually meet individual learning and disability needs. These factors include streamlining the IEP, school and parent responsibility, and the use of school-wide resources to meet learning needs that are not the result of a disability.

Streamlined IEPs

The task of streamlining the IEP process is an important focus of IDEA–2004. Streamlining the IEP process includes reducing the IEP to what is explicitly required in IDEA, not repeating IEP content,[36] eliminating benchmarks or short term objectives (or, at least, no longer requiring these by statute), expediting the Team meeting process (viz., attendance requirements[37]), reducing "the unnecessary complications and processes involved in the IEP in order to give parents greater control over the IEP and to make the process more efficient and more effective for children, their parents, and teachers,"[38] and developing model IEP forms.

Fear of litigation is one of the reasons why IEPs are bogged down by excessive detail and irrelevant information. Congress has also opined that:

> **The Act currently has no statute of limitations and leaves local educational agencies open to litigation for the entire length of time a child is in school, whether or not the child has been identified as a child with a disability. Local educational agencies are often surprised by claims from parents involving issues that occurred in an elementary school program when the child may currently be a high school student. Such an unreasonably long threat of litigation hanging over a local educational agency forces them to document every step they take with every child, even if the parents agree with the action, because they could later change their mind and sue.[39]**

This threat of litigation undermines the IEP process by establishing an atmosphere of distrust rather than one of collaboration. Most importantly, "the fear of far-removed litigation raises the tension level between the school and the parent. Prolonged litigation breeds an attitude of distrust between the parents and school personnel and has the effect of requiring school personnel to document conversations, rather than working cooperatively to find the best education placement and services for the child."[40] The House report for

IDEA–2004 also observed that "an unreasonably long threat of litigation hanging over a local educational agency forces them to document every step they take with every child, even if the parents agree with the action, because they could later change their mind and sue."[41] There is no question that fear of litigation has changed the very purpose of an IEP from a real individualized educational program to a document that records compliance with the rules and regulations . . . *ad infinitum.*

IEP Focus

Many IEP forms are a mass of regulatory guidelines, lists and information that have considerably bureaucratic import but little bearing on the development of a document to address a child's needs. Every IEP Team must focus on the primary task of providing an appropriate education to enable participation in the regular classroom and curriculum, rather giving primary attention to the bureaucratic trappings of the IEP. This is accomplished by developing IEPs that are data-based, identifying levels of performance, creating real measurable annual goals, and providing services and accommodations that address a child's educational and other needs. The child should be the focus of the IEP, and this focus is achieved by data explicating the child's various needs.

School Responsibility

Ostensible compliance with IDEA can be monitored, but ensuring that schools not only comply with IDEA but provide an appropriate education to a child is far more difficult task. Measurable annual goals can always be written that appear to be measurable but are never measured, and were not written to be measured; services can be provided that appear to meet a child's needs but do not really enable participation with nondisabled children to the maximum extent appropriate. No legislation will ensure that IEP Team members consider all measurable annual goals, services and accommodations that best meet each child's needs; and no legislation will ensure that every IEP is a real plan for providing an appropriate education. The ultimate responsibility of the school is to provide special education and related services in accordance with the child's IEP, and to make a make a good faith effort to assist the child to achieve the goals and objectives or benchmarks listed in the IEP.[42]

First and foremost, developing an appropriate IEP requires compliance with IDEA and the regulations. However, as reasoned in *Hudson v. Rowley, appropriate* also requires the above mentioned "good faith effort" to provide instruction at public expense that meets the State's educational standards, instruction that approximates regular grade levels, instruction that comports with the child's IEP as required by IDEA, and instructional plan that is reasonably calculated to provide educational benefit.[43] Contrary to the superficial interpretation of IDEA compliance that focuses on a legalistic and regulatory interpretation of compliance, a free appropriate public education requires planning, consideration of educational needs, and educational benefit.

Parent Responsibility

Parents have been given greatly enhanced responsibility in the special education process regarding services and the consent for services. Parents can refuse services, and this refusal no longer obligates schools to provide a free and appropriate public education. Most importantly, the role of parents as equal partners in the IEP process is critical. Parents have the ultimate responsibility of being their child's most important advocate, in the determination of goals, services and accommodations. Parents have been given increased responsibility concerning special education services under IDEA-2004, but the Act also requires parents to advocate for their child's needs and to voice complaints and problems in a timely manner:

> **In 1997, the reauthorization included changes designed to ensure that parents accurately notified the local educational agency of the issues they were raising in their complaint. Unfortunately, regulations issued in 1999 by the Department directly contradicted this requirement by stating that failure to comply with the notice requirement under this Act could not delay or deny the parent the right to a due process hearing. The language requiring a parent to provide a clear and specific complaint to the local educational agency is essential to making the complaint process work in a fair and equitable manner. Local educational agency officials need to know, with clarity and specificity, what the problem is that concerns the parent so they can try to remedy the problem.[44]**

The IDEA-2004 allows a parent to present a complaint "with respect to any matter relating to the identification, evaluation, or educational placement of the child, or the provision of a free appropriate public education" for "an alleged violation that occurred not more than two years before the date the parent or public agency knew or should have known about the alleged action that forms the basis of the complaint, or, if the State has an explicit time limitation for presenting such a complaint under this part, in such time as the State law allows."[45]

School Resources

The effective use of school-wide resources reduces overidentification of children with disabilities, misclassification, and helps differentiate lack of instruction from disability. Not every child who is experiencing difficulty in school has a disability. Every school has a responsibility to use school-wide resources to provide for each child's needs which can range from individualized help to a variety of remedial and school-wide programs. There is an increased emphasis on prereferral strategies and interventions to reduce the number of overreferrals and the number of misclassified children by encouraging the use of school-wide resources to enable participation in the general curriculum.

Prereferral Services

IN GENERAL–A local educational agency may use not more than 15 percent of the amount such agency receives under this part for any fiscal year, in combination with other amounts (which may include amounts other than education funds), to develop and implement comprehensive coordinated prereferral educational support services for students in kindergarten through grade 12 (with a particular emphasis on students in grades kindergarten through 3) who have not been identified as needing special education or related services but who need additional academic and behavioral support to succeed in a general education environment.

–P.L. 108–446, 613(f)(1)

Chapter 2

IEP PLANNING

The term "individualized education program" or "IEP" means a written statement for each child with a disability that is developed, reviewed, and revised in accordance with this section.[46]

The IEP is a written statement that is developed in accordance with IDEA–2004 and the regulations for IDEA contained in the Code of Federal Regulations. When the concept of a written individualized education program was first introduced in 1975 the House envisioned three basic IEP principles: (1) each child requires an educational plan that is tailored to achieve his or her maximum potential;[47] (2) all principals in the child's educational environment, including the child, should have the opportunity for input; and (3) the word "individualization" is further defined as meaning "specifics and timetables" and a periodic review of these specifics.[48]

The original rationale for the IEP centered about "planning" so that the Senate bill for IDEA–1975[49] designated "this individualized instructional planning as an 'individualized planning conference'" that would result in a written statement. The House bill for IDEA–1975[50] used the term "individualized education program" which was chosen over the Senate's concept of an "individualized planning conference" when the Senate and House bills for P.L. 94–142 were reconciled.

The definition of an IEP "means a written statement for each child with a disability that is developed, reviewed, and revised in accordance with section 614(d)."[51] In other words, the IEP must follow the IDEA guidelines provided in Section 614(d) which relate to Individualized Education Programs (and in Section 1414(d) in the United State Code). Important areas covered in Section 614(d) are shown in the chart below.

Section	Topic
614(d)(1)(A)(i)	**IEP Content**
614(d)(1)(B)	**IEP Teams**
614(d)(1)(C)	**IEP Team Attendance**
614(d)(1)(D)	**IEP Team Transition**
614(d)(2)(C)	**IEPs for Children who Transfer**
614(d)(3)	**Development of IEP**
614(d)(3)(B)	**Consideration of Special Factors**
614(d)(3)(C)	**Requirement with Respect to Regular Education Teacher**
614(d)(3)(E)	**Consolidation of IEP Team Meetings**
614(d)(3)(F)	**Amendments**
614(d)(4)	**Review and Revision of IEP**
614(d)(4)(B)	**Requirement with Respect to Regular Education Teacher**
614(d)(5)	**Multi-year IEP Demonstration**
614(d)(7)	**Children with Disabilities in Adult Prisons**

As determined in *Hudson v. Rowley*[52] the written statement of a child's educational plan or IEP must be reasonably calculated, provide educational benefit, and "formulated in accordance with the Act's requirements." The purpose of the IEP is not to *show* that a document has been developed in compliance with IDEA, but to develop a plan that actually provides educational benefit. The difference between **showing compliance** and **actually complying** with IDEA to provide an appropriate educational program is significant.

Many IEPs are simply written to show that the IEP Team and the local educational agency have complied with all the regulations to the extent that this showing of compliance results in an unwieldy document that primarily serves as a license to place a child in an alternative placement. The need to show compliance, coupled with attempts to simplify the IEP process, has resulted in meaningless IEPs that fail to provide children with an appropriate educational program. This is readily seen in the various checklists and pseudocompliance statements found in IEPs. For example, the measurable annual goal statement is intended to result in goals that are not only *measurable* but actually *measured.* Yet this elemental component of the IEP is often compromised by the creation of goals that are not measurable annual goals, are not written to be measured, and will never be measured.

In an effort to standardize the IEP process so that one IEP fits every child, many IEPs contain information that have absolutely no bearing on educational programs that will guide service providers. This includes excessive bureaucratic information (e.g., State and school codes, extensive family history), repeating information contained in other reports such as the individual evaluation, and reference to even the most tangential regulation, guideline, or area of consideration.

The IEP Team has an obligation to follow IDEA and the regulations but the task of the IEP Team is not simply to develop legal IEPs that meet the four corners of the law, but to develop IEPs that comply with IDEA to provide **a reasonably calculated plan**. All too often a fear of due process procedures (e.g., impartial hearing) and litigation becomes the motivating force for the development of the IEP. A legal IEP can be a totally useless document if the intent is to fulfill every real or perceived requirement rather than to develop a real planning document. The statement of present levels of academic achievement might be rich with scores and data but if the statement does not provide a basis or direction for educational planning and goals, no purpose has been served other than to provide a window-dressing show of compliance rather than an appropriate educational plan.

FAPE, IEPS AND LRE

The ultimate purpose of the IEP is to provide each child with a disability with an appropriate education or what is referred to as a Free Appropriate Public Education or FAPE. The final regulations for Public Law 94–142 (August 23, 1977) stated that "'FAPE' is a statutory term which requires special education and related services to be provided in accordance with an individualized education program (IEP)."[53] The goal of providing FAPE is achieved by means of an IEP that identifies levels of performance, goals to address these levels of performance and needs, appropriate services and accommodations to achieve these goals and to enable classroom participation. The focus of the IEP and how this plan is developed is the regular classroom. The purpose of FAPE is to provide an appropriate public school education, and the most appropriate public school education is to be educated with nondisabled children in the regular classroom and using the general curriculum.

For the IEP Team the development of the IEP begins with the regular classroom by considering necessary accommodations and services (or supplementary aids and services) that will enable regular classroom participation. Only when "the nature or severity of the disability of a child is such that education in regular classes with the use of supplementary aids and services cannot be achieved satisfactorily" can the IEP Team consider an alternative educational placement. The FAPE mandate requires an appropriate public school education; the IEP provides the plan for achieving FAPE; and the LRE provision permeates every element of the IEP by emphasizing the importance of the regular classroom, participating with nondisabled children and the axiomatic goal of maximizing independence to enable children with disabilities to achieve full educational potential.

The IDEA–2004 definition of FAPE is predicated on the development and implementation of a reasonably calculated plan that is provided in conformity with IDEA guidelines (i.e., the guidelines described in section 614(d)). The keyword for the IEP team is not *document, requirements,* or *paperwork,* but **appropriate**. Under IDEA the term "free appropriate public education" means special education and related services that:

1. **Have been provided at public expense, under public supervision and direction, and without charge;**

2. **Meet the standards of the State educational agency;**

3. **Include an appropriate preschool, elementary school, or secondary school education in the State involved (that is reasonably calculated to provide educational benefit to enable the child with a disability to access the general curriculum; and**

4. **Are provided in conformity with the individualized education program required under section 614(d).**[54]

Least Restrictive Environment

The LRE provision was first cited in P.L. 94–142 in 1975 as required "procedures to assure that, to the maximum extent appropriate . . ." children are educated with nondisabled children and that removal from regular education classes occurs only when supplementary aids and services are not successful.[55] This provision has been referred to as the mainstreaming provision of IDEA but "mainstreaming" suggests that the primary task is to place children from special education classes to regular education classes when possible. This can be a commendable goal, but the primary obligation of the IEP Team is to limit removal from "regular educational environments" by means of supplementary aids and services. The IEP team must not begin with the presumption that a child will be placed in special education, and that if all goes well, the child will be mainstreamed into regular classes.

The LRE Mandate

IN GENERAL–To the maximum extent appropriate, children with disabilities, including children in public or private institutions or other care facilities, are educated with children who are not disabled, and special classes, separate schooling, or other removal of children with disabilities from the regular educational environment occurs only when the nature or severity of the disability of a child is such that education in regular classes with the use of supplementary aids and services cannot be achieved satisfactorily.

–P.L. 108–446, 612(a)(5)(A)

For the IEP Team the LRE mandate provides a philosophical basis for special education, a philosophy embedded in regular classroom participation. The LRE provision provides guidance for the IEP Team in terms of accommodations, services, and where these accommodations and services should be provided. The content of the IEP underscores the importance of the regular classroom as a primary educational goal and the standard for IEP development and implementation. The statement of the child's present levels of academic achievement includes "how the child's disability affects the child's involvement and progress in the general education curriculum;" the statement of measurable annual goals is "designed to meet the child's needs that result from the child's disability to enable the child to be involved in and make progress in the general education curriculum; and the statement of the special education, services, supplementary aids and services, and the program modifications or supports places emphasis on being "involved in and make progress in the general education curriculum."[56] Of course, participating in the general curriculum is not always possible which is why the LRE provision stipulates to **the maximum extent appropriate**. This is the preference for IDEA and the **preference for mainstreaming**: for the IEP Team to develop an IEP for every child that enables participation in the regular classroom to the maximum extent possible.

The Regular Classroom Presumption

Prior to the enactment of P.L. 94–142 in 1975, the opportunity and inclination to educate children with disabilities was often in separate programs and schools away from children without disabilities. The law and this bill contain a presumption that children with disabilities are to be educated in regular classes. Therefore, the legislation requires that the IEP include an explanation of the extent, if any, to which a child with a disability will not participate with nondisabled children in the regular class and in the general education curriculum including extra-curricular and nonacademic activities.

–Senate report 105–17, IDEA–1997

The LRE mandate is not restricted educational placement but applies to every aspect of IEP content. Special education services should be as **least restrictive as possible**. If a child is able to achieve satisfactorily with two hours of consultant teacher services a week, five hours of consultant teacher services might seem like an added benefit but this would be an unnecessary restriction. If a child needs an aide one hour a day rather than three, one hour a day is more appropriate than three. Accommodations should also be as least restrictive as possible. If the IEP Team provides an array of accommodations that are not based on need but on the belief that a child with a disability needs an advantage, these accommodations would be restrictive. The LRE mandate is not easily achieved and requires careful planning and consideration by the IEP Team. Providing unnecessary goals, services or accommodations can restrict access to the general curriculum, as can the failure to provide necessary goals, services and accommodations. The task for the IEP Team is indeed difficult and entails the development of IEPs which provide what is necessary to meet each child's educational and other needs . . . no more and no less.

There is an important relationship between the IEP and LRE placement in that the least restrictive educational placement is based on the IEP. The IEP Team must first develop the IEP before considering where the IEP will be implemented. When the IEP Team considers what a child needs to participate in the regular classroom and the child's other educational needs this does not mean that the regular classroom or the regular curriculum is appropriate for every child but only that the regular classroom and general curriculum is the standard for providing an appropriate education. After the IEP has been developed the IEP team might conclude that a placement other than the regular classroom is necessary. If this is the case, the LRE standard requires the IEP Team to determine the extent a child is able to participate in the regular classroom.

Inclusion and Mainstreaming

Public Law 108–446 requires the inclusion of children with disabilities under the LRE mandate although the term *inclusion* is never actually mentioned in the law. The IDEA–2004 is deliberate in avoiding the use of the term **inclusion** and **mainstreaming** when referring to regular classroom participation. However, the Rehabilitation Act of 1973 does refer to "the goal of providing individuals with disabilities with the tools necessary to (a) make informed choices and decisions and (b) achieve equality of opportunity, full inclusion and integration in society, employment, independent living, and economic and social self-sufficiency, for such individuals."[57]

The statutory requirement, what IDEA–2004 requires, is not *inclusion* or *mainstreaming* but to educate children with disabilities with children who are not disabled to the maximum extent appropriate. Mainstreaming is an interpretation of this mandate (mostly by the courts), while inclusion is a more proactive interpretation of the LRE requirement. Unfortunately, inclusion or full-inclusion is used to suggest that all special education should be in inclusive environments. The IDEA does not require that all children be included in inclusive environments, but that all children are educated with nondisabled children to the maximum extent appropriate. Indeed, full-inclusion is contrary to the LRE mandate, the concept of a continuum of alternative placements, and IDEA.

Educational Benefit

One of the controversial areas that the IEP Team must address is the obligation to provide an individual education program that is beneficial. This does not mean that the IEP Team must configure a program that provides maximum benefit, a substantial level of benefit, but simply to provide educational benefit. The standard of maximum possible development (MPD) or maximum feasible benefit (MFB) sometimes referred to in state codes/regulations is a standard that is virtually impossible to enforce.

The standard "educational benefit" is admittedly low. As stated in *Hudson* "if the child is being educated in regular classrooms, as here, the IEP should be reasonably calculated to enable the child to achieve passing marks and advance from grade to grade." Although the standard of educational benefit is low, and the IEP team is guided by a good faith effort to develop a reasonably calculated IEP, many IEPs are developed with no intent of educational . . . either low or high.

IEP-related Acronyms

504 -	**Plan developed under the Rehabilitation Act of 1973 (e.g., Section 504 plan).**
FAPE -	**Free Appropriate Public Education**
IAC -	**Individualized Accommodation Plan (see 504)**
IEE -	**Independent education Evaluation**
IEP -	**Individualized Education Program**
IFSP -	**Individualized Family Service Plan**
IPE -	**Individualized Employment Plan**
LEA -	**Local Educational Agency (the *school* or *district*)**
LEP -	**Limited English Proficiency**
LRE -	**Least Restrictive Environment**
MDT -	**Multidisciplinary team**
PWN -	**Prior Written Notice**
PSN -	**Procedural Safeguards Notice**
SEA -	**State Educational Agency**

Planning is at the heart of every IEP, and the result of this planning is educational benefit. This is achieved by the IEP Team carefully considering each child's needs, and necessary goals, services and accommodations to meet these needs. The IEP Team must consider a variety of special factors such as the need for behavioral interventions and strategies, English as a second language, Braille, communications needs, assistive technology, physical education and nonacademic services. However, these considerations are not achieved by a series of boxes to check on the IEP form to show that the IEP Team considered each factor.

Related IEP Documents

Individualized Family Service Plan (IFSP)

The IEP required by IDEA for school-age children has a close counterpart in the individualized family service plan (IFSP) required for infants or toddlers with a disability under three years of age who need early intervention services.[58] For a child between the ages of 3 through 5 years of age the IEP Team can use the IFSP to "serve as the IEP . . . if agreed to by the agency and the child's parents."[59] Noteworthy among the elements of the IFSP is the emphasis on noncategorical difficulties (e.g., physical and cognitive development), the family's concerns, a statement of natural environments, and the identification of a service coordinator. As shown by the IFSP requirements outlined below for many children requiring an IEP, the components of an IFSP can be extremely relevant in the development of an IEP:

1. a statement of the infant's or toddler's present levels of physical development, cognitive development, communication development, social or emotional development, and adaptive development, based on objective criteria;

2. a statement of the family's resources, priorities, and concerns relating to enhancing the development of the family's infant or toddler with a disability;

3. a statement of the measurable outcomes expected to be achieved for the infant or toddler and the family, including, as appropriate, preliteracy and language skills, and the criteria, procedures, and timelines used to determine the degree to which progress toward achieving the outcomes is being made and whether modifications or revisions of the outcomes or services are necessary;

4. a statement of specific early intervention services necessary to meet the unique needs of the infant or toddler and the family, including the frequency, intensity, and method of delivering services;

5. a statement of the natural environments in which early intervention services will appropriately be provided, including a justification of the extent, if any, to which the services will not be provided in a natural environment;

6. The projected dates for initiation of services and the anticipated length, duration, and frequency of the services;

7. The identification of the service coordinator from the profession most immediately relevant to the infant's or toddler's or family's needs (or who is otherwise qualified to carry out all applicable responsibilities under this part) who will be responsible for the implementation of the plan and coordination with other agencies and persons, including transition services; and

8. The steps to be taken to support the transition of the toddler with a disability to preschool or other appropriate services.

Individualized Plan for Employment (IPE)

Both the IEP and IFSP are similar in structure to the Rehabilitation Act amendments Individualized Plan for Employment (IPE)[60] which includes services, outcomes, conditions, timelines and criteria but with an emphasis on the responsibilities of the client in the implementation of the IPE (a factor underutilized by IEPs). The IPE "affords eligible individuals the opportunity to exercise informed choice in selecting an employment outcome, the specific vocational rehabilitation services to be provided under the plan, the entity that will provide the vocational rehabilitation services, and the methods used to procure the services."[61] Although this client-centered approach is not always possible for young children, student involvement in the selection of transition goals and services should be incorporated in the IEP meeting process whenever possible. The IEP Team must remember that an underlying long-term goal is always maximizing independent skills in the development of both IPEs and IEPs. For the statement of transition services in IEPs, IPE guidelines provide direction for post-school and employment outcomes, integrated settings, and individual responsibility in the transition process. Important elements of the IPE include:

1. **A description of the specific employment outcome that is chosen by the eligible individual, consistent with the unique strengths, resources, priorities, concerns, abilities, capabilities, interests, and informed choice of the eligible individual, and, to the maximum extent appropriate, results in employment in an integrated setting;**

2. **A description of the specific vocational rehabilitation services that are needed to achieve the employment outcome, including, as appropriate, the provision of assistive technology devices and assistive technology services, and personal assistance services, including training in the management of such services; and provided in the most integrated setting that is appropriate for the service involved and is consistent with the informed choice of the eligible individual;**

3. **Timelines for the achievement of the employment outcome and for the initiation of the services;**

4. **A description of the entity chosen by the eligible individual or, as appropriate, the individual's representative, that will provide the vocational rehabilitation services, and the meth-**

ods used to procure such services;

5. A description of criteria to evaluate progress toward achievement of the employment outcome;

6. The terms and conditions of the individualized plan for employment, including, as appropriate, information describing the responsibilities of the designated State unit;

7. The responsibilities of the eligible individual, including the responsibilities the eligible individual will assume in relation to the employment outcome of the individual;

8. If applicable, the participation of the eligible individual in paying for the costs of the plan;

9. The responsibility of the eligible individual with regard to applying for and securing comparable benefits;

10. The responsibilities of other entities as the result of arrangements made pursuant to comparable services or benefits requirements;

11. The extended services needed by the eligible individual;

12. As determined to be necessary, a statement of projected need for post-employment services.

Section 504 Plans

The Rehabilitation Act of 1973 or Public Law 93–112 provides services relating to training, counseling and employment.[62] Whereas IDEA requires special education and related services as defined by an IEP, Section 504 (which refers to Title V of the Rights and Advocacy Section of P.L. 93–112) requires that children with disabilities are not discriminated against and are provided services and accommodations necessary to meet individual educational needs as adequately as nondisabled children. There is no specific plan (e.g., an IEP) that Section 504 requires only that a child with a disability is not discriminated against. This actual Section 504 requirement is simply this: "No otherwise qualified individual with a disability in the United States, as defined in section 705(20) of this title, shall, solely by reason of her or his disability, be excluded from the participation in, be denied the benefits of, or be subjected to discrimination under any program or activity receiving Federal financial assistance or under any program or activity conducted by any Executive agency or by the United States Postal Service."[63]

The Council for Administrators of Special Education (CASE) has developed a Section 504 Student Accommodation Plan which entails specifying the problem, the disability, how the disability affects a "major life activity" and reasonable accommodations.[64] Section 504 is important in that a Section **504 plan** or **Section 504 accommodation** can provide very specific and focused services. Whereas a child with a disability requires an IEP as per IDEA, a Section 504 plan can be developed using an IEP or IEP-like document, a specific service (e.g., an aide), or a specific accommodation. The regulations for Section 504 allow for the implementation of an IEP in accordance with IDEA as one means of meeting the educational needs of a child. For the majority of children Section 504 is appropriate for providing specific accommodations or services without special education, and for meeting the needs of children who are not or no longer disabled under IDEA (e.g., children who have been declassified). Although there are no regulatory guidelines for the contents of an accommodation plan, a plan under Section 504 should include all reasonable accommodations and services that a child might need as a result of a disability.

The two primary distinctions between IDEA and Section 504 concern how each defines a disability and what criteria must be met before either IDEA or Section 504 services are provided. For children with disabilities under IDEA, a child must **need special education** and have an **IDEA-defined disability** (as defined in the regulations for IDEA). These disabilities include: (1) autism, (2) deaf-blindness, (3) deafness, (4) emotional disturbance, (5) hearing impairment, (6) mental retardation, (7) multiple disabilities, (8) orthopedic impairment, (9) other health impairment, (10) specific learning disability, (11) speech or language impairment, (12) traumatic brain injury, and (13) visual impairment.[65] A child might have a hearing impairment but not need special education because the child is able to function satisfactorily in the regular classroom. However, if this child required a specific accommodation (e.g., amplification, seating preference in the classroom) but not special education, Section 504 would be used to provide the necessary accommodations.

Under Section 504 a disability "means any person who (i) has a physical or mental impairment which substantially limits one or more major life activities, (ii) has a record of such an impairment, or (iii) is regarded as having such an impairment,"[66] and the child "has a record of such an impairment means he has a history of, or has been misclassified as having, a mental or physical impairment that substantially limits one or more major life activities."[67] In contrast to the 13 specific IDEA disability categories, Section 504 disabilities include "any physiological disorder or condition, cosmetic disfigurement, or anatomical loss affecting one or more of the following body systems: neurological; musculoskeletal; special sense organs; respiratory, including speech organs; cardiovascular; reproductive, digestive, genitourinary; hemic and lymphatic; skin; and endocrine; or any mental or psychological disorder, such as mental retardation, organic brain syndrome, emotional or mental illness, and specific learning disabilities."[68]

Services provided under IDEA require both need and the determination of a specific disability, and services must conform to IEP requirements. Services under Section 504 require only that a child have a disability as defined (very broadly) under Section 504. Because Section 504 does not have specific requirements such as present levels of academic achievement or special education services, Section 504 can be used to provide a single accommodation, a specific related service, or an array of services and accommodations similar to those provide under IDEA.

Chapter 3

IEPs AND IDEA AMENDMENTS

*Since the enactment and implementation of the Education for
All Handicapped Children Act of 1975, this title has been successful
in ensuring children with disabilities and the families of such
children access to a free appropriate public education and in
improving educational results for children with disabilities.*[69]

The IEP required by IDEA has undergone several changes beginning with the first statutory guidelines for IEP content required by Public Law 94–142 in 1975. The initial version of IDEA required five basic IEP elements. From 1975 to IDEA–2004 the required content for IEPs increased considerably, as did the apparent need by schools to add both required and nonrequired content to IEP forms. In 1975, the P.L. 94–142 the requirement for services was relatively simple and straightforward:

> **(c) a statement of the specific educational services to be provided to such child, and the extent to which such child will be able to participate in regular educational programs.**

The statement of services requirement for IDEA–1997 added supplementary aids and services, the need to attain goals, to make progress in the general curriculum, and to participate with both disabled and nondisabled children:

> **(IV) a statement of the special education and related services, and supplementary aids and services, based on peer-reviewed research to the extent practicable, to be provided to the child, or on behalf of the child, and a statement of the program modifications or supports for school personnel that will be provided for the child–**

(aa) to advance appropriately toward attaining the annual goals;
(bb) to be involved in and make progress in the general curriculum in accordance with subclause (I) and to participate in extracurricular and other nonacademic activities; and
(cc) to be educated and participate with other children with disabilities and nondisabled children in the activities described in this subparagraph.[70]

Although IDEA–1997 made substantial changes to the statement of services, this is not the cause of excessive paperwork and does not result in educationally and administratively unwieldy IEPs. The statement for services for IDEA attempts to address each of the relevant services, is clearly focused, and intentionally places emphasis on the general curriculum and participation with nondisabled children. The problem of excessive paperwork occurs when schools fail to acknowledge the underlying purpose of the various services. The deficiencies regarding IEP services center about confusing services with placement, not providing supplementary aids and services, the questionable use of related services, and a failure to provide program modifications and supports.

IDEA–1975 IEP

Federal involvement in special education began with Public Law 89–750 which amended the Elementary and Secondary Education Act (ESEA) of 1965 to provide schools with grant programs for special education. Public Law 91–230 further amended the law by creating the Education of the Handicapped Act (EHA) and Public Law 93–280 in 1974 mandated "full educational opportunity" and provided the basis for the Least Restrictive Environment or mainstreaming clause ("to the maximum extent appropriate . . .") which underlies all of special education. What we now refer to as the Individuals with Disabilities Education Act amendments (or IDEA) is based on the 1975 amendments or Public Law 94–142 (Education for All Handicapped Children Act or EAHCA). This law, often referred to as simply P.L. 94–142, first outlined required IEP content which consisted of five basic components.

Required IDEA–1975 IEP Content

1. A statement of the present levels of educational performance of such child;

2. **A statement of annual goals, including short-term instructional objectives;**

3. **A statement of the specific educational services to be provided to such child, and the extent to which such child will be able to participate in regular educational programs;**

4. **The projected date for initiation and anticipated duration of such services, and;**

5. **Appropriate objective criteria and evaluation procedures and schedules for determining, on at least an annual basis, whether instructional objectives are being achieved.**[71]

IDEA-1990 IEP

Public Law 101–476 in 1990 renamed EAHCA the Individuals with Disabilities Education Act (IDEA), changed "handicap" to "disability" and added the statement of transition services to the IEP required elements:

> **a statement of the needed transition services for students beginning no later than age 16 and annually thereafter (and, when determined appropriate for the individual, beginning at age 14 or younger), including, when appropriate, a statement of the interagency responsibilities or linkages (or both) before the student leaves the school setting.**

For IDEA–1990 transition services were defined as "a coordinated set of activities "designed within an outcome-oriented process that promotes movement from school to post-school activities." These coordinated activities included instruction, community experiences and the development of employment and other post-school adult living object.[72]

IDEA-1997 IEP

The 1997 amendments to Individuals with Disabilities Education Act amendments (IDEA–1997) resulted in extensive modifications to required IEP content. First, the statement of present levels of education performance was expanded to include how the child's disability affects the child's involvement and progress in the general curriculum, for preschool children how the disability affects the child's participation in appropriate activities.[73]

The controversial "benchmarks or short-term objectives" requirement (deleted by IDEA–2004) was added to the statement for measurable annual goals in 1997. This change modified the 1990 statement from "annual goals, including short-term instructional objectives" to "a statement of measurable annual goals, **including benchmarks and short-term objectives**. . . ." More importantly IDEA–1997 measurable annual goals emphasized "meeting the child's needs that result from the child's disability to enable the child to be involved in and progress in the general curriculum; and meeting each of the child's other educational needs that result from the child's disability."[74] Added to the list of required services was **supplementary aids and services** and **program modifications** or **supports for school personnel**.[75] The IDEA–1997 emphasized the need to attain goals, "to be involved and progress in the general curriculum . . . and to participate in extracurricular and other nonacademic activities."[76]

To emphasize the need for regular classroom participation IDEA–1997 required a statement of nonparticipation which explained the extent, if any, a child will not participate with nondisabled children in the regular classroom.[77] Also new to the IDEA–1997 IEP was a statement of "**any individual modifications in the administration of State or district-wide assessments**" and if these assessments were not appropriate "how the child will be assessed."[78]

For the statement indicating the timeframe of services (viz., beginning data and duration of services), the **frequency** and **location** of services were added.[79] For transition services a distinction was made for the types of services provided at ages 14 and 16, and "an age of majority" clause was added to the transition services statement:

1. **Beginning at age 14, and updated annually, a statement of the transition service needs of the child under the applicable components of the child's IEP that focuses on the child's courses of study (such as participation in advanced-placement courses or a vocational education program);**

2. **Beginning at age 16 (or younger, if determined appropriate by the IEP Team), a statement of needed transition services for the child, including, when appropriate, a statement of the interagency responsibilities or any needed linkages; and**

3. **Beginning at least one year before the child reaches the age of majority under State law, a statement that the child has been**

informed of his or her rights under this title, if any, that will transfer to the child on reaching the age of majority."[80]

The IDEA–1997 detailed how the child's progress toward the annual goals would be measured, and "how the child's parents will be regularly informed (by such means as periodic report cards), at least as often as parents are informed of their nondisabled children's progress, of their child's progress toward the annual goals . . . and the extent to which that progress is sufficient to enable the child to achieve the goals by the end of the year."[81]

IDEA–2004 IEP

Public Law 108–446 amendments to the IDEA resulted in several changes to the required IEP content, and placed a renewed emphasis on academic achievement and streamlined IEP process and IEP form. The statement for **present levels of educational performance** was changed to a statement of the child's **present levels of academic achievement and functional performance** to emphasize the importance of the general education curriculum in providing every child with an appropriate education.[82]

Possibly one of the most significant changes to the 2004 IEP is the elimination of benchmarks and short-term objectives from the statement of measurable annual goals (and academic and functional goals). The statement of "how the child's progress toward meeting the annual goals" was repositioned in the list of required IEP content to immediately follow measurable goals.

Not all the changes to the IEP will result in a streamlined IEP process as demonstrated by the statement of services that ". . . special education and related services and supplementary aids and services, **based on peer-reviewed research to the extent practicable**, to be provided to the child. . . ." For the IEP Team the "based on peer reviewed research" clause will require more reflection as to the legitimacy of services, especially related services. Nonetheless, this peer-reviewed research clause provides an important reminder to IEP Team members that services should not be frivolous, should not be caviler, and should be based on data and an expectation that every service will result in educational benefit or to allow a child to benefit from special education.

The 2004–IEP has streamlined the IEP by clearly stating "that additional information need not be included in a child's IEP beyond what is explicitly required in this section," by providing greater flexibility regarding IEP Team attendance, and encouraging "the consolidation of reevaluation meetings for the child and other IEP Team meetings for the child."

The statement for State or district-wide test accommodations was changed to include the qualifier **appropriate** to ensure that test modifications do not invalidate the test (e.g., reading a reading test to a child). The statement now requires "a statement of **any individual appropriate accommodations** that are necessary to measure the academic achievement and functional performance of the child on State and district-wide assessments."[83]

The statement of transition services added to IEP content in IDEA–1990 required a statement of services at age 16 or before if appropriate to deal with the transition from school to post-school activities. This was further refined in IDEA–1997 to require a statement of course-related transition service before age 14, and post-school transition service before age 16. Public Law 108–446 has simplified the age distinction for the types of transition services by requiring "beginning not later than the first IEP to be in effect when the child is 16 . . . appropriate measurable postsecondary goals based upon age appropriate transition assessments related to training, education, employment, and, where appropriate, independent living skills."[84]

Effective Dates

The effective date for the implementation of IDEA–2004 requirements is July 1, 2005.[85] This date includes the implementation for Part A–General Provisions, Part B–Assistance for Education of All Children with Disabilities, and Part C–Infants and Toddlers with Disabilities requirements.

Following the passage of a law or an amended law, the regulations for the law are published in the Code of Federal Regulations (CFR) within one year. This is not always so in that the regulations for IDEA–1997 were not published until 1999. The regulations recite (especially beginning with the 1997 revision of IDEA), interpret IDEA, provide basic definitions (e.g., definitions of each IDEA disability), and guidelines for IEP Teams, IEP meetings, IEP content, due process, etc. Prior to IDEA–1997 the regulations amplified and some think (viz., Congress) created requirements, but the elimination of footnotes from the 1997 (published in 1999 regulations) resulted in guidelines that were very consistent with the Act.

Case Law

Many of the guidelines relating to IEPs can be traced to District, Appellate and Supreme Court decisions. Of foremost importance is the landmark Supreme Court decision of *Hudson v. Rowley*[86] which was the first and certainly the most influential decision concerning IDEA and IEPs. This decision involved Amy Rowley, a deaf student attending a school in the Hendrick Hudson School District in Peekskill, New York. The IEP for Amy provided for an FM hearing aid, instruction from a tutor for the deaf one hour a day, and three hours of speech services a week. Although an interpreter in Amy's kindergarten class for a two-week period indicated that his services were not needed, Amy's parents requested and received an impartial hearing. The hearing officer agreed with the school that Amy did not need a qualified sign-language interpreter in all her classes, as did an appeal to the New York Commissioner of Education. The District Court sided with the parents and found that the school did not provide Amy with FAPE because she was not given the opportunity to achieve her full potential. The Second Court of Appeals agreed with the district court. The Supreme Court decreed that the Court of Appeals erred in affirming the decision of the District Court and made the following important determinations:

FAPE: The Act's requirement of a "free appropriate public education" is satisfied when the State provides personalized instruction with sufficient support services to permit the handicapped child to benefit educationally from that instruction. If a child is being educated in regular classrooms, "the IEP should be reasonably calculated to enable the child to achieve passing marks and advance from grade to grade."[87]

Level of services: An IEP is intended to provide an appropriate education but it (the IEP) is not intended "to achieve strict equality of opportunity or services for handicapped and nonhandicapped children . . . **the Act does not require a State to maximize the potential** of each handicapped child commensurate with the opportunity provided nonhandicapped children." The primary responsibility of an IEP Team is to comply with the statutory procedures, and "then determine whether the individualized program developed through such procedures is reasonably calculated to enable the child to receive educational benefits. If these requirements are met, the State has complied with the obligations imposed by Congress" and the courts can require no more.

Courts: Contrary to a legalistic interpretation of IEPs, the IEP Team and not the courts are responsible for determining an appropriate education and IEP content. The courts must not impose "their view of preferable educational methods upon the States. Once a court determines that the Act's requirements have been met, questions of methodology are for resolution by the States."

To understand all the necessary IEP requirements, finding and accessing relevant IEP information specific to each State is essential. The specific requirements for individual States regarding IEPs can be included in the State code, rules generated by specific governing agency (e.g., State Board of Education), State policies and procedures, etc. There are generally two (or more) sources that must be identified: the State code or regulations governing IEPs and special education), and state guidelines relating to special education and IEPs (e.g., sample IEPs and guidance information).

Chapter 4

IEP: PREREFERRAL AND REFERRAL

*Providing incentives for whole-school approaches, scientifically-
based early reading programs, positive behavioral interventions
and supports, and early intervening services to reduce the need
to label children as disabled in order to address the learning
and behavioral needs of such children.*[88]

For an IEP to be effective, the IEP document must be a meaningful part of the entire special education process. The IEP does not begin with the first IEP meeting but is predicated on prereferral strategies and interventions, a focused referral, and a full and individual evaluation that determines both disability and need. When schools fail to provide every child with an opportunity to receive a free and appropriate public education, the Supreme Court's admonition in 1954 is current today: "In these days, it is doubtful that any child may reasonably be expected to succeed in life if he is denied the opportunity of an education. Such an opportunity, where the state has undertaken to provide it, is a right which must be made available to all on equal terms."[89] Special education is not an entity that exists apart from regular education; special education is intended to enable regular classroom participation. When the prereferral process is ignored, when the referral process does not take into account the purpose of special education, the result is often misclassification and the misuse of resources.

Special education is not intended to deal with all learning problems. Special education is not intended to address environmental, cultural, economic disadvantage, lack of instruction, or limited English proficiency. These are extremely important concerns that must be addressed by every school, but special education is not about lack of instruction, limited English proficiency or cultural factors if a child does not have a disability and does not need specialized instruction. If the IEP Team must develop and implement

IEPs for children who do not have disabilities, the task of developing a reasonably calculated plan for areas affected by a child's disability becomes virtually impossible. The problem of misclassification, of children with disabilities not receiving services and children not having disabilities identified as disabled and thus usually segregated from nondisabled children to some extent, is rectified by careful attention to prereferral interventions, an understanding of the role of special education, and referrals for special education that are made to enable participation in the regular classroom and general curriculum. Special education is not the placement of last resort; special education is not intended to remove children from the regular classroom. However, because special education can result in an alternative placement, this ability to by-pass the *Brown v. Board of Education* mandate "that in the field of public education the doctrine of separate but equal has no place because separate educational facilities are inherently unequal," must result in extraordinary consideration given to the responsibility of schools to prove an appropriate education, the role of special education, and the referral and identification of children who receive special education services.

An effective IEP is the logical outcome of a process that begins with the **child find** requirement to identify, locate and evaluate all children (including children in private schools).[90] Many of the problems associated with IEPs result from a failure of schools to provide every child with an appropriate education within the context of the regular classroom, a misunderstanding of the role of special education, and evaluation procedures that misidentify disability and individual need.

The prereferral period before a child is evaluated for special education is extremely important for preventing overreferrals and misclassification, and for providing the foundation for data-based IEPs. Every child has unique learning needs that are best met within the matrix of the regular classroom and regular curriculum, and special education is not the answer for problems relating to lack of instruction, cultural factors or economic disadvantage. Special education is explicitly intended for children with **IDEA-defined disabilities** and for children who **need** special education.

If a child exhibits academic problems, the regular classroom teacher should document the problems as much as possible. This could be in the form of classroom tests, samples of classroom work or observational data. If behavior is an issue, the classroom teacher should record specific behaviors that affect classroom progress (or affects the progress of other children). If the problem persists or there is an obvious need, the parents should be contacted for input. Prior to a request for an individual evaluation parent input is extremely important in that the parents might have information relating to the child's academic history, prior evaluations, or information concerning effective strategies and interventions.

Before a child is referred for an individual evaluation, classroom interventions and strategies should be attempted to accommodate the child's needs within the regular classroom. As a general rule all school-wide resources should be used such as reading, remedial mathematics, and speech and language services (but not special education speech and language), school counseling, input from specialists (e.g., reading teacher, consultant teacher), tutorial and volunteer programs, and Title I programs[91] before referral for an individual evaluation. Many schools use a child study team or student assistance team as a clearing house before a referral for special education is made. Prereferral teams focus on using school-wide resources to meet individual classroom and curriculum needs in the regular classroom.

The classroom teacher also plays an important role in the prereferral and evaluation process. Many classroom teachers view the individual evaluation as the only data source for determining the existence of a disability, but classroom data is absolutely necessary for determining the impact of disability on educational performance. Classroom data includes grades, tests, quizzes, student projects, reports, study pages, work samples, teacher evaluations, and virtually all areas that are part of the general curriculum or the curriculum used by nondisabled children. Finally, meeting with a consultant teacher, the director of special education or other individuals with expertise in the special education process should be sought to clarify individual needs, the role of the regular classroom teacher, and the need for an individual evaluation.

Input from the regular classroom teacher and parent must be sought prior to referral for an individual evaluation, and during the evaluation process. Consideration of each of these areas will reduce referrals for special education, the overidentification of children as disabled under IDEA, and promote the use of school-wide resources to address many of the educational problems that children exhibit but who are not disabled or who do not need special education. The regular classroom teacher plays an important role in identifying specific factors that a child exhibits or specific skill levels that prevent classroom participation. Input from the regular classroom teacher cannot be ignored. Also, there should be a record of strategies in the regular classroom to accommodate a child's learning needs. The regular classroom teacher is not expected to implement the types of accommodations that might be listed in a child's IEP (e.g., reading a test to a student, converting text to large print). However, the classroom teacher can provide information concerning easily implemented accommodations that might be appropriate for children with and without disabilities (e.g., providing breaks for relatively long classroom activities, classroom seating, and classroom lighting, extra time, enhanced directions, etc.). At the very least the regular classroom teacher should provide input, as much as possible, as to what accommodations might enable classroom and curriculum participation.

For children having behavioral or learning difficulties in the classroom the regular classroom teacher can provide invaluable information concerning strategies that may or may not be effective. In this sense *classroom intervention* does not mean providing special education but using a variety of activities and strategies to best meet a child's needs (e.g., small group, peer tutoring, one-to-one activities, etc.). The IDEA–2004 requires the participation of the regular classroom teacher in the development of the IEP, "including the determination of appropriate positive behavioral interventions and supports, and other strategies, and the determination of supplementary aids and services, program modifications, and support for school personnel."[92]

Before a referral for an individual evaluation there should be a record of parent involvement. A referral for special education should never be considered, and certainly not made, before a parent is informed of a child's performance and given an opportunity to provide input concerning accommodations, suggestions and strategies.

The Referral for an Individual Evaluation

Consistent with subparagraph (D), either a parent of a child, or a State educational agency, other State agency, or local educational agency may initiate a request for an initial evaluation to determine if the child is a child with a disability.

–P.L. 108–446, 614(a)(1)(B)

Teacher and Parent Referrals

Referrals will be made before or at the beginning of the school year when a child's needs are extensive or the child requires immediate attention. If a child has a severe visual, hearing, behavior or health need, input from the parent concerning the suspected disability is an essential before a referral is made. Most requests for an individual evaluation are made by the parent or the school, but the referral should always be a collaborative effort. Parent referrals are usually straightforward and will not include information relating to specific classroom problems or interventions. As a result a parent referral is often less detailed than referrals submitted by a teacher or school representative.

If the referral for an individual evaluation is made by the classroom teacher, or by the school or local educational agency at the bequest of the classroom teacher, the referral should include three elements: (1) a description of the child's academic performance and or behavior that is a cause of concern (which is also detailed in the Prior Written Notice); (2) a list of the various classroom accommodations, strategies and interventions to use in the classroom; and (3) parent input regarding the child's needs. This basic information forms the basis of the Prior Written Notice sent to parents when consent is sought to conduct an individual evaluation, helps guide the individual evaluation, and provides a basis for the development of the IEP if a child has a disability and needs special education.

Prior Written Notice

Prior Written Notice (PWN) provides parents with a statement of what the school intends to do (e.g., individual evaluation), what other options have been considered, a description of tests and evaluations used to make this decision and other relevant factors, and the parents procedural safeguard rights. If a child's needs cannot be accommodated by school-wide resources, and an individual evaluation is required to determine whether the child has a disability, the PWN indicates what action the school proposes to take (or not) and the reason for the action (or inaction). For an initial referral the "action" is the full and individual evaluation, and the "reason" for the action is a possible disability that affects academic performance.[93] Prior to evaluation the parents also receive a copy of the Procedural Safeguard Notice which is intended to clarify the parent's rights.

The PWN is required when a school proposes to initiate, or refuses to initiate, a change in identification, evaluation, placement, or in providing FAPE. The PWN serves as the springboard for the evaluation, provides parents with a clear understanding regarding why an evaluation is being conducted, and helps identify goals, services and accommodations when and if an IEP is developed. The notice should specify what it is that prevents a child from participating in the regular classroom or general curriculum without special education. The initial evaluation provides an in-depth link between the problem described in the PWN and the development of the IEP (if an IEP is necessary).

The prior written notice should be an extension and elaboration of the referral for evaluation and should always be considered by the IEP Team prior to developing the IEP. An unfortunate practice by schools is to downplay the importance of the PWN by simply sending parents a copy of the referral as well as a copy of the procedural safeguards. The referral generally does not contain the required PWN content and the list of procedural safeguards is difficult to understand.

The PWN should always be considered by the IEP Team because this notice indicates specific areas of concern that affect participation in the classroom or curriculum. The role of the IEP Team is not to discover the child's disability but use all available information and data that prompted the referral to determine if a child does have a disability. The PWN identifies other options considered by the school for dealing with the problem (e.g., using school-wide resources), a description of each evaluation procedure, test, record, or reports, and a description of any other factors that are relevant. The PWN includes the following elements:

1. **A description of the action proposed or refused by the agency;**

2. **An explanation of why the agency proposes or refuses to take the action and a description of each evaluation procedure, assessment, record, or report the agency used as a basis for the proposed or refused action;**

3. **a statement that the parents of a child with a disability have protection under the procedural safeguards of this part and, if this notice is not an initial referral for evaluation, the means by which a copy of a description of the procedural safeguards can be obtained;**

4. **Sources for parents to contact to obtain assistance in understanding the provisions of this part;**

5. **A description of other options considered by the IEP Team and the reason why those options were rejected; and**

6. **A description of the factors that is relevant to the agency's proposal or refusal.**[94]

Resources and individuals with expertise who are not affiliated with the school should be identified by the school district to assist parents in understanding the PWN or the procedural safeguards. In addition schools should have a list of persons or organizations who can advocate for the parent, especially at the IEP meeting "at the discretion of the parent or the agency" an individual who has special knowledge or expertise.

EVALUATIONS, ELIGIBILITY DETERMINATIONS, INDIVIDUALIZED EDUCATION PROGRAMS, AND EDUCATIONAL PLACEMENTS.

In any case for which there is an absence of consent for an initial evaluation . . . or for which there is an absence of consent for services . . . (aa) the local educational agency shall not be required to convene an IEP meeting or develop an IEP under this section for the child; and (bb) the local educational agency shall not be considered to be in violation of any requirement under this part (including the requirement to make available a free appropriate public education to the child) with respect to the lack of an initial evaluation of the child, an IEP meeting with respect to the child, or the development of an IEP under this section for the child.

–P.L. 108–446, 614(a)(1)(D)(ii)(III)

Procedural Safeguards Notice (PSN)

After a referral has been made by the parents, teacher, or school representative, the parents are sent a Procedural Safeguards Notice (PSN) listing their rights. The PSN for IDEA–1997 required the notice be given to parents upon initial referral for evaluation, "upon each notification of an IEP meeting," reevaluation, and receipt of a due process complaint.[95] The PSN describes the various procedural safeguards that must be provided to parents. Every IEP Team member should be aware of the procedural safeguards which parents are entitled to ensure that parents and school personnel participate in IEP meetings on a more or less even footing. The PSN must be given to parents upon initial referral for an individual evaluation (or when parents request an evaluation) but only once each year, or upon the first occurrence of the filing of a complaint.[96]

The major change in the PSN for IDEA–2004 is to limit the number of times the notice must be given to parents by no longer requiring the list of safeguards "upon each notification of an individualized education program meeting and upon reevaluation of the child."[97] The PSN details various rights that parents have and is "written in the native language of the parents, unless it clearly is not feasible to do, and written in an easily understandable manner" and includes the following:

A. Independent educational evaluation;

B. Prior written notice;

C. Parental consent;

D. Access to educational records;

E. The opportunity to present and resolve complaints, including (i) the time period in which to make a complaint; (ii) the opportunity for the agency to resolve the complaint; and (iii) the availability of mediation;

F. The child's placement during pendency of due process proceedings;

G. Procedures for students who are subject to placement in an interim alternative educational setting;

H. Requirements for unilateral placement by parents of children in private schools at public expense;

I. Due process hearings, including requirements for disclosure of evaluation results and recommendations;

J. State-level appeals (if applicable in that State);

K. Civil actions, including the time period in which to file such actions;

L. Attorney's fees.[98]

Parental Consent

The initial purpose of the IEP was the documentation of the partnership between school and parents to provide a child with an appropriate education. This partnership sometimes dissolves into a litigious and contentious relationship. Often this shaky relationship between school and parents becomes apparent when consent is required for the evaluation or services. Prior to IDEA–2004 consent was required for evaluation and services, and lack of consent often resulted in a complaint, mediation or due process hearing.

The receipt of parent consent for the individual evaluation begins the formal timeline for the conduct and completion of the full and individual evaluation. Public Law 108–446 has made an important distinction between parental consent for the initial evaluation and parental consent for services.

A school can but is not required to override a lack of consent for the initial evaluation.

> **The bill clarifies the rights of parents with regard to initial evaluation and services for their child. Parents have the right to refuse both the initial evaluation of their child as well as the provision of services to their child under the Act. However because of the obligation to conduct child find, the law permits, but does not require, the local educational agency to override parental consent for the limited purpose of the initial evaluation.**

As was the case with IDEA–1997, IDEA–2004 permits schools to challenge the lack of consent for evaluation, but this is not the expectation, especially in view of the right of parents as per IDEA–2004 to refuse services. There is no point in conducting an individual evaluation if parents have indicated that all services resulting from such an evaluation will be refused.

> **The Committee does not expect local educational agencies, as part of the required child find process, to feel compelled to override the refusal of a parent to consent to an evaluation if the parent has clearly indicated their refusal to consent to an initial evaluation and their intention to refuse the offer of special education and related services for their child.**

Prior to IDEA–2004 schools were required to provide a child with an appropriate education, and if parents refused services, a due process hearing often resulted. The IDEA–2004 empowers parents by stipulating that lack of consent for services cannot be overridden. An interesting corollary to this is an expectation by the Committee that a school is not expected to override lack of consent for an initial evaluation if a parent clearly indicates that services will be refused.

> **The bill strengthens parental consent provisions to ensure that parental consent is required, and cannot be overridden, when it comes to the provision of services. This provision clarifies the distinction between the ini-**

**tial evaluation and the provision of services.
This bill further clarifies that local educational agencies are not required to draft an IEP
for a child if the parent has refused their consent for services.**[99]

As was the case with earlier versions of IDEA, parents continue to play a role in the determination of educational need and whether their child has a disability. However, the new IDEA guidelines for parental consent exemplify the importance of parent participation and input in the IEP process. For IDEA–1997 parental consent focused on the individual evaluation so that consent was required before an evaluation was conducted. If a parent refused consent, the school *could* pursue mediation or due process (i.e., impartial hearing).[100] Public Law 108–446 enhances the responsibility for parents (and limits the responsibility of schools) so that "if the parent of such child does not provide consent for services . . . the local educational agency shall not provide special education and related services to the child through the procedures described in section 615."[101] When parent consent is lacking for either an individual evaluation or services, the school is not required to convene an IEP meeting, develop an IEP or to otherwise provide a free appropriate public education.[102]

IEP Timeframe

Parental consent provides the initial benchmark for the timeframe from evaluation to IEP implementation. The purpose of instituting a timeframe is to evaluate children in a "timely manner"[103] and to discourage schools from delaying evaluations, and the development and implementation of the IEP. Reasons for delay can range from parent-school disagreements, other factors (e.g., foreign born children), and availability of services.

The regulations for IDEA–1990 contained a requirement that an IEP must be developed within 30 days after the determination of eligibility is made, and that implementation of the IEP as soon as possible following the IEP meeting.[104] This provision was expanded by the regulations for IDEA 1997 to further require that "within a reasonable period" of time, following parent consent, the initial evaluation is conducted.[105]

State guidelines often vary from Federal guidelines and a typical State timeline might be 45 days from consent for evaluation to IEP development, or sixty days from consent to services.[106] Idaho has a 60-day rule (calendar days) from the time parent consent for the evaluation is received to the implementation of the IEP.[107] Idaho also has a 30-calendar day rule from the determination of eligibility to the development of the IEP and LRE placement. In Massachusetts the school district is required to arrange for the individual evaluation by a multidisciplinary team within 30 school days,[108] and "within forty-five (45) school working days after receipt of the parent's written consent to an initial evaluation" the school district must conduct an evaluation, convene a Team meeting, determine the need for special education, and develop an IEP if required.[109] The timeline between receipt for parental consent and the IEP meeting in California is 50 days.[110] In Vermont an Evaluation and Planning Team is "convened without undue delay," an evaluation shall be completed and the report issued within 60 calendar days from either,[111] and an IEP is developed within thirty days of a determination that the child is eligible for special education."[112] In New York State "for a student not previously identified as having a disability, the committee on special education shall provide a recommendation to the board of education which shall arrange for the appropriate special education programs and services to be provided to the student with a disability within 60 school days of the receipt of consent to evaluate."[113] New Hampshire requires that the evaluation process and written summary report "be completed within 45 days after receipt of parental permission for testing or, if testing is ordered by a court, the process shall be completed within the time limit set by the court,"[114] and that the IEP must be developed within 30 days following the determination that a child has a disability under IDEA. In Illinois the IEP meeting must "be completed within 60 school days after the date of referral or the date of the parent's application for admittance of the child to the public school," and "the IEP meeting shall be conducted within 30 days after the child is determined eligible.[115]

Evaluation Timeframe

PROCEDURES–Such initial evaluation shall consist of procedures–(i) to determine whether a child is a child with a disability (as defined in section 602) within 60 days of receiving parental consent for the evaluation, or, if the State establishes a timeframe within which the evaluation must be conducted, within such timeframe; and (ii) to determine the educational needs of such child.

–P.L. 108–446, 614(a)(1)(C)

The IEP and Misclassification

Before a child receives services under IDEA the evaluation team must determine that the child has a **disability** and the child must **need** specially designed instruction. Eligibility for services is important to ensure that children who are disabled receive services and are thus able to participate in the regular classroom and curriculum to the maximum extent appropriate; to ensure that children who are not disabled are not restricted from participating in the regular classroom and curriculum; and to provide focus for the development of the IEP. When a learning problem is the result of environmental, cultural, economic disadvantage, or lack of instruction, a child is not disabled under IDEA. For a child to have a specific learning disability the child must have a problem in one of seven specifically defined areas, and the problem must not be the result of limited English proficiency or lack of instruction.

The House version of Public Law 108–446 (HR 1350) included a *Sense of Congress* that underscores the problem with IDEA disability determination and how this determination can invalidate the development of a meaningful IEP. That is, an IEP cannot meet the needs that result from the child's disability if the child does not have a disability, or the disability is misunderstood by the evaluation team. Congress observed that certain of the categories of disability are vague and not scientifically determined which results in children not having disabilities identified as disabled. Definitions such as emotional disturbance are often "vague and ambiguous" and children so identified could be better served "through classroom-based approaches involving positive discipline and classroom management." Also, many children receive substandard instruction in "fundamental skills like reading" and then inappropriately identified as having a disability. The result of this is that the educational future of these children is harmed as well as "reducing the resources available to serve children with disabilities."[116] An early version of IDEA–2004 required that "the Comptroller General of the United States shall conduct a review of variation among States in definitions, and evaluation processes, relating to the provision of services" under IDEA for "the terms 'emotional disturbance,' 'other health impairments,' and 'specific learning disability'; and the degree to which these definitions and evaluation processes conform to scientific, peer-reviewed research."[117] Although the vagueness of IDEA disability definitions is undeniable, many evaluation teams confound the problem by ignoring existing criteria for the various definitions. This is certainly so with respect to specific learning disabilities, other health impairments, emotional disturbance and mental retardation.

The development of an IEP for a child who is not disabled draws resources away from children who are actually disabled. An erroneous determination of a disability can result in segregative practice and discrimination. For example, the rate of mental retardation among blacks is 20.6 while the rate among whites is 7.5. Many authorities, including Congress, have long recognized that this "disproportionality," and States are required to have "policies and procedures designed to prevent the overidentification or disproportionate representation by race and ethnicity of children as children with disabilities.[118] For lower achieving students, many are overidentified and misidentified as disabled because of vague and ambiguous criteria.

For children who are overidentified and do not have disabilities under IDEA, services are provided that are not needed, children are segregated from the mainstream (as is the case for many black children mistakenly identified as mentally retarded), services that might otherwise be provided for children with actual disabilities are misdirected, and school resources that should deal with real learning needs are not utilized. For children who are not identified as disabled but who do have a disability under IDEA the lack of services might deprive these children of an appropriate education and, if so, the misclassification is discriminatory. What all this means is that the determination of eligibility is extremely important, and this determination provides the foundation for an effective IEP. The development of an IEP that is the result of a misinterpretation of disability or vague disability guidelines, not only serves to limit services to children who have actual disabilities, but can be segregative in the sense that these children receive services that prevent inclusion in the regular education mainstream. An IEP founded on misclassification is little more than an outline for the misuse of services and school resources, and amounts to *de jure* segregation or segregation sanction by law.

Four areas that are especially prone to misclassification include specific learning disabilities, emotional disturbance, mental retardation and other health impairments. These disability categories account for approximately 74 percent of all children who are receiving services under IDEA–2004. Every evaluation team member should be aware of each of these categories, the criteria for determining a disability for each, and how each category can result in misclassification. Inclusion in regular classes must begin with a strong commitment to providing services to children who are actually disabled under IDEA. Providing IDEA services to children whose poor academic achievement is the result of environment, cultural factors, or poor instruction is inappropriate, often discriminatory, and a misuse of local, State and Federal resources.

If a child has a disability under IDEA but does not need special education, the child does not have an IDEA disability. If the child has a hearing, visual, or physical impairment but has no need for special education and is able to participate satisfactorily with nondisabled children, classroom accommodations or modifications might be necessary but these would be provided under Section 504 of the Rehabilitation Act of 1973 and not IDEA–2004. On the other hand, if a child needs special education (i.e., specially designed instruction) because of lack of prior instruction or limited English proficiency but does not have a disability under IDEA–2004 or Section 504, services must be provided using other school resources such as remedial and Title I programs.[119]

If the IEP Team has only a vague notion of a child's disability and actual needs, there is a small likelihood that that an IEP will be developed to address individual needs. The problem is exacerbated when the already vague criteria are simply ignored. As much as IDEA and the regulations have emphasized the importance of using a variety of criteria to determine a disability, many children are determined to be disabled (especially mentally retarded) because of one score (viz., an IQ score) while at the same time disregarding causative cultural and environmental factors. For IEPs based on such faulty decision making, no amount of care regarding process or content will overcome the fact the IEP is inherently flawed and, even worse, will probably serve as a license to exclude children from the general curriculum.

Decreasing Overrepresentation

Possible the lengthiest (or endured) litigation in the United States was begun in 1963 with *Lee v. Macon* to force desegregation of Macon County Public Schools.[120] The Lee v. Macon Consent degree addressed "the overrepresentation of African-American students in the mental retardation and emotional disturbance special education classifications and the under representation of African-American students in the specific learning disabilities and gifted and talented special education classifications." In order to eliminate racial disparities in special education, and to end this ongoing litigation the State Superintendent of Education and other state officials must "vigorously and fully comply with the proposed consent decree so that, at the end of the period outlined in the decree, there will be no doubt whatsoever that the court should terminate this litigation as to special education and finally return to the Alabama State Board of Education the full responsibility of the operation of the state school system as to this issue. Alabama State Department of Education agreed to implement the following to resolve the issue of racial disparities."[121]

1. Awareness training: "Design awareness training with the Southeastern Equity Center to address the overrepresentation of minorities in the areas of mental retardation and emotional disturbance and underrepresentation in the area of specific learning disabilities."

2. Prereferral teams: "Expand existing training on the Building Based Student Support Teams (BBSST) model that will be phased in throughout the state no later than four years after entering his Consent Decree. Following this phase-in period, the BBSST will be mandatory. The structure for building-based professionals . . . includes encouraging parent participation, to use their individual professional strengths in solving instructional and behavioral issues of students."

3. Prereferral interventions: "A prereferral form that documents severity and duration of academic and behavior problems, interventions attempted with results achieved, and a functional assessment of the classroom environment has been included in the BBSST model. Training on conducting a functional assessment will be included in the expanded training on the BBSST model. The DOE commits to employing additional staff (two educational specialists) to provide statewide BBSST training and requiring administrators and teachers to attend a training session "and to change a sentence in the *Alabama Administrative Code,* 290-8-9-.1(2), so that it will read: 'Before a child is referred for special education services, prereferral intervention strategies must be implemented in the general education program and monitored by BBSST or other designated staff for at least six weeks or longer, depending on the problem, and be determined unsuccessful.'"

4. Referral Process: "The Alabama Administrative Code will be revised to require that a referral form will be completed each and every time a student is suspected of having a disability," and "the severity/duration of the problem with subsequent prereferral interventions, including functional assessment of the classroom environment, must now be a part of the information collected and attached to the referral form."

5. Teacher training: "Provide training to all teachers and evaluators on the revised special education student referral form, referral process, and on conducting a functional assessment of the classroom environment. The functional assessment includes a structured observation that examines teacher and student behaviors and how these behaviors influence academic performance."

6. Evaluation: "The DOE will revise the *Code's* eligibility criteria for mental retardation to quantify the criteria for adaptive behavior. The revised Code will state that: 'Total score on an adaptive behavior scale or two sub-composite scores on an adaptive behavior scale must be at least two standard deviations below the mean (usually 70 or below). A school version of an adaptive behavior assessment is required. When the parent participates in the meeting to discuss the referral, a home version of the adaptive behavior assessment will be completed by the parent/guardian at that time. The parent/guardian may complete the scale or it may be administered by conducting a parental interview. If the parent/guardian does not attend the meeting to discuss the referral, a home version of the adaptive behavior assessment will be sent home. The local education agency must make at least two attempts, and document such attempts, to have the parent or guardian complete the home version of the adaptive behavior assessment within the 90-day referral process. However, the absence of a home version of the adaptive behavior assessment may not delay the 90-day referral to placement process. The school version and the home version of the adaptive behavior assessment must be conducted using the same test instrument.'"

7. Evaluating criteria: "The DOE will revise the *Code's* eligibility criteria for mental retardation to require that 'information must be gathered as part of the referral to determine if there are any environmental, cultural, language or economic differences that might mask a student's true abilities and thereby affect the student's performance in the areas evaluated. Tests and evaluative materials selected and administered should be sensitive to environmental, cultural, linguistic, and economic differences.'"

Preventing Misclassification

The following are several guidelines for evaluation and IEP Teams for reducing misclassifications:

- **Discuss classification procedures and problems prior to actual IEP Team determinations.**

- **Ensure parent participation.**

- **Provide parents, when appropriate and certainly when requested, with an advocate (other individuals who have knowledge or special expertise) who is aware of IDEA classifications and corresponding problems.**

- **Carefully consider IDEA criteria for each disability.**

- **Determine that the disability affects educational performance.**

- **Remember that a child is not eligible for IDEA services because of lack of scientifically based instruction in reading, lack of instruction in mathematics; or limited English proficiency.**

- **Eligibility for services requires both an IDEA disability and the need for special education.**

- **As is the case for specific learning disabilities environmental, cultural, and economic disadvantage mitigate against eligibility for services.**

Chapter 5

IEP TEAMS AND MEETINGS

. . . promoting collaboration between IEP Team members.[122]

Three teams are involved in the determination of an IDEA disability and IEP: **Prereferral team**, **Evaluation team**, and **IEP Team**. Informal teams may or may not be defined in State code or regulations but these teams are important for reducing overreferrals and using school-wide resources to address individual needs. If a child is referred for an individual evaluation, information provided by the prereferral team is invaluable for providing direction for the evaluation team and data and information that can be used in the development of the IEP by the IEP team.

Prereferral Teams

Individualizing a child's educational program does not always require special education and certainly not an IEP. Schools have the responsibility to accommodate every child's needs within the regular classroom to the maximum extent possible. Prior to a formal referral for an individual evaluation the regular classroom teacher should consult with parents, other teachers and school personnel who might have specific input concerning a child's academic performance and other needs. Often schools have teams for specific grades comprised of regular classroom teachers, teacher assistants or aides, related service personnel (viz., speech and language specialist), and possible special education personnel such as a consultant teacher. If a teacher is isolated from school resources and other teachers, when there is no sense of cooperation among school personnel, the only logical recourse for many regular classroom teachers is a referral for an individual evaluation. In the absence of a collaborative educational environment, special education becomes the primary, if not only solution for many academic and classroom problems.

There is no statutory requirement for a prereferral team but best practice has shown that referral to a Child Study Team (CST) is often acknowledgement that a child is exhibiting needs that require special consideration (but not necessarily special education). Usually the CST is a quasi-formal group of school personnel, but the CST can also be empowered by the State to have very specific functions or even as another name for the IEP Team (as is the case in New Jersey described below). The CST, Child Assistance Team (CAT), Instructional Support Team (IST), Student Study Team (SST) might include the regular classroom teacher, a special educator, and a school representative. Unlike IEP teams where parent participation is mandated by IDEA, parent participation in CST meetings is not required or necessary but parent input should be sought for children having serious classroom needs. Even if the CST does not include a parent member, best practice indicates that parents should be invited to a CST meeting that might impact a child's performance or results in referral for evaluation. Child Study Team meetings are often held when needed or on a weekly basis. Even if there is no pressing academic problem, informal teams should meet periodically to discuss concerns, strategies, and interventions.

The CST can serve as a screening mechanism to ensure that all school-wide resources have been used to accommodate a child in the regular classroom prior to. If a referral for special education is deemed necessary, prereferral interventions and strategies help identify levels of academic achievement, the effectiveness of accommodations and interventions for allowing classroom participation, and for identifying specific skills and behaviors that require an individualized education program. Many states are beginning to recognize that prereferral interventions are important for reducing over-referrals and misclassifications, while providing excellent data and information for an individual evaluation if necessary and the development of an IEP. Idaho requires that "if the student shows adequate progress with prereferral activities–modifications and interventions–a referral to consider a special education evaluation may be unnecessary. However, if modifications and interventions must be provided on an ongoing basis, or if the student shows limited or no progress, a referral to consider a special education evaluation is warranted."[123] North Dakota uses a Building Level Support Team (BLST) as a support group for the regular classroom teacher. A summary of BLST prereferral interventions must accompany the request for an individual evaluation. If a child is referred without documenting the need for an individual evaluation, "the evaluation planning process should address modifications and adaptations to the various natural and learning environments" (p. 5).[124]

Alabama requires that "before a child is referred for special education services, prereferral intervention strategies must be implemented in the general education program and monitored by the Building Based Student

Support Team (BBSST) or other designated staff for at least six weeks or longer, depending on the problem and be determined unsuccessful." Prior to a referral "a prereferral form and functional assessment of the classroom environment" is completed."[125] This rule is waived for children with certain disabilities (e.g., severe learning problems) and children referred by the parents. To ensure that referrals are necessary Idaho requires "a team process to problem solve and plan general education interventions" and before a child is referred "modifications and instructional interventions must be attempted in the general education classroom."[126] In New York a referral submitted by persons other than the parent, student or a judicial officer requires the following:

1. **State the reasons for the referral and include any test results, records or reports upon which the referral is based that may be in the possession of the person submitting the referral;**

2. **Describe attempts to remediate the student's performance prior to referral, including any supplementary aids or support services provided for this purpose, or state the reasons why no such attempts were made; and**

3. **Describe the extent of parental contact or involvement prior to the referral.**[127]

Evaluation Teams

The conduct of the individual evaluation is critical for the development of a meaningful IEP. The evaluation team must focus on the task of integrating prereferral information, data and interventions with the collection of addition data to determine eligibility, the need for special education, and the development of the IEP. The determination of eligibility identifies important disability-related needs, the affect of a child's disability on educational performance, and other needs to enable regular classroom and curriculum participation to the maximum extent appropriate. The individual evaluation is often coordinated or managed by the director of special education, chairperson of the IEP Team, or a person with expertise relating to assessment and special education.

The evaluation team is comprised of **qualified individuals and the parents**. For the evaluation team and the IEP team parents are important members who *should* play a meaningful role in the determination of the child's disability, the need for special education and the contents of the IEP.

Report language: "Conferees intend the evaluation process for determining eligibility of a child under this Act to be a comprehensive
process that determines whether the child has a disability, and as a
result of that disability, whether the child has a need for special education and related services. As part of the evaluation process, conferees expect the multi-disciplinary evaluation team to address the educational needs of the child in order to fully inform the decisions made
by the IEP Team when developing the educational components of the
child's IEP. Conferees expect the IEP Team to independently review
any determinations made by the evaluation team, and that the IEP
Team will utilize the information gathered during the evaluation to
appropriately inform the development of the IEP for the child."
                      –Conference report, H.R. 1350, Nov. 17, 2004, p. H9945

The regulations for IDEA–1990 describe the evaluation team as a **multidisciplinary team**[128] (or MDT), while IDEA–1997 required an evaluation
conducted by a team of qualified professionals and the parent of the child.viii
In Illinois the IEP Team reviews existing data and information and determines the specific assessments needed to evaluate a child.[129] North Dakota
uses a multidisciplinary team for developing an assessment plan, analyzing
data and preparing an Integrated Written Assessment Report,[131] and Arizona
relies on a Multidisciplinary Evaluation Team (MET) process.[132] In Ohio an
evaluation team (including the parents) an evaluation team chairperson
develop and evaluation plan, conduct a "multifactored evaluation" determine eligibility and generate an Evaluation Team Report.[133] In Montana the
CST is equivalent to an evaluation team and is responsible for determining
"whether the student has a disability which adversely affects the student's
involvement and progress in the general curriculum and because of that disability needs special education," preparing a written report, and identifying
a disability category.[134]

Wisconsin has a well-defined group that comprises the M-team (or
Multidisciplinary evaluation **team**) comprised of at least one teacher or other
specialist licensed in or with knowledge of the suspected disability, two members who have expertise in assessment and programming, an employee of
the district residence, "for every referral concerning a minority child, a member of that minority is allowed input into the M-team's decision-making
process," an occupational or physical therapist if these are suspected areas of
need, "if the child is suspected of having a learning disability, at least one
team member other than the child's regular teacher observes the child's academic performance in the regular classroom setting. In the case of a child of

less than school age or out of school, a team member observes the child in an environment appropriate for a child of that age."[135]

Parents must receive a copy of the evaluation report before the IEP meeting if the determination for disability is made at the IEP meeting. Presenting the parents with a copy of an evaluation report at the meeting, without an opportunity to consider what is often technical data, is unfair and intimidating.

Consolidated Teams

The IEP Team can serve the simultaneous role of evaluation team and the team responsible for developing an implementing the IEP (e.g., New York State's Committee on Special education or CSE[136]). However, the responsibilities of a consolidated evaluation/IEP Team must have clearly differentiated responsibilities. The determination of eligibility is made before the IEP is developed, and the IEP is developed before services are provided. If "the team of qualified professionals and the parent of the child" is separate from the IEP Team, the placement decision should be made after the IEP Team meeting and not when eligibility is determined.

Consolidated IEP meetings are primarily a matter of preparedness and efficiency. Necessary evaluation materials should be available prior to the IEP meeting, parents should understand the evaluation report and be aware of possible options, and all team members who can make a meaningful contribution should be present. Parents must have an opportunity "to examine all records relating to such child and to participate in meetings with respect to the identification, evaluation, and educational placement of the child, and the provision of a free appropriate public education to such child, and to obtain as appropriate an independent educational evaluation of the child."[137] If the determination of eligibility and the IEP meeting is consolidated, the meeting must be conducted in two parts. First, the determination of eligibility is made by a "team of qualified professionals and the parent."[138] In making this determination, "a copy of the evaluation report and the documentation of determination of eligibility shall be given to the parent."[139]

Efficiency and streamlining should not be used to deprive parents of the right to understand the evaluation and provide input to the development of the IEP. Best practice indicates the appropriateness of separate evaluation team meetings (at least when disability is determined) and meetings to develop the IEP. However, the regulations for IDEA–1997 (Appendix A, Question #19) provide some guidance concerning consolidated meetings. The meetings for determining disability and the development of the IEP may be held at the same if the school follows the necessary regulations "including appropriate notification to the parents." Upon completion of the individual evaluation a determination is "made by a team of qualified professionals and the parent" to determine whether the child has a disability under IDEA. If the determination and IEP meeting are held at the same time, the parent should have the evaluation report well before the meeting. To give a fairly detailed individual report immediately prior to the development of the IEP is disingenuous and hardly offers the parent an opportunity to understand the evaluation report, or to consider needs that should be incorporated in the IEP. In addition, if the eligibility determination and IEP meeting are held at the same time, parents should be aware of this dual purpose and that they are participants in both eligibility determination and IEP development.[140]

In New Jersey the CST is similar to the dual function Committee on Special Education (CSE) in New York which is responsible for determining disability and developing the IEP. In New Jersey the CST is responsible for the "identification, evaluation, determination of eligibility, development and review of the individualized education program, and placement."[141] Child Study Team members are employees of a district board of education and include a school psychologist, a learning disabilities teacher-consultant and a school social worker. An IEP case manager from the CST is assigned to each child to coordinate the individual evaluation. Often the special education teacher serves as the *de facto* case manager, but assigning an identifiable case manager eliminates any ambiguity as to who is responsible for the implementation of the IEP, coordinating "the development, monitoring and evaluation of the effectiveness of the IEP" and facilitating "communication between home and school" and coordinating "the annual review and reevaluation process."[142] New Jersey recognizes that the IEP case manager requires a time commitment so that "an apportioned amount of time for case management responsibilities; and be responsible for transition planning."

Multidisciplinary Teams

The regulations for IDEA–1990 required that an individual "evaluation is made by a multidisciplinary team or a group of persons, including at least one teacher or other specialist with knowledge in the area of the suspected disability."[143] This was modified somewhat by IDEA–1990 in that the determination of eligibility was changed to "a group of qualified professionals and the parent."[144] The IDEA–2004 now uses the term multidisciplinary team in reference to the development of an individualized family service plan,[145] but variations of the multidisciplinary team are used by individual states in reference to evaluation and/or IEP development. In Wisconsin the M-team is responsible for the individual evaluation, and the IEP is developed at an IEP meeting in which the M-team report is considered.[146] Ohio refers to a more elaborate Intervention-based Multifactored Evaluation (IBMFE), and New York relies on a Committee on Special Education (CSE) to oversee the evaluation and IEP development.

Evaluation Team Decisions

The determination as to whether a child has a disability under IDEA is made "by a team of qualified professionals and the parent of the child.[147] Following the evaluation and determination of eligibility "a copy of the evaluation report and the documentation of determination of eligibility" is given to the parent.[148] The evaluation report provides the basis for many of the IEP team's decisions relating to goals, services, and accommodations. If the IEP Team ignores the evaluation report or the evaluation report is an uninterpretable collection of subtest scores, there is no basis for developing an IEP that will realistically address a child's needs. The evaluation report must identify a child's disability, and "the content of the child's individualized education program, including information related to enabling the child to be involved in and progress in the general curriculum."[149] The evaluation report is not merely a collection of scores but must also contain information relating to specific levels of performance and/or behaviors that will provide the beginning benchmarks for measurable annual goals, appropriate modifications, and other supports that a child might need to become involved in the general curriculum.

The individual evaluation provides data and information relating to medical (e.g., asthma, diabetes), sensory (e.g., auditory or visual impairment), and specific disability-related needs (e.g., mental retardation, autism, emotional disturbance and specific learning disabilities). The disability should be sufficiently identified so that the IEP Team is able to focus on specific behaviors and needs. For example, a child does not simply have a specific learning disability but a specific learning disability in writing, oral expression, etc.

The adverse affect on academic performance documented in the evaluation report should include information to guide the IEP Team, the effect on specific classroom performance as indicated by grades, classroom tests and quizzes, observational data, classroom behavior, and samples of classroom work. The evaluation report should cite accommodations that have been used in the classroom and on tests, and accommodations and interventions that have been successful or are likely to be successful. The first consideration of test accommodations should not be at the IEP meeting, but should be based on information gathered during the prereferral and individual evaluation. The IEP Team should know "if an assessment is not conducted under standard conditions, a description of the extent to which it varied from standard conditions (e.g., the qualifications of the person administering the test, or the method of test administration) must be included in the evaluation report."[150] Performance on State and district-wide tests should be included as important academic benchmarks. To this end the individual evaluation is not a summary of a psychological evaluation, or a report of IQ test subtest scores, but a wide-range evaluation encompassing all areas relating to the disability, classroom performance, and ability to participate in the general curriculum. A primary function of the IEP Team is to create measurable annual goals. This cannot be accomplished without specific areas of classroom and/or academic performance included in the evaluation report. Specific levels of performance must address significant needs, and must be measured and not just measurable.

Specific Learning Disability Report

Often IEPs for children identified as having a specific learning disability are deficient because basic information required during the individual evaluation is neither collected nor considered. For children identified as having a specific learning disability a report is required that documents the following:

Specific Learning Disability Report Contents

- **Whether the child has a specific learning disability;**

- **The basis for making the determination;**

- **The relevant behavior noted during the observation of the child;**

- **The relationship of that behavior to the child's academic functioning;**

- **The educationally relevant medical findings, if any;**

- **Whether there is a severe discrepancy between achievement and ability that is not correctable without special education and related services;**

- **The effects of environmental, cultural, or economic disadvantage.**[151]

The report supporting the determination of a specific learning disability must also include a written certification by each team member "whether the report reflects his or her conclusion. If it does not reflect his or her conclusion, the team member must submit a separate statement presenting his or her conclusions."[152]

IEP Teams

Of the many changes in IDEA–2004, considerable attention has been given to reducing IEP Team meeting inefficiency. This task is accomplished by streamlining the IEP document (discussed in detail below), and increasing the ability of the IEP Team to address individual needs. The IEP Team participants include the following:

1. **The parents of a child with a disability;**

2. **Not less than one regular education teacher of such child (if the child is, or may be, participating in the regular education environment);**

3. **Not less than 1 special education teacher, or where appropriate, not less than 1 special education provider of such child;**

4. **A representative of the local educational agency who—**

   a. **is qualified to provide, or supervise the provision of, specially designed instruction to meet the unique needs of children with disabilities;**
   b. **is knowledgeable about the general education curriculum; and**
   c. **is knowledgeable about the availability of resources of the local educational agency;**

5. **An individual who can interpret the instructional implications evaluation results, who may be a member of the team described in clauses (ii) through (vi);**

6. **At the discretion of the parent or the agency, other individuals who have knowledge or special expertise regarding the child, including related services personnel as appropriate; and**

7. Whenever appropriate, the child with a disability.[153]

The IEP is a partnership between the school and parents and if parents have little or no input in the development of the IEP that partnership is one-sided. Input from parents should be sought concerning strengths and weaknesses that might assist in the development of the IEP, specific areas of performance that should be addressed, possible measurable annual goals, accommodations that have been effective, and other strategies to assist the in regular classroom participation. Finally, parents must participate in the selection of appropriate services and, after the substantive areas of the IEP have been development, the least restrictive environment for providing those services. The methodology for meeting a child's needs can be controversial. For a child who is deaf, oral language development, American Sign Language (ASL), and total communication are all possibilities. Likewise, the Braille needs of a child with a visual impairment, the instructional needs of a child with ADHD, and the augmentative communication needs of a cerebral palsy can be met in a variety of ways. In all instances parents should understand the issues, the reason for services and accommodations, and the reason for selecting the service or methodology.

If a parent is not able to understand any or all of the IEP content, the school should provide assistance to interpret or help parents understand exactly what is being considered by the IEP Team. The obligation of schools to help parents participate in the IEP process is consistent with the schools obligation to include parents in meetings and placement decisions by various means (e.g., video conferencing),[154] and the prior written notice requirement which states that schools must provide "sources for parents to contact to obtain assistance in understanding the provisions" of the notice.[155]

Parents

Parents might be reluctant to contribute to the IEP meeting; parents might be intimidated by the IEP Team process; or parents might be completely satisfied that all the services that have been or are currently being considered. Nonetheless, the chairperson must go beyond a general query to all Team members if "anyone has anything to add" and actively seek input from the parents. Public Law 108–446 includes an IDEA–1997 regulation that requires detailed record-keeping and "if neither parent can attend, the public agency shall use other methods to ensure parent participation, including individual or conference telephone calls."[156] This need to "ensure participation" goes beyond attendance at IEP meetings. Because the IEP is an agreement between the school and parents, schools must be flexible in order to encourage parent participation.

IEP Parent Participation

The IEP process can be improved and problems of disproportionate placements addressed by enhancing the role of parents in the IEP decision-making process. Section 672(b) of IDEA–2004 provides for parent and community training and information centers to assist parents to better understand the nature of their children's disabilities and their educational, developmental, and transitional needs; to communicate effectively and work collaboratively with personnel responsible for providing special education, early intervention, transition services, and related services; and to participate in decision making processes and the development of individualized education programs under part B and individualized family service plans.

Parent participation is not only necessary at IEP meetings but the IEP document can encourage participation via parent counseling and training to "(i) assisting parents in understanding the special needs of their child; (ii) providing parents with information about child development; and (iii) helping parents to acquire the necessary skills that will allow them to support the implementation of their child's IEP or IFSP."[157] In addition, the 1997 regulations provide an entire section (34 CFR 300.345) relating to Parent Participation which includes the requirement that "the public agency shall take whatever action is necessary to ensure that the parent understands the proceedings at the IEP meeting, including arranging for an interpreter for parents with deafness or whose native language is other than English."[158]

The need for parent participation in IEP meetings described above indicates that IEPs develop without the parents, or IEPs developed by a single individual (including computer generated IEPs) are inherently flawed. The inappropriateness of an IEP developed apart from the IEP Team is not mitigated by a caviler statement that the IEP is only a *recommendation* that is easily changed. If practice shows one person is the IEP author, then the IEP brought to the IEP meeting is usually a *fait accompli* and not in compliance with either the spirit or the letter of IDEA.

Teachers

Because every child receiving services under IDEA requires specially designed instruction, the special education teacher providing this specially designed instruction should attend the meeting. In addition, a person knowledgeable about school resources for addressing all of a child's educational and disability-related needs. The Senate report for IDEA–2004 expressed a concern that "many IEP meetings are conducted without a member present who is knowledgeable about the availability of resources of the local educational agency. Many disagreements arising at IEP meetings could be resolved if this person were in attendance instead of intervening only after a parent has filed a complaint."

Because of the importance of regular classroom participation, "a regular education teacher of the child, as a member of the IEP Team shall, to the extent appropriate, participate in the development of the IEP of the child, including the determination of appropriate positive behavioral interventions and supports, and other strategies, and the determination of supplementary aids and services, program modifications, and support for school personnel consistent."[159]

IEP Meeting Attendance

The regular classroom teacher participating in the IEP meeting is the regular classroom teacher of the child being considered by the IEP Team and not a representative of all classroom teachers. Participation of a regular classroom teacher is required if the child is or might be participating in regular education classes. If a child has more than one regular education teacher, the school determines which teacher or teachers will attend the meeting. New to IDEA–2004 is the provision that "a member of the IEP Team shall not be required to attend an IEP meeting, in whole or in part, if the parent of a child with a disability and the local educational agency agree that the attendance of such member is not necessary because the member's area of the curriculum or related services is not being modified or discussed in the meeting."[160] For classroom teachers, this should not be used to excuse the regular classroom teacher from attending IEP meetings when participation in the classroom is being considered.

For the regular classroom teacher, IEP meeting attendance is not required (involving issues not related to the child's participation in the regular education environment). Likewise, multiple regular education teachers for a child are not required to attend IEP meetings unless, of course, several teachers have unique input relating to regular classroom participation. However, the regular education teacher is expected to "participate in the development of the IEP of the child, including the determination of appropriate positive behavioral interventions and supports, and other strategies and the determination of supplementary aids and services, program modifications, and support for school personnel."[161] There might be occasions when several regular classroom teachers attend the meeting, although this is not a requirement, but the focus should be to obtain substantive input from the regular classroom teacher rather than having one or more a classroom teachers attend an

IEP meeting for the sake of attending the meeting.

The mandatory attendance of the entire IEP Team has also been modified so that the parents and school may jointly excuse a member of the IEP Team from attending if that member's participation is not necessary. If a member is excused who does have input for the IEP, there is an expectation that the IEP Team will obtain any possible input prior to the meeting.[162] Public Law 108–446 has attempted to reduce the number of IEP meetings by encouraging consolidated IEP meetings,[163] using alternatives to traditional IEP meetings such as video conferences and conference calls, "and by allowing multi-year IEPs when appropriate.[164]

> **ATTENDANCE NOT NECESSARY.–A member of the IEP Team shall not be required to attend an IEP meeting, in whole or in part, if the parent of a child with a disability and the local educational agency agree that the attendance of such member is not necessary because the member's area of the curriculum or related services is not being modified or discussed in the meeting.**
>
> **–P.L. 108–446, 614(d)(1)(C)**

Other Individuals

There are occasions when the augmentation of the IEP Team with "other individuals who have knowledge or special expertise regarding the child" is essential. The House report for IDEA–2004 reasoned that "the IEP Team should consider including a bilingual or English as a second language teacher in IEP Team meetings as appropriate, based on the individual child's needs to address the special language development needs of a limited English proficient child with disabilities."[165] For schools (and States) where race is a significant factor in the determination of a disability (especially mental retardation and emotional disturbance) school districts should adopt a policy whereby parents are provided with IEP meeting advocates to ensure that disability and need, rather than race, are the determining factors in all decisions relating to evaluation and IEPs. Of particular importance in the "other individual" category are related service providers (e.g., social worker, occupational therapist) who might offer essential services, be involved in developing measurable annual goals and provide important accommodations. In addition, a representative from placements where services are provided should attend all IEP meetings, and this includes private school placements if services are provided to eligible private school children. As noted in the regulations for IDEA–1997 "if a child with a disability is enrolled in a religious or other private school and receives services IDEA services the local educational agency is required to "initiate and conduct meetings to develop, review, and revise a services plan for the child . . . and ensure that a representative of the religious or other private school attends each meeting. If the representative cannot attend, the LEA shall use other methods to ensure participation by the private school, including individual or conference telephone calls."[166]

The Child

In most situations the child does not attend the IEP meeting although IEP Teams can have photographs, videotape or recording of the child to personalize the development of the IEP. When transition services are being considered, the student should attend the meeting if at all possible. The purpose of this requirement is to ensure that the student's preferences and interests are considered. If the student is not able to attend the IEP meeting, and if transition services are being considered, the school must take steps to ensure that the preferences and interests of the student are considered.

IEP Team In-service

Often school resources are not used effectively, and supports not provided, because of a misunderstanding of the process for referring for an individual evaluation, the individual evaluation, the determination of a disability and the need for special education or the IEP and placement process. Overreferrals, misclassification and the failure to use available school resources can be addressed by in-service training for all teachers and school personnel. Essential areas that should be considered by in-service training include the referral process, the purpose of special education, IDEA disabilities, and eligibility. The IEP Team must be aware of the full range of program options such as physical education, art, consumer education, homemaking, industrial arts, music, vocational education, and nonacademic services (e.g., clubs, athletics, etc.). The IEP Team should be aware of commonly used accommodations, modifications and assistive technology devices and services: preferential seating, practice tests/materials, magnification and amplification aids, large print, Braille materials, extended time, test/curriculum breaks, curriculum/test modifications, shortened assignments, assignment notebooks.

IEP Meetings

IEP Consensus

The IEP is a collaborative effort between the school and parents, where each is an equal partner, and IEP decisions are by consensus rather than a vote.[167] The interpretation of "consensus" for IDEA–1997 was always weighted in favor of the school because the ultimate responsibility for providing an appropriate education was that of the school. Public Law 108–446 has balanced the role of school and parents by giving parents a very strong voice in the decision-making process concerning services. Parents are now able to preclude the provision of services, and curtail the responsibility of a school to provide FAPE by not consenting to a service or services. For IDEA–2004 if the parent does not provide consent for services, or fails to respond to a request to provide the consent, "the local educational agency shall not provide special education and related services to the child through the procedures described in section 615." Most importantly, "in any case for which there is an absence of consent for an initial evaluation . . . or for which there is an absence of consent for services . . . the local educational agency shall not be required to convene an IEP meeting or develop an IEP . . . and the local educational agency shall not be considered to be in violation of any requirement under this part (including the requirement to make available a free appropriate public education to the child) with respect to the lack of an initial evaluation of the child, an IEP meeting with respect to the child, or the development of an IEP."[168]

As noted by the Nebraska Department of Education "when one considers the magnitude of the charge given to the IEP Team, it is vital to consider the processes the team uses to make decisions. To assist the IEP Team in making decisions, best practice is to use **consensus** building.[169] In a similar vain the Iowa Department of Education recommends that "the IEP team should work toward consensus. It is not appropriate to make IEP decisions based upon a majority vote. Every effort should be made to resolve difference through voluntary mediation (pre-appeal or Resolution Facilitator process)."[170] In spite of the acknowledged need for consensus, prior to IDEA–2004 the primary source of decision-making power was the IEP chairperson. For example, in Vermont "if the team cannot reach consensus, the LEA Representative on behalf of the school district shall determine the contents of the IEP pursuant to Rule 2363.8 and shall notify the parents of their rights to seek mediation, file an administrative complaint or request a due process hearing.[171]

Part of the rationale for empowering parents to unilaterally reject services for special education concerns the ultimate responsibility for a child's education. The law is now clear: parents have this responsibility. The IEP Team should collaborate, compromise, and otherwise work as a Team. The regulations for IDEA–1997 indicated that "the IEP team should work toward consensus, but the public agency has ultimate responsibility to ensure that the IEP includes the services that the child needs in order to receive FAPE. It is not appropriate to make IEP decisions based upon a majority 'vote.'"[172] The ultimate responsibility for services has been assigned to parents in IDEA–2004, but the goal to achieve consensus without mediation or a due process hearing is an important ingredient for an effective partnership between school and parents.

Non-team IEPs

The practice of assigning the actual writing of the IEP to one person (e.g., the special education teacher) and then presenting the completed IEP to meetings has several variations, all of which are contrary to IDEA. The regulations for IDEA–1997 were abundantly clear in stating that the IEP could not be completed prior to the IEP meeting:

> **Agency staff may come to an IEP meeting prepared with evaluation findings and proposed recommendations regarding IEP content, but the agency must make it clear to the parents at the outset of the meeting that the services proposed by the agency are only recommendations for review and discussion with the parents. Parents have the right to bring questions, concerns, and recommendations to an IEP meeting as part of a full discussion, of the child's needs and the services to be provided to meet those needs before the IEP is finalized. Public agencies must ensure that, if agency personnel bring drafts of some or all of the IEP content to the IEP meeting, there is a full discussion with the child's parents, before the child's IEP is finalized, regarding drafted content and the child's needs and the services to be provided to meet those needs.**

In spite of the admonition that IEPs are not to be completed prior to the IEP meeting this is exactly what is often done. Variations of this practice include the development of IEP proposals that are in every way the final IEP, secondary IEPs, and computerized IEPs. Secondary IEPs and IEP proposals are favored by nonregular classroom placements, separate schools and residential placements. An IEP proposal is an IEP developed apart from the IEP Team and then presented to the Team as a "proposal." If the "proposal" is developed apart from the school (e.g., in a separate placement), when the IEP Team considers the plan actual concerns or IEP modifications are difficult if not impossible to make. A secondary IEP means that the local educational agency develops the primary IEP, but the separate placement develops a secondary IEP (that may or may not be related to the primary IEP) which is used to provide services. In both instances the service providers may never attend the actual IEP meeting but will develop the *de facto* IEP in the separate location and, more likely than not, completely ignore the IDEA-mandated IEP, or IEP developed by the local educational agency.

Amending an IEP

During the course of the year a child's IEP might need to be amended. This can occur when a needed accommodation or service has not been included in the IEP, or measurable annual goals are either too easy, too difficult or do not address all of the child's needs. Public Law 108–446 allows the parent and the local educational agency to "agree not to convene an IEP meeting for the purposes of making . . . changes, and instead may develop a written document to amend or modify the child's current IEP."[173] The school and parents can also agree not to reconvene the entire IEP Team in order to amend the IEP in writing after the annual IEP meeting and that "upon request, a parent shall be provided with a revised copy of the IEP with the amendments incorporated."[174] This is an important change because the efficient updating or amending of measurable annual goals, and services or accommodations during the school year will better meet a child's changing educational needs. Of course, this process of expediting the IEP process should not be used to by-pass the IEP meeting process so that a factually new IEP is developed by modification and amendment, including placement, without IEP Team consideration.

Streamlining IEP Meetings

Just as the IEP document has been streamlined, IDEA–2004 has also focused on implementing procedures to streamline the IEP meeting and to reduce the bureaucratic requirements concerning meetings and meeting participation. Many of the changes relating to flexible IEP Team meetings and member participation, alternative meetings and amending IEPs relate to the bureaucracy that has come to personify the IEP process. The need to reduce the burdensome bureaucracy in favor of a modicum of common sense to better meet individual needs is the underlying rationale for these changes: "The committee heard testimony that, often, common sense changes developed by a teacher and a parent to improve the child's educational services cannot be implemented without reconvening an IEP meeting, which requires coordinating the schedules of a number of people, and often forces a parent to take off work to attend. Such a process is so burdensome that often changes that could benefit a student are simply not made."[175]

The ways in which an IEP meeting can be streamlined and made more efficient include the following:

- **Collaboration among IEP members**

- **Planning IEP agendas**

- **Understanding rules and regulations**

- **Developing effective communication techniques**

- **Conflict resolution among IEP members**

- **Developing IEP meeting outcomes**

- **Encouraging participation**

- **IEP problem solving**

- **Learning to reach consensus**

Section 504 Teams

There is not a requirement for a Section 504 Team but only a stipulation in the 504 regulations to provide FAPE and that the "implementation of an individualized education program developed in accordance with the Education of the Handicapped Act is one means of meeting the standard established" by Section 504.[176] A Section 504 accommodation or service can be provided by the local educational agency (LEA), or the IEP Team can assume the role of the Section 504 Team. For a child who has been declassified or who has a disability but no longer needs special education, a group or individual other than the IEP Team can develop the plan or statement of accommodations/services that a child requires. Good practice suggests that the IEP Team is best situated to determine whether IDEA services are appropriate, and if not, how services and accommodations required by Section 504 should be implemented.

Under IDEA an IEP Team is not allowed to provide only a related service or a specific accommodation without special education. If a child does not need special education under IDEA the IEP team must provide or recommend needed Section 504 services or accommodations, or make a referral to school personnel responsible for meeting a child's Section 504 needs. Because a child can have a disability under Section 504 and not IDEA, Section 504 is not restricted regarding permissible services that are or are not permitted. If a child has been declassified or misclassified, the child has a disability under Section 504 and is entitled to any and all special education services, related services or accommodations resulting from the former, perceived or disability of record. Unlike IDEA which first requires the need for special education services, Section 504 can be used to provide special education, a specific related service (without special education) or one or more accommodations. In Vermont if a child has a disability but is not eligible for special education, the Evaluation and Planning Team (EPT) recommends "accommodations, as needed, in such areas as assessment procedures, curriculum, material or programmatic adaptations, behavior management interventions, and supplemental aids and services " and "if the EPT determines that the student has a disability, but is not eligible for special education, it may proceed to operate as a Section 504 team to determine whether the child is eligible for reasonable accommodations under Section 504."[177]

To this end the IEP Team must be flexible concerning how a Section 504 accommodation or service is documented. For children requiring no services or a specific accommodation (e.g., large print, reader, aide, etc.), a simple IEP statement might be sufficient. Section 504 services can be provided by means of a Section 504 plan, a statement of accommodations and services or even an IEP.

Chapter 6

IEP INDIVIDUAL EVALUATION

. . . use a variety of assessment tools and strategies that may assist
in determining whether the child is a child with a disability; and
the content of the child's individualized educaiton program.[178]

The full and individual evaluation provides the planning substance for a child's IEP. This will not be achieved if the individual evaluation does not take into consideration areas that will provide the basis for a child's IEP. This occurs when the evaluation does not identify specific educational needs, classroom performance, beginning levels of performance, and effective services and accommodations. Most important, the IEP Team must consider the individual evaluation when the IEP is developed.

The individual evaluation is conducted by using "a variety of assessment tools and strategies to gather relevant functional, developmental, and academic information, including information provided by the parent" to "assess the relative contribution of cognitive and behavioral factors, in addition to physical or developmental factors, " and to determine whether a child has a disability and "the content of the child's individualized education program, including information related to enabling the child to be involved in and progress in the general education curriculum, or, for preschool children, to participate in appropriate activities."[179]

Essential Evaluation Requirements

1) Test and evaluation materials are not discriminatory, and "are provided and administered, to the extent practicable, in the language and form most likely to yield accurate information on what the child knows and can do academically, developmentally, and functionally;

2) The child is assessed in all areas of suspected disability;

3) Assessment tools and strategies that provide relevant information that directly assists persons in determining the educational needs of the child are provided.

–P.L. 108–446, 614(b)(3)(A)–(C)

The problem of gathering relevant information during the evaluation process is especially important for children with behavioral and emotional needs. A child is classified as having an emotional disturbance or Attention Deficit Hyperactivity Disorder (which is included under Other Health Impairments), but specific data relating to the behavior is not collected. This usually occurs when the purpose of the determination of disability is not to enable classroom participation, but to remove the child from the regular classroom.

No Child Left Behind (NCLB)

The No Child Left Behind act has placed a renewed emphasis on the participation of children with disabilities in State and district-wide assessments. The NCLB act requires "challenging academic content standards, coherent and rigorous content that encourage advanced skills and are aligned with the State's academic content standards."[180] The change from a statement of Present Level of Performance to a statement of Present Levels of Academic Achievement in IDEA–2004 also highlights the importance of regular curriculum progress in the evaluation of children with disabilities. This statement requires "how the child's disability affects the child's involvement and progress in the general education curriculum; for preschool children, as appropriate, how the disability affects the child's participation in appropriate activities; and for children with disabilities who take alternate assessments aligned to alternate achievement standards, a description of benchmarks or short-term objectives."[181] For the vast majority of children (99%) the evaluation of student progress in the general curriculum can be determined by assessments used with all children with no accommodations, assessments used with accommodations that do not change what assessments are intended to measure, and for a small percentage of children (1%) alternate assessments can be used to measure proficiency.

The 1% NCLB Alternate Assessment Cap

An alternate achievement standard is an expectation of performance that differs in complexity from a grade-level achievement standard. These regulations clarify that a State is permitted to use alternate achievement standards to evaluate the performance of students with the most significant cognitive disabilities and to give equal weight to proficient and advanced performance based on the alternate standards in calculating school, district, and State AYP, provided that the number of proficient and advanced scores based on the alternate achievement standards does not exceed 1.0 percent of all students in the grades tested at the State or LEA level. The Secretary may approve an exception for a specified period of time for a State (or a State may approve a higher limit for an LEA.).
      –Federal Register, 12/9/2003, Rules and Regulations, p. 68699.

For children with disabilities assessment has an added importance because of the NCLB emphasis on providing all children opportunities to meet State standards. The following are several NCLB guidelines concerning school-wide reform strategies that are particularly pertinent for children with disabilities that are readily apparent in IDEA–2004:[182]

NCLB School-wide Reform Strategies

1. **provide opportunities for all children to meet the State's proficient and advanced levels of student academic achievement;**

2. **use effective methods and instructional strategies that are based on scientifically based research that strengthen the core academic program in the school;**

3. **increase the amount and quality of learning time, such as providing an extended school year and before- and after-school and summer programs and opportunities, and help provide an enriched and accelerated curriculum;**

4. **include strategies for meeting the educational needs of historically underserved populations;**

5. include strategies to address the needs of all children in the school, but particularly the needs of low-achieving children and those at risk of not meeting the State student academic achievement standards.

Evaluation and the IEP

There must be a close link between the individual evaluation and the development of the IEP. The individual evaluation provides the framework for the IEP, the basis for creating measurable annual goals, and for providing appropriate services and reasonable accommodations. The data gathered during the evaluation helps discern classroom and curriculum needs and includes (1) existing evaluation data on the child, (2) evaluations and information provided by the parents of the child; (3) current classroom-based, local, or State assessments, and classroom-based observations; (4) observations by teachers and related services providers,[183] and (5) "whether any additions or modifications to the special education and related services are needed to enable the child to meet the measurable annual goals set out in the individualized education program of the child and to participate, as appropriate, in the general education curriculum."[184] The data collected during the individual evaluation is then used to determine whether a child has a disability, "the present levels of academic achievement and related developmental needs of the child;" and "whether the child needs special education and related services, or in the case of a reevaluation of a child, whether the child continues to need special education and related services."[185]

CONDUCT OF EVALUATION

In conducting the evaluation, the local educational agency shall–(A) use a variety of assessment tools and strategies to gather relevant functional, developmental, and academic information, including information provided by the parent, that may assist in determining-

(i) whether the child is a child with a disability; and

(ii) the content of the child's individualized education program, including information related to enabling the child to be involved in and progress in the general curriculum, or for preschool children, to participate in appropriate activities.

–P.L. 108–446, 614(b)(2)

The Determination of Disability

The purpose of determining whether a child has a disability is not (although it often is) to label a child for the sake of labeling a child. The purpose is to determine children with disabilities receive services and, just as important, children who do not have disabilities are not segregated from the regular classroom or regular curriculum. In addition, the determination of a disability provides focus for determining IEP needs and all other areas affected by the child's disability.

Each of the over five million children receiving services under IDEA must have an IEP in effect at the beginning of each school year.[186] As shown in Table 6.1, the *high-incident disabilities* (viz., specific learning disabilities, speech and language impairments, mental retardation, emotional disturbance and other health impairments) account for 92.8 percent of children receiving services under IDEA while the remaining eight categories and developmental delay account for 7.2 percent of children receiving services under IDEA. Because of the inclusion of Attention deficit Disorder or Attention Deficit Hyperactivity Disorder ("a heightened alertness to environmental stimuli, that results in limited alertness with respect to the educational environment"[187]) the Other Health Impairments category has increased from 1.3 percent in 1990–91 to 5.05 percent in 2000–01.

Table 6-1.
Number and Percent of Children Ages 6–21 Served Under IDEA in 2000–2001[188]

Disability	2009–2001	
	N	%
Specific Learning Disability	2,879,445	49.96
Speech or Language Impairment	1,092,105	18.95
Mental Retardation	611,878	10.61
Emotional Disturbance	472,932	8.20
Other Health Impairments	291,474	5.05
Multiple Disabilities	121,954	2.11
Autism	78,717	1.36
Orthopedic Impairment	73,011	1.26
Deafness and Hearing Impairment	70,662	1.22
Developmental Delay	28,683	0.49
Visual Impairment	25,927	0.44
Traumatic Brain Injury	14,829	0.25
Deaf-blindness	1,318	0.02
All	5,762,935	100%

For the IEP Team the determination of disability provides direction for IEP development and the identification of academic, disability and other needs. A child identified as having a specific learning disability does not simply have a learning disability but a specific learning disability in oral expression, listening comprehension, written expression, basic reading skill, etc. Likewise, a child who identified as having an other health impairment could have leukemia, a chronic health problem, attention deficit hyperactivity disorder, or countless other specific disabilities that can affect academic performance.

Every category of disability is comprised of specific disabilities that are manifested by very unique needs. Within the Other Health Impairment category one child with ADHD might be unable to focus on tasks, while another child with ADHD needs might lack organizational skills. As much as possible the evaluation report should explicate the disability and disability-related needs as much as possible so that the IEP Team is able to use this information as a guide for the development of an appropriate IEP.

The evaluation team must determine the existence of a disability but this task is confounded by definitions that are used to label rather than explicate need. Not only are there many subcategories for each disability, and many ways for each of these subcatgeories to be manifested, but several IDEA disability definitions are vague and inconsistently interpreted by States. An initial version of IDEA went as far as requiring "the Comptroller General of the United States shall conduct a review of variation among States in definitions, and evaluation processes, relating to the provision of services" under IDEA for "the terms 'emotional disturbance,' 'other health impairments,' and 'specific learning disability'; and the degree to which these definitions and evaluation processes conform to scientific, peer-reviewed research."[189] Although the vagueness of IDEA disability definitions is undeniable, many evaluation teams exacerbate the problem by ignoring existing criteria and guidelines for the various definitions. This is certainly so with respect to specific learning disabilities, other health impairments, emotional disturbance and mental retardation.

Specific Learning Disabilities

A specific learning disability is defined as a "disorder in one or more of the basic psychological processes involved in understanding or in using language, spoken or written, which disorder may manifest itself in the imperfect ability to listen, think, speak, read, write, spell, or do mathematical calculations" and is a "learning problem that is primarily the result of visual, hearing, or motor disabilities, of mental retardation, of emotional disturbance, or of environmental, cultural, or economic disadvantage."[190]

Public Law 108–446 has changed the requirement that a specific learning disability is the result of a discrepancy between intellectual ability and academic achievement so that "when determining whether a child has a specific learning disability as defined in section 602, a local educational agency shall not be required to take into consideration whether a child has a severe discrepancy between achievement and intellectual ability in oral expression, listening comprehension, written expression, basic reading skill, reading comprehension, mathematical calculation, or mathematical reasoning."

A determination that a child has a specific learning disability without designating a "specific" area of need is contrary to IDEA and is a misuse of the term. In addition, the stipulation that a child does not have a disability because of "environmental, cultural, or economic disadvantage" should be closely examined by the evaluation team. This will not only reduce the number of children misidentified as having specific learning disabilities, but will result in a better utilization of special education and school-wide services. Furthermore, IDEA–2004 now allows a local educational agency to use "a process that determines if the child responds to scientific, research-based intervention as a part of the evaluation procedures"[191] when determining the existence of a specific learning disability.

This new interpretation of a specific learning disability (research-based intervention) can present a problem for the IEP Team. As noted by the Council for Exceptional Children (CEC) "the use of scientific research-based intervention cannot determine whether a child is or is not learning disabled! Instead, students who do not display meaningful gains and who appear to be unresponsive to intervention are candidates for referral for special education evaluation," and that "the concept of discrepancy or intra-individual differences remains a hallmark of specific learning disabilities."[192] Although the CEC cautionary note concerning the specific learning disability criteria is on point, identification of successful interventions can assist the IEP Team in the selection of goals, accommodations and services.

Specific learning disabilities has become a catch-all for providing IDEA services for children who do not fit other categories, including children with general educational needs (not specific), children who have not received adequate instruction, and children who have very definite educational needs because of socioeconomic, cultural, and environmental factors. All this has resulted in specific learning disabilities becoming a behemoth category accounting for approximately 50 percent of all children receiving IDEA services in spite of criteria that should limit this number.[193]

SPECIAL RULE FOR ELIGIBILITY DETERMINATION

In making a determination of eligibility . . . a child shall not be determined to be a child with a disability if the determinant factor for such determination is—
(A) lack of scientifically based instruction in reading;
(B) lack of instruction in mathematics; or
(C) limited English proficiency.[194]

Mental Retardation

The term mental retardation is used to indicate means "significantly subaverage general intellectual functioning, existing concurrently with deficits in adaptive behavior and manifested during the developmental period that adversely affects a child's educational performance."[195] The problem is not identifying children with severe cognitive deficits, and certainly an IQ test is not necessary to identify a child with limited language, self-help skills, etc., but to use an IQ score as the primary if not sole criterion[196] for determining mental retardation in spite of the prohibition against this practice.[197]

In the determination of mental retardation most States use the two standard deviation criterion as the cutoff for mental retardation. In South Carolina a child's IQ score for mild retardation must be between 48 and 70, moderate retardation between 25 and 48, and severe retardation less than 25.[198] Vermont is one of the few states that has apparently abandoned the term mental retardation in favor of "a learning impairment or delay in learning" which is defined as "of sufficient magnitude to cause a student's performance to fall at or below -1.5 standard deviations from the mean of a test of intellectual ability and the student shall show concurrent deficits in adaptive behavior."[199]

Emotional Disturbance

Emotional disturbance is defined as "a condition exhibiting one or more of the following characteristics over a long period of time and to a marked degree that adversely affects a child's educational performance:"

1. **An inability to learn that cannot be explained by intellectual, sensory, or health factors.**

2. **An inability to build or maintain satisfactory interpersonal relationships with peers and teachers.**

3. **Inappropriate types of behavior or feelings under normal circumstances.**

4. **A general pervasive mood of unhappiness or depression.**

5. **A tendency to develop physical symptoms or fears associated with personal or school problems.**

The term *emotional disturbance* includes schizophrenia, but "the term does not apply to children who are socially maladjusted, unless it is determined that they have an emotional disturbance."[200] Not all children who exhibit behavior problems in the classroom are emotionally disturbed, and the determination of emotional disturbance is not to exclude the child from the regular classroom but to meet all the child's needs that are caused by the emotional disturbance. As shown in Table 6.2 many children identified as emotionally disturbed receive services outside of the regular classroom. Congress has suggested indicated that "African-American children are identified as having mental retardation and emotional disturbance at rates greater than their white counterparts."[201] Whether the cause is vague definition, lack of behavioral specificity, a desire to exclude a child from the regular classroom, or segregative intent, the IEP Team must be diligent when providing supplementary aids and services, and when considering the placement of children identified as having emotional disturbance.

Table 6-2.
Percent of Children Served Outside of the Regular Classroom[202]

Disability	<21%	21–60%	>60%	PUBLIC SEPAR	PRIVATE SEPAR	PUBLIC RESID	PRIVATE RESID	HOME HOSP
Speech-language	87.4	6.7	5.2	0.24	0.16	0.04	0.02	0.05
Visual	49.1	19.5	17.6	4.57	1.12	6.46	0.92	0.64
SLD	45.3	37.8	15.7	0.37	0.31	0.10	0.08	0.18
OHI	44.9	33.2	17.2	0.88	0.74	0.13	0.20	2.67
OI	44.3	21.9	27.7	3.49	0.65	0.13	0.14	1.59
HI	40.3	19.3	24.4	5.39	1.64	8.02	0.56	0.23
TBI	31.0	26.6	31.6	2.55	4.61	0.37	0.88	2.30
ED	25.8	23.4	32.7	7.50	5.50	1.50	1.99	1.51
Autism	20.6	14.4	49.9	7.90	5.39	0.17	1.08	0.45
Deaf-Blind	14.7	10.1	39.6	13.82	3.42	12.21	4.20	1.74
MR	14.0	29.5	50.4	4.06	0.87	0.36	0.24	0.43
MD	11.2	18.7	43.0	15.03	6.77	1.31	1.39	2.49

For the evaluation team the task is to carefully examine whether inappropriate behavior rises to the level of emotional disturbance, and whether many classroom and behavioral problems that do not rise to the level of emotional disturbance could be accommodated through classroom management techniques and using school-wide resources.

For the IEP Team the task is to use the evaluation report to help determine what factors, what behaviors, what "inabilities" (e.g., maintain satisfactory interpersonal relationships) affect classroom participation. For many children identified as having emotional disturbance, the identification of specific needs is secondary to placement. The first consideration is not given to what goals, accommodations and services will enable regular classroom participation, but what placement will enable removal from the regular classroom.

> **According to the Study of Personnel Needs in Special Education, over half of beginning teachers who serve primarily students with emotional disturbance are not fully certified for their positions, and the vast majority of regular education teachers receive little to no training in how to help special needs students with behavioral and emotional problems.**
>
> **–Senate report 108–185, p. 59**

Other Health Impairments

At one time (before IDEA–1997) the term Other Health Impairment (OHI) was reasonably specific but the addition of a single and exceedingly vague phrase has resulted in a steady increase in the use of this term: "having limited strength, vitality or alertness, **including a heightened alertness to environmental stimuli**, that results in limited alertness with respect to the educational environment, that is due to chronic or acute health problems such as asthma, attention deficit disorder or attention deficit hyperactivity disorder, diabetes, epilepsy, a heart condition, hemophilia, lead poisoning, leukemia, nephritis, rheumatic fever, and sickle cell anemia; and adversely affects a child's educational performance."[203]

The key to the appropriate use of the term for OHI, especially for ADD/ADHD, is specificity. This type of specificity is not suggested by the vague definition in IDEA–1997 regulations (heightened alertness to environmental stimuli[204]) but the DSM–IV does cite such specific behaviors as making careless mistakes, inattention, organizational problems, not listening, not finishing tasks, avoiding sustained efforts, not being prepared, easily distracted, and forgetfulness. If a child is identified as having ADD/ADHD, the evaluation team must carefully determine whether the disability (viz., OHI) affects educational performance to the extent that special education is needed. If a child requires only an accommodation for testing and not special education, Section 504 should be used to provide services and not IDEA.

Reducing Misclassification

If special education is provided for children who actually have disabilities and need special education, the IEP Team case load is reduced and greater attention can be devoted to children who actually need IEPs. This is accomplished by prereferral interventions and by excluding children who do not have disabilities from the IEP process. Reducing the number of IEPs is accomplished by a renewed effort by the evaluation team to identify legitimate IDEA disabilities, and identifying educational needs that require specialized instruction. Children should not be identified as having a specific learning disability because of cultural or environmental factors; children should not be identified as mentally retarded because of a single IQ score; and children should not be identified as disabled because of lack of instruction in reading, mathematics, or because of limited English proficiency. The IEP Team can promote appropriate classifications by providing feedback to the evaluation team (if these teams are separate) concerning disability and educational need, by developing a philosophy of regular classroom and general curriculum participation, and by always considering the need for special education and the possibility of declassification on an annual basis.

The Determination of Educational Need

Determining the need for special education requires that the evaluation team and the parents make a determination that the child's disability affects academic performance. If a child has a disability but does not need special education and academic performance is not affected, the child does not have a disability under IDEA. If a child has a disability and needs a specific accommodation, but not specially designed instruction, this specific need should be met using Section 504. A child with a hearing impairment might function quite well in the regular classroom but nonetheless require certain accommodations (e.g., amplification device, classroom seating). If the disability does impact educational performance, the effect must rise to the level that specially designed instruction is required.

The various needs that the IEP Team must consider when developing the IEP include all areas that affect educational performance. This includes disability-related needs, academic achievement and other developmental needs (e.g., when appropriate self-help skills, communication, etc.), accommodations to meet these needs in the classroom, and specific levels of performance (e.g., a reading comprehension of 30% of grade level material, a fourth grade student who is able to identify 20% of primary addition facts). The individual evaluation provides essential information relating to "all areas of the suspected disability, including, if appropriate, health, vision, hearing, social and emotional status, general intelligence, academic performance, communicative status, and motor abilities."[205] If there is one prohibition relating to the evaluation it is the use of a "single procedure, measure, or assessment as the sole criterion for determining whether a child is a child with a disability or determining an appropriate educational program for the child. The individual evaluation might require a physical examination, psychological evaluation, social history, observation, and other assessments related to a child's disability (e.g., functional behavioral assessment, audiological evaluation)."[206] In Vermont the evaluation procedures are quite lengthy and include: physical characteristics (vision, hearing, etc.); social, behavioral, or emotional characteristics; adaptive behavior across settings; relevant life circumstances; speech and language; intellectual or cognitive characteristics; areas of concern in the basic skills areas (oral expression, listening comprehension, etc.); vocational needs and assistive technology needs; and the student's current level of performance in all curriculum areas. In New York the individual evaluation includes a physical examination, an individual psychological evaluation (except when a school psychologist determines that an evaluation is unnecessary), a social history, an observation of the student in the current educational placement, and other appropriate assessments or evaluations (including a functional behavioral assessment when necessary).[207]

The IDEA–2004 requires that a child is assessed to determine "the relative contribution of cognitive and behavioral factors, in addition to physical or developmental factors,"[208] that the child "is assessed in all areas of suspected disability,"[209] and assessment tools and strategies are used "that provide relevant information that directly assists persons in determining the educational needs of the child are provided."[210] These tests must not be discriminatory and tests must be "provided and administered, to the extent practicable, in the language and form most likely to yield accurate information on what the child knows and can do academically, developmentally, and functionally, unless it is not feasible to so provide or administer"[211]

If a child is believed to have a disability or needs special education, some aspect of the child's educational performance must be affected. The evaluation process and the development of the IEP are predicated on the need for specially designed instruction in order to receive an appropriate education. The regular classroom provides an important source for determining educational needs, the effectiveness of interventions, and/or the effectiveness and need for classroom and curriculum accommodations. The evaluation report

should contain not only information relating to standardized test performance, but curriculum-based assessments, reports of classroom behavior and
other information that will explicate why and how a child is not successful in
the classroom.

Standardized Scores

Normative and curriculum-based information are both important for
determining a child's educational needs. Standardized scores provide a general idea of a child's academic performance in relation to other children, and
are important for determining the need for special education. A child might
be having difficulties in the regular classroom but standardized test performance indicates that these needs do not rise to the level that "adversely affects
a child's educational performance." On the other hand, standardized test
performance might not only corroborate classroom performance but provide
insights as to specific areas of academic need.

The evaluation team must not confuse the role of standardized scores and
curriculum-based assessments. Standardized test scores (e.g., stanines, percentile ranks, grade equivalents) provide one basis for understanding academic need, and to what extent a child is achieving in relation to other children. Standardized test scores (especially district-wide achievement scores
and statewide assessments) provide an overall understanding of student
progress, but standardized test scores are not the only source for determining academic performance. The determination of academic needs and other
needs that a student might have should include a consideration of all data,
grades, reports, curriculum-based assessments, rating, teacher observations,
and diagnostic assessments.

Standardized assessments evaluations provide an understanding of **general academic need**; curriculum-based assessments provide an understanding of **specific academic need**. A district-wide assessment might
reveal a deficiency in reading or in mathematics, while a curriculum-based
assessment identifies important classroom skills as well as beginning levels of
performance. The standardized assessment is one method for considering
how a child's disability adversely affects educational performance, while curriculum-based assessments identify meaningful benchmarks for improving
performance (e.g., the child is able to recognize 37 sight words).

The role of the IEP Team is not to reinterpret the individual evaluation but
Team members should be aware of general areas of need as indicated by
standardized test scores. A frequently used rule of thumb is that a standardized score should be approximately **one standard deviation below the
mean** to indicate an area of need. For percentile ranks, this is equivalent to
a score 16 or less, and for IQ-type scores of 85 or less (where the mean is 100

and the standard deviation is 15). In Table 6.3 the term z score simply indicates the number of standard deviations a score is above or below the mean. Obviously, this is not an absolute guide for interpreting standardized scores but, generally speaking, scores in the less than one standard deviation range warrant consideration.

Table 6-3.
Interpreting average and below average standardized scores

Category	Percentile Rank	z score	IQ-Type Score
Average	77	.74	111
	50	0	100
	23	-.74	89
Below Average	22	-.77	89
	16	-.99	85
	4	-1.75	74
Low	3	-1.88	72

Standardized scores are easily misinterpreted, and also easily misused. A seemingly low percentile rank of 30 (see Table 6.3) is actually within the average range. The IEP Team must also be wary of grade equivalents because these scores do not necessarily indicate a child is achieving at a specific grade level but only that a score is similar to score at that grade level. Grade equivalents must always be substantiated by curriculum-based assessments. Also, the standard deviation for grade equivalents increases with increasing age so that a larger grade equivalent disparity is needed as a child advances from grade to grade. For example, a child in the third grade would need a grade equivalent about one year below grade level to indicate a significant discrepancy between grade level and grade level score, while a child in the sixth grade would need a grade level score of about 1.5 below grade level.[212]

In addition to districtwide tests such as the Stanford Achievement Test, many schools use wide-range tests as part of the individual evaluation. A test such as the Wechsler Individual Achievement Test has a series of subtests that corresponds to the various specific learning disabilities categories (e.g., oral expression, written expression) and therefore is useful for establishing a discrepancy between mental ability and achievement. Wide-range tests are useful because these tests assess a wide range of content and are therefore able to provide a normative score for children with a wide-range of abilities (as is the case for children with disabilities). Another attractive feature of a wide-range test is that most can be given in a relatively short period of time. This attribute, however, also results in scores that provide, at best, a very general sense of a child's normative performance and do not result in an explication of specific academic needs or beginning levels of performance that are suitable for use with measurable annual goals.

Rather than using a district-wide test **out-of-level**, wide-range tests allow for the determination of a standardized score for an age range that might vary from kindergarten to twelfth grade. An out-of-level assessment (e.g., using a third-grade assessment with a student in the 8th grade) will never be valid and the results will always be virtually impossible to interpret. A wide-range test provides a type of alternative assessment to district-wide tests but with several provisions. Unlike district-wide assessments most wide-range tests are not re-standardized on a regular basis, norms are often not up-to-date, local norms are generally not available for wide-range tests, and test content is limited.

Alternate Assessments

The wording of the statement of Present Levels of Academic Achievement has caused some confusion because of the section relating to alternate assessments which requires that for children who take alternate assessments that the assessments include benchmarks or short-term objectives. Recall that IDEA–1997 required benchmarks and short-term objectives for measurable annual goals so the difference between benchmarks and short-term objectives as part of the Present Levels of Academic Achievement or as part of measurable annual goals has not been clear. The initial wording of IDEA–2004 (House bill 1350) stipulated "the inclusion of benchmarks or short-term objectives in the child's IEP for students taking alternate assessments aligned to alternate standard."[213] The conference for IDEA–2004 accepted the Senate version which required that "for children with disabilities who take alternate assessments aligned to alternate achievement standards, a description of benchmarks or short-term objectives." The change from "the inclusion of . . ." to "a description of . . ." suggests the use of benchmarks and short-term objectives as an assessment device rather than a method for delineating specific measurable annual goals. In other words, benchmarks and short-term objectives are used to show how an alternate assessment is aligned to state standards, and how a child participates in the general curriculum.

In New York, the Standard (#1) for Mathematics, Science and Technology requires "students will use mathematical analysis, scientific inquiry, and engineering design, as appropriate, to pose questions, seek answers and develop solutions." The alternate level for this student is described as Mathematical Analysis and includes the following performance "use mathematics and symbolism to communicate in mathematics" and "compare and describe quantities. Sample tasks for these performance indicators include "draw 5 apples and 5 oranges and compare the quantitative similarity" and "set the table by counting out sets of 5 dishes, spoons, etc." Although these performance indicators and sample tasks could be short-term objectives included with measurable annual goals, the intent here is to provide an assessment to indicate progress in the general curriculum. This assessment could be used with a variety of children and so are unlike benchmarks and short-term objectives that are specifically designed "to gauge, at intermediate times during the year, how well the child is progressing toward achievement of the annual goal"[214] which was the purpose of benchmarks or short-term objectives for IDEA–1997.

Evaluation: Determining IEP Content

An important function of the individual evaluation is to assist in determining the "content of the child's individualized education program, including information related to enabling the child to be involved in and progress in the general education curriculum or, for preschool children, to participate in appropriate activities."[215] An insurmountable error committed by the evaluation team is not to evaluate or identify specific needs. When this occurs, the IEP is more a confirmation of placement rather than a real planning document to address individual needs.

A mistake made by many IEP teams is to simply ignore the evaluation report. This is unfortunate in that the IEP is not developed out of thin air but is based, in part, on the information contained in the evaluation report. The evaluation report should provide information relating to successful interventions, strategies, and accommodations used in the regular classroom, or accommodations and interventions necessary for a child to receive an appropriate education.

Disability Needs

The disability determined by the evaluation team often indicates important needs for the IEP Team to consider. For a child with health concerns (such as asthma) accommodations might be needed to allow the child to participate in the regular classroom (e.g., air purifier, rest periods). A student with an orthopedic impairment might receive services relating to the use of augmentative communication, instruction in the general curriculum using augmentative communication, and, if necessary, remedial instruction involving the general curriculum using augmentative communication. A child with a disability is entitled to all the services and programs that are available for children who are not disabled. However, just as a child cannot be denied remedial instruction because special education is provided, remedial instruction cannot replace special education unless the service is specifically provided as *specially designed instruction.*

For a child with a hearing or visual impairment, the evaluation of the child's disability provides specific information regarding extent of the disability, the degree of residual hearing or vision, as well as information relating to Braille and communication needs. A child might receive instruction in how to use Braille, instruction in the general curriculum using Braille, or remedial instruction involving the general curriculum.

As shown in Table 6-4 a child's disability often provides the IEP Team with direction concerning disability needs that should be considered. Severe cognitive needs often indicate the need for language, social development and self-help skills; a hearing impairment often indicates the need for amplification or nonverbal communication.

The distinction between disability need and educational need is not always clear, and for many children the disability and academic need are one and the same. This is the case for most children identified as having specific learning disabilities. If a child has specific disability in reading comprehension, reading comprehension is both the source of the disability and the primary academic need. For a child with a specific learning disability in written expression, the disability (written expression) and educational need (written expression) are one and the same. For low-incidence disabilities such as visual and hearing impairments, specific health impairments (Other Health Impairments) and traumatic brain injury, the effect of the disability on academic performance is relatively straightforward. However, for disabilities such as emotional disturbance and mental retardation, the cause/effect relationship between academic performance and disability is far from clear. A child's determined disability never completely explicates academic performance, and an important responsibility of the evaluation team and the IEP Team is to identify academic needs that result from the disability. For the evaluation team the responsibility is to collect data and information that can be used by the IEP Team to develop appropriate IEP content; for the IEP Team the task is to use the data and information provided by the evaluation team to develop a coherent and reasonably calculated plan to provide an appropriate education.

Not only can disability and academic need be one and the same, there are occasions when a determination cannot be made whether the disability caus-

Table 6-4.
Disability and Disability-related Needs

Disability	Possible Need
Specific Learning Disability	Reading comprehension, Writing
Speech or Language Impairment	Receptive language, Expressive language, Voice, Articulation
Mental Retardation	Functional and self-help skills
Emotional Disturbance	Classroom behavior, Social, Interpersonal needs
Other Health Impairments	Medication, ADHD needs, Hospital
Multiple Disabilities	Extensive special education needs
Autism	Language and social needs
Orthopedic Impairment	Assistive technology, Health needs, Accommodations
Deafness and Hearing Impairment	Communication
Developmental Delay (ages 3–9)	A delay in physical development, cognitive development, communication development, social or emotional development, or adaptive development
Visual Impairment	Braille visual correction, mobility training
Traumatic Brain Injury	Functional and psychosocial needs
Deaf-blindness	Extensive communication needs

es the academic problem or the academic problem results in behavior that is interpreted as a disability (e.g., emotional disturbance). For a child having behavior problems, whether the primary need is behavior or academic performance, and whether poor academic performance causes the behavior problem or vice versa, is often not clear. In this situation the IEP Team must first address the disability as determined by the evaluation Team (e.g., emotional disturbance, ADHD) and then consider all other areas affected by the disability (viz., academic and specific classroom needs).

Specific Academic Needs

Information must be gathered relating to specific academic needs that affect participation in the general curriculum. Observational reports, checklists, classroom teacher input, grades, tests, quizzes, standardized scores, State competency tests, reports from specialists, observations from aides, input from related service providers, etc. are all used to determine what is needed for successful classroom participation. Areas that might affect classroom performance include (but are not limited to) specific classroom behaviors that affect academic performance, language needs, reading and writing, study skill, mathematics, and other problems that affect content area performance.

A child might be below average on a standardized test in reading comprehension, but this standardized score does provide the basis for a measurable annual goal to improve performance. To compliment the standardized test score a curriculum-based assessment must be conducted to determine a benchmark for improving reading comprehension. This could be accomplished by reading several grade-level passages to the student, followed by a series of questions, to determine the approximate percent of reading comprehension. A standardized test score might be 1.5 standard deviations below the mean, and a curriculum-based assessment reveals that reading comprehension is approximately 40 percent of grade level material. The standardized test score indicates a general need in reading comprehension, and the measured beginning level of performance provides a frame of reference or benchmark for an annual goal to improve reading comprehension to 70 percent, 80 percent, etc.

There is no correspondence between a standardized score and specific ability level, and the standardized score provides no basis for the beginning level of performance. Reading comprehension at the 85 percent level seems a reasonable goal, but less reasonable if the beginning level of reading comprehension is 0 percent or 80 percent. More importantly, because there is no actual measurement of the initial percent of reading comprehension, there will be no actual measurement of the percent of reading comprehension at the end of the year. At best a teacher might check-off whether the goal was achieved, and then this vague and meaningless goal will be repeated the next year, and the next, and so on.

A disability need is addressed to mitigate the effect on academic performance. A child learns Braille, an amplification device increases ability to develop language skills, or a Functional Intervention Plan is developed to improve a child's behavior that is a result of emotional disturbance. The real task of the IEP Team is to identify what **it** is in the regular classroom that affects performance and requires specially designed instruction.

Specific Levels of Performance

A major problem in the field of assessment is a false dichotomy that has been created between standardized and curriculum-based assessments. Standardized and curriculum-based assessments are not alternative forms of assessment that can be selected based on one's philosophy of quantitative and qualitative methodology, but are inextricably related in the determination of disability, educational need, and appropriate IEP content. If a child is suspected of having a disability, standardized assessments indicate general academic need; the specific areas of academic need are determined by both standardized (e.g., subtests) and nonstandardized input (e.g., informal tests, reports, grades, classroom-based assessments); informal assessments and curriculum-based assessments identify specific levels of performance that can be used to gauge the effectiveness of specially designed instruction as defined in a child's IEP.

The individual evaluation must result in data that establishes beginning levels of performance in areas of need that relate to disability-related needs (e.g., using an augmentative communication device), academic performance, functional needs, and other needs. In many ways the beginning levels of performance, which are the basis for developing annual goals, provide the essence of the IEP by identifying areas of specialized instruction. The evaluation team is not responsible for developing measurable annual goals, but the team should collect data that will identify how participation in the regular classroom and curriculum can be improved.

Identifying IEP Accommodations

Public Law 108–446 requires that tests "are administered by trained and knowledgeable personnel" and "are administered in accordance with any instructions provided by the producer of such assessments."[216] Most assessments provide guidance for permissible accommodations, and virtually every State that administers a State proficiency examination has guidelines for accommodations. The IEP Teams must not make cavalier accommodations from a list of possible accommodations included on an IEP form. The task of the IEP Team is not to select accommodations to validate the IEP process (the IEP team believes that every IEP must have accommodations) but to identify IEP accommodations that are needed and "to thoroughly review and consider which accommodations are appropriate for the individual child to ensure that the assessment is meaningful and valid for the child."[217]

The determination of accommodations by the IEP Team must take into consideration the evaluation report, and what accommodations have been used in the regular classroom, and what accommodations are needed to mitigate the effects of the disability. The evaluation team must provide guidance concerning both classroom accommodations and test accommodations, and this task should not be confined to a checklist of items on the IEP form with no consideration given to data-based needs. The evaluation report should document all accommodations or modifications used to evaluate a child, and accommodations and modifications used in the regular classroom.

"High Expectations" and Alternate Assessments

School personnel should be aware of the emphasis on assessments and high expectations for all students. This has resulted in the recognition that State and district-wide assessments must be available to **"all students"** and that "reasonable adaptations and accommodations for students with disabilities (as defined under section 602(3) of the Individuals with Disabilities Education Act) necessary to measure the academic achievement of such students relative to State academic content and State student academic achievement standards" are made.[218] This emphasis on participation of assessments is reiterated in IDEA so that

> **All children with disabilities are included in all general State and district-wide assessment programs, including assessments described under section 111 of the Elementary and Secondary Education Act of 1965, with appropriate accommodations, where necessary and as indicated in their respective individualized education programs.**

To ensure participation in State or a district-wide assessment, the local educational agency must develop and implement guidelines for permissible accommodations, and guidelines for the participation of children with disabilities in alternate assessments.[219] The importance of including children with disabilities in State and district-wide assessments is emphasized throughout IDEA. If an alternate assessment is selected for a child with a disability, the assessment must be "aligned with the State's challenging academic content standards and challenging student academic achievement standards" and "if the State has adopted alternate academic achievement standards permitted under the regulations promulgated to carry out section 1111(b)(1) of the Elementary and Secondary Education Act of 1965, measure the achievement of children with disabilities against those standards."[220] If a child is not able to participate in a State or district-wide assessment, the IEP Team must state "why the child cannot participate in the regular assessment" and "the appropriate alternate assessment that is selected."[221]

Rigorous Alternate Assessments

The bill also encourages States to develop and implement appropriate and rigorous alternate assessments aligned to State standards for students that cannot participate in the regular assessment. However, since many States have failed to implement this existing provision, the Committee encourages the Secretary to take this failure into consideration for compliance purposes.

–Senate report 108–77, p. 97

Evaluation: Integrated IEP Content

An IEP is integrated when every section is logically related to every other section. The individual evaluation must provide the framework for developing IEPs that are logically consistent and integrated. The individual evaluation, when viewed as a separate entity from the IEP process, is flawed. For every IEP the individual evaluation determined not only the need for an IEP but IEP content and the presentation of that content in the form of a meaningful and logically constructed educational plan. The following are several examples of areas which detract from IEP content integration:

Levels of performance that have no basis in the evaluation report: The evaluation report is replete with standardized scores, but no data or rational is given for behavioral goals (e.g., improve classroom behavior).

Levels of performance not cited in the measurable annual goals: Achievement data might indicate a need relating to mathematics but there is no corresponding goal in the IEP.

Test accommodations that have no basis in fact: The best example of this is the frequent use of extended time without a determination that extended time will actually mitigate the effects of a disability. A child with ADD/ADHD might need smaller blocks of time to complete a test or breaks during a test period rather than the perfunctory extended time accommodation.

Measurable annual goals that have no beginning levels of performance: If a child is expected to read grade-level material with 70 percent comprehension by the end of the school year, the degree the child can read grade level material at the beginning of the year is essential. When this obvious and necessary data is not present, the individual evaluation is either being ignored or the evaluation did not consider all of the child's needs.

Services that are based on a child's disability and not need: States cannot use "a funding mechanism on the basis of the type of setting in which a child is served" that violates the LRE mandate.[222] As explained in the Conference Committee for IDEA the IEP process is to "make placement decisions that are individually determined on the basis of each child's abilities and needs. The new provisions in this section were added to prohibit States from maintaining funding mechanisms that violate appropriate placement decisions, not to require States to change funding mechanisms that support appropriate placements decisions."[223]

Services are provided that fail to consider actual needs: A child might not need a full-time aide to participate in the regular classroom, or a full-time aide might actually distract from meaningful classroom participation. In the case of assistive technology, the IEP Team cannot logically consider AT needs at the IEP meeting when there is no information in the individual evaluation report based on classroom performance as to what assistive technology services or devices are most appropriate.

Chapter 7

STREAMLINING THE IEP

*. . . a streamlined, straightforward, expression of
only the requirements mandated by this Act.*

Too often the IEP process involves what is referred to in *Doe v. Defendant I* as a "laundry list of items" rather than full participation by all parties.[224] The primary problem with a "laundry list of items," especially a very long list, is that every item is considered for every child. The list dictates what is considered by the IEP Team rather than the child's individual needs guiding the selection of appropriate accommodations, services and supports. Because the list is the motivating force rather than individual needs, items not on the list are not considered and items that are completely irrelevant are dutifully noted for each and every child.

The Senate report for IDEA–2004 expressed a "desire for a streamlined, straightforward, expression of only the requirements mandated by this Act."[225] Many IEPs are repetitious, contain information that have little bearing on a child's program of study, lack important information (e.g., beginning levels of performance, real measurable annual goals), and are presented in a sequence that is confusing. Developing a "streamlined and straightforward" IEP is achieved by including relevant IEP content and eliminating information that does not impact the IEP, less "bureaucratic paperwork" (to cite the Senate report 108–185 for IDEA–2004), and the development of a logically sequenced IEP that focuses entirely on the development of a reasonably calculated educational and appropriate plan.

Relevant IEP Content

Relevant IEP content must be considered when developing the IEP form, and when considering IEP content during the IEP Team meeting. A major impediment to the development of an efficient and valid IEP is a form that cites virtually every rule in the regulations or IDEA to show that everything has been considered, every *t* crossed, and every contingency considered by an array of checklists and checkboxes. There is no mystery what Congress envisions as a relevant IEP and what the IEP content should contain. First, the IEP must specify levels of academic achievement and other functional levels of performance, and show how progress toward achieving these goals will be reported to parents. Next, the IEP must include measurable annual goals. This provides the plan for the specially designed instruction; goals represent the basis for providing an appropriate education. Third, the IEP must specify services, related services, transition services, school supports and accommodations that enable goals to be achieved and for a child to participate with nondisabled children. Fourth, the IEP must provide "individual appropriate accommodations" for participating in state and district-wide assessment or alternative assessments. Last, the IEP must show when services begin, and the frequency, location and duration of services. If a child is not able to participate with nondisabled children, this must be explained in the IEP. This is the relevant content that must be included in every IEP. All the information contained in the evaluation report need not be repeated in the IEP; checklists of accommodations are not required; a listing of every regulation pursuant to the development of an IEP need not be detailed; and every possible service need not be cited in the IEP, ranging from Braille to extended school year services, if these services are not relevant to a child's needs.

Individualized education programs should be *individualized*. When an IEP is designed to meet every conceivable contingency, the form cannot be anything but a cluttered and cumbersome planning document. The IEP Team must not develop IEPs with the intent to show that IEPs comply with IDEA, but to develop IEPs that provide an appropriate education. Yes, compliance with IDEA is important but this is not the goal: for the IEP Team the goal is the development of IEPs which comply with the laws and, to use the Supreme Court *Hudson v. Rowley* phrase, to develop reasonably calculated IEPs that will provide educational benefit.

Less "Bureaucratic Paperwork"

One of the reasons for eliminating benchmarks and short-term objectives is the unfortunate fact that benchmarks often did result in "bureaucratic paperwork" rather than meaningful milestones for meeting a child's needs. School personnel constructed elaborate IEPs to show what evaluation procedures *could* be used to measure performance (e.g., tests, work samples, grades, portfolios, oral tests, teacher observation, logs, charts), and when the evaluation *could* be made (e.g., daily, weekly, etc.). The IEP Team often went to great (and creative) lengths to fill IEPs with benchmarks and short-term objectives that did not break down goals into manageable parts and "measurable, intermediate steps (short-term objectives) or major milestones (benchmarks) that will enable parents, students, and educators to monitor progress during the year, and, if appropriate, to revise the IEP consistent with the student's instructional needs."[226] The "statement of measurable annual goals, including benchmarks or short term objectives" was changed in IDEA–2004 to "a statement of measurable annual goals, including academic and functional goals." Although some experts believe that this change detracts from IEP planning, IEP sans benchmarks or short-term objectives may not only reduce the amount of required paperwork but also place more emphasis on the development and actual measurement of measurable annual goals.

The goal was noble but benchmarks and short-term objectives became synonymous with bureaucratic paperwork rather than an effective way for monitoring goals and reporting progress to parents. The lesson to be learned from IEP benchmarks and short-term objectives is that if an emphasis is placed on bureaucratic compliance rather than actual needs, paperwork will result. For measurable annual goals the IEP form often contains a neat little section of columns or boxes showing the type of evaluation that *might* be conducted, who *might* conduct the evaluation, how progress *might* be measured. This is nothing but paperwork, IEP busywork, and work that detracts from providing a child with an appropriate education. Rather completing the IEP forms to provide pro forma goals (which will probably not affect actual educational performance), each measurable goal should begin with a simple statement of the beginning level of performance and a brief description of how the trait, skill, or ability was measured.

The IEP should focus on **appropriate** and not **compliance**. Of course regulations must be followed; of course, the IEP Team and the local educational agency must keep track of timelines, meetings, and procedural tasks; but the IEP should focus on appropriate planning and not compliance for the sake of compliance, and bureaucratic record-keeping. This emphasis on a **show of compliance** rather than **actual compliance** is the primary cause of overly bureaucratic and difficult to follow IEPs. The IEP need not replicate the child's personnel folder and include every data point and even the most tangential personal information. The IEP should have one purpose and that is to focus on the development of an individualized program that will address the child's disability, educational needs affected by that disability, and other needs. The purpose of the IEP is not to create a document that is bureaucratically useful but to develop a reasonably calculated plan that addresses a child's needs. The IEP form should not be burdened with every requirement, consideration and regulation; the IEP should focus on a child's educational plan.

Reduce paperwork by simplifying measurable annual goals; make goals meaningful; eliminate trivial goals. The development of meaningful goals will eliminate much of the excessive paperwork commonly associated with IEPs. For each goal there should be a beginning level of performance, and an expected level of annual performance. This will eliminate many of the vacuous goals, traditionally found in IEPs such as the venerable "to improve classroom behavior by the end of the year" or "to improve reading performance to 80 percent as determined by teacher observation by the end of the year." If the goal is to improve classroom behavior by the end of the year, the measured level of classroom behavior at the beginning of the year must be cited. If the goal is to improve reading performance to 80 percent as determined by teacher observation, the **reading performance to 80 percent as determined by teacher observation** must be determined; that is, reading performance must actually be **measured** at the beginning of the year. If the overused "teacher observation" method is cited, a beginning level of performance requires that the teacher observation be quantified to some degree. At the very least, some type of rating scale would be needed to quantify teacher observation or to translate teacher observation to a percentage.

The IDEA–2004 has made the reduction of paperwork, especially bureaucratic paperwork, a primary goal. To this end, two years after the enactment of IDEA–2004 "the Secretary shall submit an annual report to the Committee on Education and the Workforce of the House of Representatives and the Committee on Health, Education, Labor, and Pensions of the Senate regarding the effectiveness of the program" relating to reducing the paperwork burden on teachers, principals, administrators, and related service providers, and the noninstructional time spent by teachers, and enhancing longer-term educational planning.[227]

IEP Forms

As described in P.L. 94–142 (or IDEA–1975) the IEP statement has become the essence of the IEP process, and the IEP form describes the required content for providing FAPE, equal opportunity, and nondiscriminatory educational participation. Yet, as early as 1980 many IEPs were found not to contain all of the mandated information, or a direct link between areas of need and services (p. 15).[228] More recently Bateman concluded that "most IEPs are useless or slightly worse" and nothing more than "a quasi-legal document to be filed away with the expectation it won't be seen again except, heaven forbid, by a monitor or compliance officer."[229] Contrary to what many think, the task is not to write legally correct IEPs, but to develop IEPs that follow regulations and provide an appropriate education. Simplistic and disingenuous goals might be legally correct, but goals that do not afford a child an appropriate education are not only meaningless but harmful because goals that can provide an appropriate education are not developed.

All too often the IEP form and not IEP content is the paramount concern to the extent that irrelevant and misleading information is readily accepted because the only concern is completing the form and not completing the form to provide an appropriate education. Indeed, one of the greatest needs realized by Congress in amending IDEA is a streamlined IEP that is designed to meet a child's needs and not designed to show line-by-line compliance with IDEA. The impact of the IEP form on services is certainly not new. In 1978, Schipper and Wilson noted that ". . . the form itself is an important factor in eliciting the type and quality of information which is appearing in IEPs. If two lines are provided for 'statement of educational performance,' IEP developers will tend to fill that space only. This follows the old adage, unfortunate in this case, that 'structure dictates function,' rather than the reverse" (p. 12).[230]

In an early evaluation of the P.L. 94–142 process Pyecha (1980) found that many IEP forms restricted the number of goals that could be listed. The implication then, and what is even now often the case, is that form dictates content. Give one page for goals, there will be a single page of goals; give three lines for levels of performance, there will be three lines.[231] In *Doe v. Defendant 1* the court recognized that technical detail (and "deviations" from this detail) exalts "form over substance."[232] This is paperwork: complete emphasis on completing the IEP document and a virtual disregard for actual needs, goals and services.

The IEP Team must use the form decided upon by the local educational agency, but the IEP Team can eliminate a great deal of extraneous information by developing guidelines for including questions about compliance and factors to consider, and appending lengthy reports and information to the IEP. If the local educational agency (or the IEP team) feels that additional information, checklists for ensuring that the IEP is in compliance, or other bureaucratic data or codes is necessary, this should be part of a document entitled IEP Team Guidelines that is provided to every Team member. These guidelines can be tailored to meet LEA (Local Educational Agency), State and Federal requirements, and provide explicit information for the development of the IEP. Many of the factors that the IEP Team must consider should not be listed in the IEP document for the simple reason that this trivializes the IEP if the factor being considered has no bearing on a child's needs. If limited English proficiency (LEP) is not a major concern for a district, there is no need for the IEP Team to routinely check an IEP form box that indicates "in the case of a child with limited English proficiency, consider the language needs of the child as such needs relate to the child's IEP." If a child has LEP needs, and the IEP Team checks "Yes," this does not necessarily mean that LEP needs were really considered. The intent of the requirement to consider special factors by the IEP Team is not to check a box on an IEP document but to actually consider the special factors. For most children (children who do not have LEP needs) there will be no mention of LEP in the document, no item to check that this was considered. On the other hand, the IEP Team Guidelines could contain a checklist, or a list of items that must be considered, or whatever else enables the Team to comply with the regulations.

The IEP form is essential for the meeting a child's needs, but as evidenced by actual practice, the IEP has been transformed from this written statement of appropriate educational services to an officious nitpicking document replete with secondary and tertiary information. The "appropriate educational services" envisioned by the Congress has become secondary to a show compliance by reciting a law, rule, or regulation in the IEP form.

Following the passage of IDEA–1997 many states provided a wealth of IEP-related forms and information. Alabama, Georgia, Massachusetts, New York, North Dakota, Illinois, Ohio, Vermont, Washington State are among the many states that have made IEP forms, guidelines and regulations available to all interested in the development of IEP forms and instructions. What

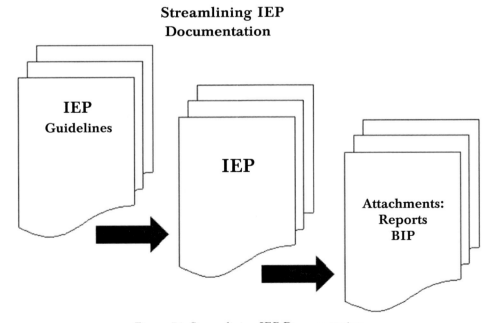

Figure 7.1. Streamlining IEP Documentation

has been learned from the various IEP forms and related documents is that there is not one form that is appropriate for all states, but that each IEP form must reflect each State's interpretation of IDEA and the regulations and the particular needs and demographics of the local educational agency or unit developing the IEP.

Public Law 108–446 has recognized the importance of the IEP form and requires that "not later than the date on which the Secretary publishes final regulations . . . shall publish and disseminate widely to States, local educational agencies, and parent training and information centers" model forms for the Individualized Education Program, the procedural safeguards notice described in section, and the Prior Written Notice.[233]

There are many factors that determine the appearance and length of an IEP form including State regulations, the perceived importance of IEP content, and the needs of the local educational agency. To this end the IDEA–2004 requires the development of model forms for IEPs, IFSPs, procedural safeguards, and prior written notice.[234] The purpose of a model form for each State is described in the House report for IDEA–2004 as follows:

> **The Committee understands that the paperwork forms associated with the Act are greatly varied from State to State and district to district. A standard IEP in one State could be seven pages while in a neighboring State that same child's IEP would be eighteen pages. While some of this variance is related to State or local policy, most of the differences relate to confusion regarding what the Act requires. The bill requires the Secretary to develop model forms for the IEP, prior written notice, and procedural safeguards notice. Each of these model forms will help inform local educational agency efforts as they develop their own forms and will result in decreased paperwork burdens while still ensuring that all of the requirements of the Act are met.[235]**

Technology and Forms

Although computer technology can provide data banks and templates for quickly generating IEPs, many attempts to computer generate IEPs have failed because one individual, and not the IEP Team, is responsible for gen-

erating the IEP, accommodations are often selected without due consideration given to real need; and measurable annual goals are not generated based
on beginning levels of performance. For example, a computerized IEP goal
might be "the ability to recognize 80 sight words" rather than the "increasing sight word recognition from 30/100 to 80/100" or some variant of this
goal to take into account the beginning level of performance.

> **The Committee has heard from hundreds of
> teachers, principals, and parents who have
> concerns that local educational agencies do
> not have the ability to use modern technology
> for record keeping, data collection, and devel-
> oping IEPs. Mr. Gregory J. Lock, principal of
> Oak View Elementary School in Fairfax,
> Virginia, testified to the Subcommittee on
> Education Reform that the Act should 'pro-
> vide for the use of technology to automate the
> written components of the IEP process in
> order to reduce the time spent on the prepa-
> ration of the IEP.'**[236]

One of the objectives of IDEA–2004 is to reduce the paperwork burden
so that teachers can devote more time to instructional activities. Paperwork
reduction is the reason for eliminating benchmarks and short-term objectives, and for adding a "Paperwork Reduction" section to IDEA–2004
(609[a]) that describes a pilot program for States "to identify ways to reduce
paperwork burdens and other administrative duties that are directly associated with the requirements of this title, in order to increase the time and
resources available for instruction and other activities aimed at improving
educational and functional results for children with disabilities."

Paperwork can be reduced, but the quest for efficiency should not be used
to abandon the IEP decision-making process, to make IEP decisions from
easily used pull-down menus, or to use technology to further obfuscate the
determination of real goals and the measurement of goal progress.

The IDEA–2004 envisions technology as another means for reducing
paperwork by supporting "paperwork reduction activities, including expand-
ing the use of technology in the IEP process."[237] Computerized IEPs are
deceptively simple to use and far easier to abuse. A computerized IEP might
be generated by a teacher, administrator or secretary, and the product is a
lengthy list of goals and accommodations that were not decided by the IEP
Team and the parents. The technology of the computerized IEP lends an

aura of authenticity to the IEP, but this type of IEP is even less likely to outline an appropriate educational plan.

IEP Redundancy

The regulations for IDEA–1997 included a proviso that "nothing in this section shall be construed to require the IEP team to include information under one component of a child's IEP that is already contained under another component of the child's IEP." To reduce redundancy IDEA–2004 stipulates that nothing in section 614(d) "shall be construed to require additional information be included in a child's IEP beyond what is explicitly required in this section; and the IEP Team to include information under one component of a child's IEP that is already contained under another component of such IEP."[238] This provision is intended to confine the development of the IEP to what is included in IDEA and to "indicate to States and local educational agencies that these requirements are all that is required for an IEP to comply with this Act. While States and local educational agencies may add their own additional requirements, such requirements should be identified as State- or locally-mandated."[239] If supplementary services are provided as part of a general services category, or as part of special education services, there is no need to include a special supplementary aids and services category. If test accommodations are included under classroom accommodations, there is no need to repeat this information under a different category such as assistive technology.

Overlap can occur between assistive technology and accommodations, between AT services and special education services, and between accommodations and services. Reading content area passages to a student in order to measure academic performance is not only a service, but a service that requires some degree of preparation and training. Providing a relatively straightforward large print accommodation might entail simply obtaining the large print form of a test, but this service will require considerably more time if a test or other classroom material must be changed to large print. For the most part, many accommodations require minimal or little effort on the part of the service provider. Providing extended time requires little more than being available. If extended time requires a different location, the demands on the service provider are increased. Providing a book stand, preferential seating in the classroom, or installing an air purifier places more weight on the accommodation itself rather than the expertise of the service provider.

There is always the possibility of overlap between services and between services and accommodations. Indeed, often a service and accommodation will be one and the same such as when a student requires a scribe for all written tasks. Inherent in each IEP component will be a degree of overlap with other components and this cannot be avoided. Nonetheless, by considering each IEP element in a logical order, and the relationship between these various elements, much can be done to eliminate unnecessary overlap and redundancy.

Multi-Year IEPs

A multi-year IEP is a demonstration project that is potentially useful for reducing paperwork by eliminating unnecessary IEP modifications and IEP meetings by means of long-term comprehensive planning. However, there must be a balance between reducing paperwork and the IEP process and generating an IEP that meets individual needs. A multi-year IEP is an option that can be offered to parents. The multi-year IEP is optional, is not to exceed 3 years, and is "designed to coincide with the natural transition points for the child." Natural transition points would be the transition from preschool o elementary, elementary to middle school, middle school to junior high, high school to post-school transition services.[240]

Natural Transition Points

As used in this paragraph, the term 'natural transition points' means those periods that are close in time to the transition of a child with a disability from preschool to elementary grades, from elementary grades to middle or junior high school grades, from middle or junior high school grades to high school grades, and from high school grades to post-secondary activities, but in no case longer than 3 years.

–P.L. 108–446, 614(d)(5)(C)

The proposal for a multiyear IEP must include measurable annual goals that coincide with natural transition points, a description of the process for the review and revision, an annual review of the child's IEP progress and whether annual goals are being achieved, and a requirement to amend the IEP to enable the child to continue to meet IEP goals.[241]

Two potential problems with multi-year IEPs concern the development and review of **measurable goals** rather than **measurable annual goals**, and the appropriate use of multi-year IEPs. For measurable annual goals, whether measured annually or every three years, a serious problem occurs when goals are carried from one year to the next with no review, consideration or modification.

The use of a multi-year year must be very selective, and must not detract from an annual review of the IEP. The multi-year IEP requires a review at natural transition points, and "in years other than a child's natural transition points, an annual review of the child's IEP to determine the child's current levels of progress and determine whether the annual goals for the child are being achieved, and a requirement to amend the IEP, as appropriate, to enable the child to continue to meet the measurable goals set out in the IEP."[242] For children identified as having specific learning disabilities, emotional or attention-related needs, an annual review, as well as new goals and services, is essential for meeting a child's needs.

Reducing Paperwork

Public Law 108–446 has addressed the problem of excessive paperwork by underscoring the need to focus "resources on teaching and learning while reducing paperwork and requirements that do not assist in improving educational results[243] and to recognize that "teachers, schools, local educational agencies, and States should be relieved of irrelevant and unnecessary paperwork burdens that do not lead to improved educational outcomes."[244]

Excessive paperwork is unnecessary, detracts from instructional activities, and is a burden to teachers. The Senate report suggests that teachers are "leaving the profession out of frustration with the overwhelming and unnecessary **paperwork** burden, contributing to what is becoming a chronic shortage of quality teachers in special education."

> **The Committee has even heard from teachers who have been required to hand write all of their IEPs, and rewrite IEPs from the beginning whenever any changes are made to the IEP. The Act does not contain any such requirements or prohibit the appropriate use of technology. The Committee encourages local educational agencies to use technology appropriately in implementing this Act. To further this goal, the bill allows local educational agencies to use funds under the Act to purchase appropriate technology to improve the administration of the Act and to reduce the paperwork burden on teachers.**

Suggested remedies for this problem include modified IEP requirements, the use of model IEP forms, alternate IEP meeting formats (e.g., teleconferencing, video conferencing), multi-year IEP. Requiring teachers to complete meaningless IEP forms is certainly excessive paperwork, but the problem is not the paperwork but how the paperwork is completed. The sentiment is to reduce paperwork but the Senate committee's "interest in reducing the **paperwork** burden on teachers, schools, local educational agencies, and States" by calling "for an independent review of the **paperwork** requirements under the Act to determine which requirements are responsible for causing the burden" sidesteps the fundamental problem: developing meaningless documents.

How to Reduce Paperwork

Excessive paperwork can be reduced by thoughtfully developing the IEP form, careful consideration of required IEP content, and developing IEPs to provide an appropriate education rather than to show compliance. Oftentimes the IEP Team is so burdened with mindless paperwork that more time is expended developing what appears to meet IEP requirements than the time required to actually develop a meaningful educational plan.

Case in point: measurable annual goals. For the IEP Team developing meaningful measurable annual goals is time-intensive, does require a careful consideration of a child's needs, and does require work . . . paper or otherwise. Measurable annual goals provide the substance of the **plan** in IEP, and "are critical to the strategic planning process used to develop and implement the IEP for each child with a disability."[245] The deletion of benchmarks and short-term objectives might reduce paperwork, but there will be no net time gain if the resulting measurable annual goals sans benchmarks or short-term objectives are fictitious. Indeed, often more time is expended developing pretend goals than the time required to develop real goals. Of course, if the task is reduced to computer generated goals that have even less bearing on real needs, the time requirement is reduced although the amount of paperwork is increased.

The following are several steps that the IEP Team can take to reduce paperwork when developing IEPs:

- **Eliminate an excess of standardized scores,**

- **Eliminate redundant IEP content,**

- **Eliminate bureaucratic codes and compliance content.**

- **Eliminate irrelevant detail,**

- **Eliminate trite goals,**

- **Eliminate pretend goals,**

- **Eliminate goals that are not measurable.**

By focusing on real needs, needed accommodations and goals and services that address real needs, the paperwork quagmire will disappear. Most will fault a document that is completed to meet compliance standards and nothing more; few will fault a real plan to meet a child's needs

A Minority View

Reducing the amount of paperwork associated with IEPs should result in less cluttered and easily developed and implemented IEPs. However, a minority viewpoint in the House report for IDEA–2004 stated that "the paperwork reduction pilot program in H.R. 1350 has absolutely no restrictions on what paperwork could be waived. Under this program as it is currently written, a state could propose to waive IEPs or due process notices as a way of reducing paperwork. Such broad discretion will only harm efforts to improve services for children with disabilities."[246] This cautionary note is well taken in that reducing the amount of burdensome paperwork is laudable, but there are limits . . . and that limit occurs when paperwork is needed to define a child's free and appropriate public education program.

Chapter 8

IEP DEVELOPMENT

O ther than the need to include in each child's IEP all the IEP elements specified in IDEA–2004 , there is no requirement concerning in what order each component is considered by the IEP Team. An IEP requires eight basic components, and these components should be integrated into an IEP document to provide a logical educational program for meeting a child's needs. Although the sequence for considering IEP components is not addressed in IDEA, the order of these components as listed in IDEA–2004 provides a basic format for developing the IEP. For IDEA–1997 these eight components were listed in IDEA (Section 614[d][1][A])

1. **PLEP:** present levels of educational performance.

2. **MAG:** measurable annual goals, including benchmarks or short-term objectives.

3. **Services:** special education, related services, supplementary aids and services, program modifications or supports for school personnel.

4. **Nonparticipation:** an explanation of the extent, if any, to which the child will not participate with nondisabled children.

5. **Modifications:** any individual modifications in the administration of State or district-wide assessments, and a statement of needed alternative assessments.

6. **Timeframe:** projected date for the beginning of services and modifications, and the anticipated frequency, location, and duration of these services and modifications.

7. **Transition:** beginning at age 14 a statement of the transition service needs that focuses on the child's courses of study, and beginning at age 16 a statement of needed transition services including a statement of the interagency responsibilities or any needed linkages. Also, beginning at least one year before the child reaches the age of majority under State law, a statement that the child has been informed of his or her rights.

8. **Progress:** how progress toward the annual goals will be measured and reported to parents.

The regulations for IDEA–1997 subdivided IEP content into two sections (a & b) so that Section 34 CFR 300.347(a) included: 1. PLEP, 2. MAG, 3. Services, 4. Nonparticipation, 5. Modifications, 6. Timeframe, and 7. Progress and Section 34 CFR 300.347(b) included Transition services, Transfer of rights, and students with disabilities in adult prisons.

For IDEA–2004, Section 614(d)(1)(A)(I), the sequence of IEP components is as follows:

1. **PLAA:** present levels of academic achievement and functional performance.

2. **MAG:** measurable annual goals, including academic and functional goals.

3. **Progress:** how progress toward the annual goals will be measured and reported to parents.

4. **Services:** special education, related services and supplementary aids and services, based on peer-reviewed research to the extent practicable, and program modifications or supports for school personnel.

5. **Nonparticipation:** an explanation of the extent, if any, to which the child will not participate with nondisabled children.

6. **Modifications:** any individual appropriate accommodations that are necessary to measure the academic achievement and functional performance of the child on State and district-wide assessments, and a statement of needed alternate assessments on a particular State or district-wide assessments.

7. Timeframe: projected date for the beginning of services and modifications, and the anticipated frequency, location, and duration of these services and modifications.

8. Transition: beginning not later than the first IEP to be in effect when the child is 16–appropriate measurable postsecondary goals based upon age appropriate transition assessments related to training, education, employment, and, where appropriate, independent living skills; the transition services (including courses of study) needed to assist the child in reaching those goals; and (cc) beginning not later than 1 year before the child reaches the age of majority under State law, a statement that the child has been informed of the child's rights under this title, if any, that will transfer to the child on reaching the age of majority.

In this book the recommended order for the sequence of IEP elements is for the IEP Team to identify PLAAs, select appropriate classroom and test **modifications**, and then identify measurable annual **goals**. As indicated in IDEA–2004 (see above) the statement of **progress** is part of Measurable Annual Goals. Finally, the statement of **transition** services is part of the general **service** component. The recommend sequence for developing the IEP is as follows:

1. PLAA: present levels of academic achievement and functional performance.

6. Modifications: any individual appropriate accommodations that are necessary to measure the academic achievement and functional performance of the child on State and district-wide assessments, and a statement of needed alternate assessments on a particular State or district-wide assessments.

2. MAG: measurable annual goals, including academic and functional goals.
  (**3. Progress:** how progress toward the annual goals will be measured and reported to parents.)

4. Services: special education, related services and supplementary aids and services, based on peer-reviewed research to the extent practicable, and program modifications or supports for school personnel.

(**8. Transition:** beginning not later than the first IEP to be in effect when the child is 16 appropriate measurable postsecondary goals based upon age appropriate transition assessments related to training, education, employment, and, where appropriate, independent living skills; the transition services (including courses of study) needed to assist the child in reaching those goals; and (cc) beginning not later than 1 year before the child reaches the age of majority under State law, a statement that the child has been informed of the child's rights under this title, if any, that will transfer to the child on reaching the age of majority.)

5. **Nonparticipation:** an explanation of the extent, if any, to which the child will not participate with nondisabled children.

7. **Timeframe:** projected date for the beginning of services and modifications, and the anticipated frequency, location, and duration of these services and modifications.

The order for addressing IEP components, as cited in IDEA–2004, should begin with a general discussion of the disability and disability related needs, and how the disability impacts academic achievement. Next, the IEP Team should identify specific areas of performance (viz., the present levels of academic achievement or PLAA) that will serve as the basis for the measurable annual goals. Immediately following the determination of PLAAs, the IEP Team should identify classroom and test accommodations. Following the determination of levels of modifications, measurable annual goals should be identified and how the progress toward each goal will be measured. Based on PLAA, modifications and MAG, all necessary services and support are determined. For each service the frequency and duration of the service should be specified but not the location of services. The location where services are provided should be part of the placement component of the IEP process so that placement does not become tantamount to service (i.e., a child is placed in a self-contained classroom as the "service"). Finally, all decisions relating placement are made following the determination of services. The signature page should be the last task of the IEP Team, and all appropriate albeit supplemental reports and documents should be appended to the IEP if necessary for service providers to implement the IEP.

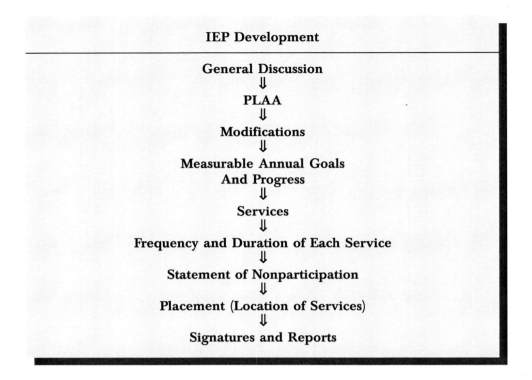

IEP Development

General Discussion
⇓
PLAA
⇓
Modifications
⇓
Measurable Annual Goals
And Progress
⇓
Services
⇓
Frequency and Duration of Each Service
⇓
Statement of Nonparticipation
⇓
Placement (Location of Services)
⇓
Signatures and Reports

General Discussion

The IEP Team must consider the academic needs that prevent participation in the classroom and general curriculum, and what the child does or does not do in the classroom that prevents participation with nondisabled children. The role of the IEP Team is not to address the entire curriculum, or at least not to address that part of the curriculum in which special education is not needed. The identification of academic needs, as well as needs in nonacademic areas that are affected by the child's disability, should be specific and focus on areas affected by the disability. The identification of academic needs should culminate in the determination of specific levels of academic performance which will provide the basis for the appropriate modifications, goals and services.

Before addressing the IEP form, the IEP Team should engage in a general discussion relating to academic needs, strengths and weaknesses, and regular classroom participation. Specifically, Public Law 108–446 requires several areas that must be considered by the IEP Team:

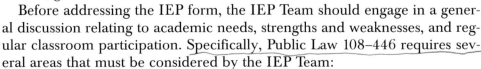

- **The strengths of the child;**

- **The concerns of the parents for enhancing the education of their child;**

- **The results of the initial evaluation or most recent evaluation of the child;**

- **The academic, developmental, and functional needs of the child;**[247]

- **Regular education teacher input;**[248]

- **Special factors which include, when appropriate, behavior, limited English proficiency, Braille and communication needs, and assistive technology.**

Strengths and Weaknesses

Identifying strengths and weaknesses has always been an important task for the IEP Team. The Team is required to consider "the strengths of the child;"[249] transition services must be "based on the individual child's needs, taking into account the child's strengths, preferences, and interests;[250] and every child's IFSP must include "a multidisciplinary assessment of the unique strengths and needs of the infant or toddler and the identification of services appropriate to meet such needs."[251] As noted by the Conferees for IDEA–2004 "the uniqueness of each child help guide . . . decisions, including the child's strengths, characteristics, and background when developing the IEP."[252]

Strengths and weaknesses provide insight into needs that affect educational performance, discerning levels of performance, and determining appropriate goals and services.[253] The strengths of the child includes strengths between abilities or skills (e.g., reading and mathematics, sociability and attention), and within ability or skills strengths (e.g., strengths in reading and weaknesses in reading). When behavior is a factor, not only is the identification of specific weaknesses (i.e., behaviors) essential, but strengths should be considered in relation to improvement and areas of behavior which are not a problem. In this regard strengths and weakness help identify beginning instructional levels and to better select appropriate and/or motivating interventions. If a child is hyperactive, exactly how this hyperactivity is manifested in the classroom must be determined. If a child has a problem with mathematics, the child's strength (e.g., ability to do primary addition) and weakness (e.g., and inability to do subtraction) must be ascertained. If the child has a problem in basic reading, what the child cannot do is just as important as what the child can accomplish. Not being able to recognize 100 sight words might be a weakness, but being able to recognize 35 sight words is a strength.

Identifying strengths and weaknesses is also useful when selecting interventions that are effective for improving performance or behavior. For example, outside interests (which are strengths) might be useful for selecting reading strategies or as part of an overall behavioral intervention plan. Parents and teachers are extremely important when identifying strengths and weaknesses, but an IEP form that relegates strengths and weaknesses to an IEP checkbox (usually quoted verbatim from either the Act or the regulations) is not.

> **Yes   No   Consider the strengths of the child and the concerns of the parents for enhancing the education of their child.**

Teacher and Parent Concerns

Parents can provide important information concerning behavior, effective strategies and interventions, and factors that affect performance. Parent input is especially important for needs involving behavior and teaching methodologies. For classroom behavior, parents might have information or experience for successful interventions in other environments or at home for dealing with certain behaviors. Unfortunately, parents and regular education teachers are sometimes reluctant to become active participants in the IEP development process.

Every IEP should include the concerns of the parents and the regular classroom teacher. The chairperson of the IEP Team must actively seek input from the classroom teacher and parents. The regular classroom teacher must play an active role in the identification of strengths and weakness, areas of need, and methods for ensuring classroom participation. On a similar basis, parent involvement is essential for developing a partnership between school and parents concerning the development of an appropriate educational plan. The regulations for IDEA–1997 indicates that "the regular education teacher who is a member of the IEP team must participate in discussions and decisions about how to modify the general curriculum in the regular classroom to ensure the child's involvement and progress in the general curriculum and participation in the regular education environment."[254] The classroom teacher should provide information relating to the general curriculum, the effectiveness of accommodations that have been used, or the need of different accommodations to enable classroom participation. Most importantly, the regular classroom teacher provides the focus that the regular classroom is the frame of reference identifying goals, accommodations, services and supports.

Discuss the Evaluation Report

The individual evaluation report, and the report for specific learning disabilities, provides the basis for many of the decisions made by the IEP Team. If the evaluation report is a mass of standardized test scores, the IEP Team will have a difficult task developing an IEP based on data and relevant information. The evaluation report must not only substantiate the general need for special education, but must provide information relating to modifications and accommodations, beginning levels of performance, and specific information concerning classroom and curriculum participation. This does not require a public reading of the evaluation report by the IEP Team but elements of the report that have a bearing on the development of the IEP should be reviewed either by the chairperson, the IEP case manager, or a member familiar with assessment and the evaluation report.

Academic Needs

The IEP team should identify specific areas of academic performance and functional performance and "how the child's disability affects the child's involvement and progress in the general curriculum."[255] The IEP team must identify both academic needs and then consider specific-disability related needs that affect academic performance. If a child is identified as ADD/ADHD, a need might be to increase attention or other attention-related behaviors (e.g., being on-task); if a child has a problem involving reading comprehension, goals might be necessary to improve reading comprehension and to improve performance in specific content areas. Likewise, for children with speech/language impairments, hearing impairment or visual impairment, specific goals might be necessary to improve speech, language, communication skills or Braille.

A child's disability cannot be understood apart from the impact the disability has on academic performance. All children with specific learning disabilities, orthopedic impairments or sensory impairments do not have similar academic needs. After the IEP Team has identified how academic performance is affected, the Team is able to consider the various factors that might affect performance.

Consideration of Special Factors

There are two categories of special concerns that the IEP Team must consider. First, the Team should review all medical alerts, medical needs, successful strategies or interventions or other factors that should be known to service providers. Second, many IEPs include a section entitled **consideration of special factors** (behavior, limited English proficiency, Braille instruction, communication needs and assistive technology) as an IEP document requirement so that the IEP Team dutifully checks off each of the special factors for all to see. This is another example of how IEPs become muddled in an attempt to show compliance rather than developing an IEP that represents a sincere plan to provide an appropriate education. The IEP Team must consider the various special factors but there is no need to show or otherwise document this consideration (e.g., by means of a checklist). If one of the special factors must be addressed by the IEP Team, obviously pertinent information will be included in the IEP (e.g., necessary positive behavioral interventions, special assistive technology accommodations or services).

There is no need to include a page in the IEP devoted to "special factors" or a checklist for special factors. If one of the IDEA–2004 special factors is relevant, the factor can be addressed in the student profile, or as a part of accommodations or services.

When the five special factors were added to IDEA–1997,[256] the intent was not to add paperwork by creating a new section in each child's IEP, but to consider, **when appropriate**, extremely important areas that could affect a child's academic success but to ensure that these factors are "reflected in the contents of the child's IEP, including as appropriate, the instructional program and services provided to the child, the annual goals, and the child's involvement in and progress in the general curriculum."[257]

Inappropriate behavior is often the one factor that can prevent regular classroom participation. The discussion of classroom behavior is an opportunity for the classroom teacher to identify specific behaviors that affect classroom performance, and thus identify specific behaviors that can be addressed by a measurable annual goal or accommodation. Because behavior can severely limit classroom participation the IEP Team must give high priority to behavior that affects classroom performance, and attempt to understand the purpose of the behavior (e.g., a Functional Behavior Assessment or FBA) might be a necessary supplement to the IEP, or a Behavioral Intervention Plan (BIP) might be appended to the IEP to outline modifications, goals, services and supports. As does Vermont many states require the consideration of "appropriate positive behavioral interventions and strategies" which includes social skills, anger management and conflict resolution.[258]

If a child's primary language is not English, the IEP Team must consider (and identify) the child's primary language and attempt to solicit input from a qualified bilingual specialist, and then develop goals and services based on the child's primary language or English language needs. This might require the IEP chairperson or case manager to augment the IEP Team with an additional qualified member.

For children who are visually impaired the IEP Team must consider Braille needs. In New Hampshire a "presumption" is made by the IEP Team that for a functionally blind pupil "proficiency in Braille reading and writing is essential for the pupil's satisfactory educational progress" and "every functionally blind pupil shall be entitled to Braille reading and writing instruction unless all members of the pupil's special education team concur that instruction in Braille or the use of Braille is not appropriate for the pupil."[259]

Finally, for all children communication needs should be considered, and for a child who is deaf or hard of hearing the IEP Team should consider direct instruction in the child's language and communication mode.[260]

The IEP Team's "consideration" of the special factors when appropriate:

1. The consideration of a child's behavior that impedes his or her learning or that of others with positive behavioral interventions and supports is intended to be a "proactive approach" that results in reduced "behavior problems and disciplinary referrals, as well as improved educational results" (see SR–108–185).

2. The IEP Team must consider the language needs of the child in relation to the IEP, but services cannot be denied a child with a disability because English is not the primary language.

3. For children with visual impairments the IEP Team must evaluate a child's reading and writing skills and the need for instruction in or the use of Braille. The IEP Team should also consider "when appropriate, instructional services related to functional performance skills, orientation and mobility, and skills in the use of assistive technology devices, including low vision devices" (see SR–108–185).

4. For a child who is deaf or hard of hearing the IEP Team should consider the family's preferred mode of communication, opportunities for direct communication with peers and professional personnel in the child's communication mode, academic level, linguistic needs, and the potential for using residual hearing.

5. The IEP Team must consider on an individual basis needed assistive technology devices and services but this "consideration" need not be documented in the IEP or result in additional paperwork.

Discuss Levels of Performance

As part of the general discussion the IEP Team will consider needs, strengths and weakness and information from all IEP members relating to regular classroom performance. The Present Levels of Academic Achievement (PLAA) translates this general discussion into an outline of Academic and other function needs that provided the basis for identifying modifications, selecting goals and providing services. The PLAA entails both general academic needs and specific levels of performance. If PLAAs are vague and not based on data, the IEP will be flimsy and ineffectual. Data-based PLAAs indicate that the IEP has substance, that an effort has been made to determine specific needs, and that all services that follow have direction and purpose. When levels of performance are not specific and not data-based, the placement becomes the paramount concern rather than improving educational performance.

The IEP Team must identify *relevant* standardized test scores to be included in the PLAA, and other information that affects classroom performance. If a child is identified as having a specific learning disability in reading comprehension, standardized scores relating to reading comprehension would be appropriate. However, the IEP Team should also identify specific levels of reading comprehension, and the effect of reading comprehension in the general curriculum (e.g., how reading comprehension affects performance in social studies, mathematics, etc.).

Discuss Modifications

Following PLAAs the next IEP component should focus on all necessary, yet reasonable, accommodations and modifications. This section should include general curriculum accommodations, test accommodations, and accommodations to State and district-wide tests. The purpose for considering modifications immediately following the statement of levels of academic performance is to identify accommodations and modifications already being used in the classroom and for assessment, and to provide input for the determination of goals and services. If a child requires a reader or scribe for curriculum participation and testing, measurable annual goals to develop reading skills or to develop the ability to effectively use a reader or scribe might be addressed in the next section. By and large accommodations will often be less restrictive (e.g., extended time, using special scissors, etc.) than services (e.g., one-to-one instruction) and thereby provide the foundation for more restrictive services and activities that involve specific goals and services to achieve these goals. To reduce redundancy, accommodations should include general classroom accommodations, test accommodations, and program accommodations and modifications.

Another reason for considering accommodations prior to goals and services is the consideration of regular classroom needs. When the task of the IEP Team is to consider what accommodations have been used and are needed to enable regular classroom participation, the overriding goal of the IEP Team for maximizing regular classroom participation becomes clear.

Classroom accommodations and modifications often provide the foundation for achieving measurable annual goals and for providing services to enable participation in the general curriculum. The accommodations that the IEP Team should discuss include classroom accommodations, assistive technology, and test accommodations. As is the case with special education services (viz., special education, related services and supplementary aids and services) there is often overlap between the various types of accommodations. The accommodations already being used will provide a guide as to what is effective (or not) for participation in the classroom and the curriculum. Classroom accommodations can include curriculum format modifications (using a scribe, reader, large print, Braille), response accommodations (e.g., an interpreter, augmentative communication device, length of time to respond), environment accommodations (e.g., humidifier, lighting, air purifier), or access accommodation (e.g., furniture, special desk, classroom seating). Many accommodations could also be classified as assistive technology (AT) devices or services in that AT entails any item or device that enables regular classroom participation, and determining needed AT devices and services is a logical part of classroom accommodations, supports or services.

To enable participation in the general curriculum, and in State and district-wide assessments, reasonable adaptation, and accommodations are often necessary. The wording in IDEA–2004 for state and district-wide assessments was changed from simply "individual modifications" in IDEA–1997 to "any individual appropriate accommodations" . . . that are necessary to measure the academic achievement" so that modifications are not made that affect or otherwise compromise a test's validity.[261] The Senate report's rationale for this is that "in the testing field today, a 'modification' to a test may affect the validity of that test, while an 'accommodation' to a test will not affect the test's validity" is not exactly correct, the need for "accurate and valid" testing is well worth noting.[262] A more accurate distinction between the terms "accommodation" and "modification" would be that an accommodation is a range of interventions provided to mitigate the effects of disability which can range from enhanced test instructions to test exemptions (the most extreme accommodation); a test modification is anything that actually modifies the test or the administration of a test. Although accommodations and modification are variously defined, and often used interchangeably, a modification is a type of accommodation (see Burns, 1998), and both accommodations and modifications can affect a test's validity. The extent to which each affects validity depends on the test, the accommodation, the content area and the disability for which the accommodation is being made. The result of the most recent evaluation should provide information relating to "reasonable adaptations and accommodations" (NCLB wording) that enable the child to participate with nondisabled children, and general and specific levels of performance.

Discuss Possible Goals

Measurable annual goals should be considered before services, and should not be developed apart from the IEP Team. Every measurable annual goal should include a beginning level of performance as well as the annual or end-of-the-year level of performance.

Because the No Child Left Behind Actx[263] requires that "all students will meet or exceed the State's proficient level of academic achievement on the State assessments within the State's timeline,"[264] many IEPs become a litany of curriculum goals. Specifically, the measurable annual goals developed for the IEP are intended

- **To meet the child's needs that result from the child's disability;**

- **To enable the child to be involved in and make progress in the general education; curriculum;**

- **To meet the child's other educational needs that result from the child's disability."**[265]

Measurable annual goals provide the substantive foundation for every IEP. A quick review of measurable annual goals will quickly determine whether the intent of the IEP is to provide a reasonably calculated plan or to document compliance. Goals which are vague or have no initial measurement is a good indication that the IEP is an officious document to show compliance and not to plan an appropriate education. A typical compliance goal is to "to improve _____ to 80% accuracy as determined by teacher observation," but there is no beginning percentage, no measurable behavior and certainly no attempt will ever be made to use teacher observation to measure performance.

The beginning levels of performance required for every measurable annual goal must be included in the evaluation report, or must be provided at the IEP meeting (e.g., regular classroom teacher input, a curriculum-based assessment). Whether the goal is to improve a specific behavior, decrease a behavior, increase reading comprehension, or develop a study skill, stating a goal without knowing the beginning level of performance is meaningless.

The measurable annual goals and the description of how progress toward meeting annual goals will be measured and periodic reports on progress (e.g., report cards) should follow the statement of accommodations. The section on services should follow measurable annual goals but this section should begin a new page within the IEP form so that additional goals can be added to the IEP document. Exactly how services are considered by the IEP Team, and the order of consideration, requires a careful examination of the purpose of each of the IEP service elements. Services should include supplementary aids and services, other special education and related services, program modifications, supports for school personnel, transition services, and nonacademic services.

> **The measurable annual goals section should begin a new page and not overlap with services so that additional pages are easily inserted into the IEP document.**

Progress

Historically, the statement concerning reporting progress to parents has been the last element in the IEP. However, this statement has been repositioned in IDEA–2004 required content to immediately follow the statement of goals because of the obvious and inextricable relation between goals and the progress toward achieving goals. The statement of progress must indicate how the child's progress toward meeting the annual goals will be measured, and when periodic reports will be provided.[266] An early version of IDEA–2004 (House bill 1350) also included the stipulation that a child's parents will regularly be informed "at least as often as parents are informed of their nondisabled children's progress, of the sufficiency of their child's progress toward the annual goals."[267]

Discuss Services

When determining services the IEP Team must make a distinction between services and educational placement. As stated in *Oberti*[268] "in collaboration with the Family, a school district must make a threshold determination as to what special services a child with a disability needs and must then determine whether those needs can be met within the matrix of a regu-

lar classroom setting with the provision of supplementary aids and services."
To this end services must be discussed that are specific to needs, modifications and goals. Thus, a service might be three hours of specialized instruction daily, or one hour of specialized instruction three days a week. The IEP
must first focus on the specialized instruction and services necessary to meet
a child's needs. After this determination has been made, the IEP then considers related services that enable a child to benefit from special education.
Classroom supports should be determined after special education and related services have been determined less a classroom support (e.g., one-to-one
aide) be assigned in lieu of special education.

Discuss Services before Placement

Discussing placement before the IEP has been developed can result in a
bias toward a placement, a placement not being based on relevant needs and
services, or the placement deemed tantamount to providing a service.
Services are always considered before placement. Placement is not a service;
placement is where a service is provided. For example, a child is said to need
a self-contained classroom without considering what will be provided in that
restricted environment (which are the real services being offered).

Assigning a child to a special education classroom is not a service but a
placement. The first obligation of the IEP Team is to determine what services and supports a child will need to participate with nondisabled children
and in the general education curriculum. This first and extremely important
task which the IEP Team must undertake for every child with a disability
cannot be achieved if the child is first placed in an alternate educational
placement.

By clearly differentiating specific services to meet specific needs from
placements which presume to provide services, the IEP Team will help
ensure maximum participation in the regular classroom and the regular curriculum. Thus, two hours of individualized help in mathematic is a service,
and two hours of pull-out special education is a placement; three hours of
special education a week is a service, and three hours of special education a
week in a resource room is a placement; five hours of instruction using an
assistive technology device is a service, and five hours of AT instruction in a
special classroom is a placement; 20 hours of intensive individualized
instruction a week is a placement, and instruction in a self-contained classroom is a placement.

The importance of differentiating services and placements becomes
apparent when the placement decision is made. If a child requires two hours
of help in mathematics, the presumption is that this service will be provided
in the regular classroom. If every special education service is pull-out or a

resource room service, this is easily (and often) ignored. If a child requires 20 hours of intensive individualized instruction in a 25 hour school week, the IEP Team then must consider where this instruction can be provided. The team might conclude, based on the child's needs, that 15 hours of specialized instruction requires a special location but five hours of specialized instruction can be provided in the regular classroom in addition to the five hours of classroom instruction that does not require individualized help. Separating services and placement allows the IEP team to consider the maximum extent a child can participate in the regular classroom and not be deceived by the presumption that a placement will provide all appropriate and necessary services.

Discuss Supplementary Aids and Services

Because IDEA requires "a statement of the special education and related services, and supplementary aids and services," many IEP forms include a separate section for each of these services cited in IDEA. The misunderstanding is that supplementary aids and services are somehow unique from special education, related services and other modifications and supports. In actuality, supplementary aids and services include special education, related services, accommodations and other supports that enable a child to participate in the regular classroom successfully. When the IEP Team considers supplementary aids and services, there is no need to list every potential service and/or accommodation that might enable regular classroom participation.

When the IEP Team first considers services, the task is to consider services that enable regular classroom participation and then services that meet the child's other needs. In other words, supplementary aids and services are always considered first and foremost because these services are necessary to determine whether a child can satisfactorily participate in the regular classroom. Supplementary aids and service are not a distinct group of services, different from special education, related services, etc., but include all services and accommodations that enable regular classroom participation. The essence of supplementary aids and services is not to have a specific category in the IEP but to identify all services that are needed for a child to achieve satisfactorily in the regular classroom. The following illustrates the range of services that the IEP Team should consider to enable regular classroom participation:

- **Special Education**

- **Related Services (e.g., speech and language, physical therapy, etc.)**

- **Supplemental Services (e.g., resource room)**

- **Transition Services**

- **Support Services (e.g., teacher aid or teacher assistant)**

- **Specialized Services (e.g., remedial reading, adaptive physical education)**

- **Nonacademic Services**

- **Assistive Technology Services**

- **Nonacademic Services**

- **Test Accommodations Services (e.g., scribe, reader)**

The IEP Team is not required to list every conceivable service in the IEP form, but to identify and include appropriate services. The IEP Team should identify each service that is necessary to provide an appropriate education; the IEP Team should not include services that have no bearing on a child's educational program.

Transition Services

The statement of transition services should be part of the general statement of special education, related services and supplementary aid and services. Transition services can include special education, related services and supplementary aids and services but what distinguishes these services from other school-based services is the emphasis on post-secondary outcomes related to training, education, employment, and independent living skills.[269] If a separate transition service report is necessary, this should be appended to the IEP.

Related Services

Related services should be identified following the determination of special education services. One new consideration for the IEP team is the requirement that "special education and related services and supplementary aids and services, based on peer-reviewed research to the extent practicable. . . ." Unfortunately, there is a dearth of research relating to "peer-reviewed" research, and what research is available is often ignored (e.g., the research relating to facilitated communication). Because of this, many IEP Teams will rely on the "extent practicable" when considering services. The National Center for Learning Disabilities provides a very *practical* view of peer-reviewed research "that this new provision seeks to establish an expectation for strong evidence of effectiveness when selecting curricula, interventions, related services, supplementary aids and services."[270]

Supports for School Personnel

Supports such as aide, specific direct or indirect consultant teacher services, in-service training, volunteer services, school-wide resources should be identified by the IEP Team after special education and related services have been determined. When identifying supports for classroom teachers, the IEP Team must not select a support in lieu of special education. If a child requires a full-time aide, the aide is not responsible for planning or implementing the IEP. If appropriately trained, the aide can assist in the implementation of the IEP but only under the direct supervision of a special education teacher.

Discuss Nonparticipation

The IEP must include the beginning date of services, and the frequency, duration and location of services. This requirement often results in the determination of placement rather than services. After the IEP Team determines what services a child needs, the frequency and duration of these services is determined. One child might need two hours of special education twice a week, while a second child might require 3 hours of special education every day. In both cases this indicates the type, frequency and duration of services.

The statement of nonparticipation and the statement of frequency, duration and location of services should be considered by the IEP Team following the identification of all services. After services and supports have been specified the IEP Team should complete the statement of nonparticipation or "an explanation of the extent, if any, to which the child will not participate with nondisabled children in the regular class." If the IEP then decides that a child can participate 100 percent of the time in the regular classroom, this affects where all services are provided. If the IEP Team decides that a child is able to receive all special education in the regular classroom, but would need pull-out services to supplement the regular classroom or to allow the child to benefit from special education (viz., the use of related services), the statement of nonparticipation could take this into account. Finally, the statement of nonparticipation can highlight factors that are particularly important for either including or not including a child in the regular classroom. For a child with extensive communication needs (e.g., using assistive technology or a language board to communicate) the statement of nonparticipation might indicate that the child requires extensive direct, indirect supplemental and support services. For a child with behavioral needs, the IEP Team might conclude that participation in the regular classroom must be based on progress toward the development of appropriate behavior in a more restrictive setting.

When the statement of nonparticipation follows the statement of services, the IEP Team is provided with an opportunity to reflect on the appropriateness of services outside of the regular classroom, and services in the regular classroom for that matter. The statement of nonparticipation should not be reduced to a perfunctory check box indicating that for every child that participation in the regular classroom is not possible because goals cannot be achieved in this placement. We can do better than this.

> **Prior to the enactment of P.L. 94–142 in 975, the opportunity and inclination to educate children with disabilities was often in separate programs and schools away from children without disabilities. Therefore, the legislation requires that the IEP include an explanation of the extent, if any, to which a child with a disability will not participate with nondisabled children in the regular class and in the general education curriculum including extracurricular and nonacademic activities.**
>
> **–Senate report 105–17, IDEA–1997**

Placement (Location)

The actual educational placement decision is always based on the child's IEP. The last section of the IEP should begin with the statement of nonparticipation, followed by the location of services. Because the frequency and duration of services have already been specified, the IEP Team then determines where these services can be provided. If a child needs individualized instruction three days a week for two hours a day, how this service is provided during the school day is determined. The determination of location of services is the actual placement and for all children the presumed location for services is always the regular classroom.

When determining where services will be provided, the first consideration and the presumption is that every service will be provided in the regular classroom. If the IEP Team decide that the regular classroom will not (or has not) result in satisfactory performance, a decision might be made that the services needed to participate in the regular classroom must be provided in an alternative setting but to the **minimum extent appropriate**. A child with a disability should participate in the regular classroom and general curriculum to the maximum extent appropriate; correspondingly, a child with a disability should participate in an alternative setting to the minimum extent appropriate.

The considerations by the IEP Team regarding educational placement should emphasize the importance of the regular classroom. The IEP Team should maximize the amount of time a child participates in the regular classroom, and minimize the amount of time the children is removed from the regular classroom. If a child is not able to participate in the regular classroom, two additional factors must be considered. The degree a child can participate in the general curriculum in the alternate setting; and the extent the child can be mainstreamed in the regular classroom. The educational placement cannot preclude regular classroom participation (although it often does). Situations where placements curtail classroom participation include residential settings which make regular school participation *inconvenient;* a nonsense philosophy that a child must earn the right to participate in the regular classroom; and mainstreaming a group of children with disabilities in the same classroom and thereby creating a *de factor* special education class but under the guise of a regular classroom placement.

Signatures and Reports

The final business of the IEP Team is to sign the IEP and include all relevant supplemental reports and documents. The signature page documents IEP meeting participation and should be signed following the meeting rather than as a preface to the IEP document. Supplemental reports can be appended to the IEP but these should be kept to a minimum and all appended reports should have a direct bearing on the achievement of goals and/or providing services (e.g., related service reports, Assessments reports and abstracts, Functional Behavioral Assessments [FBA], Behavioral Intervention Plans [BIP]).

Chapter 9

IEP STUDENT INFORMATION

The IEP should include "only the requirements mandated by this Act."

For Student Information, less is more. The IEP is intended to serve as a plan for an appropriate education and not a checklist for every conceivable statutory requirement, suggestion or consideration. The Student Information section of the IEP should focus on data and information relevant to the development of an individualized educational program, and should not be a restatement of the child's educational file.

The first section of the IEP, the Student Information page, should provide sufficient personal data to identify the child and only information that is essential for the implementation of the IEP. Student information should not replicate every data point in the child's record and individual evaluation. The key to an effective IEP is to focus on the essential purpose of the IEP and that is to provide an appropriate educational program. This focus is easily lost if the IEP becomes a document to consolidate all reports and information relating to a child, the child's parents, and every IEP Team consideration, regulatory guideline, suggestion and rule.

The IDEA–1990 indicated that "the IEP is a compliance/monitoring document which may be used by authorized monitoring personnel from each governmental level to determine whether a child is actually receiving the free appropriate public education agreed to by the parents and the school." Unfortunately, the intent of the IEP as a compliance document has supplanted the IEP as a planning document so that bureaucratic codes and checkboxes have become more important than identifying needs, goals and services secondary.

Student information is important but the focus of the IEP is always the provision of an appropriate educational program, and data that detracts from this objective should be avoided. The IEP provided by New Jersey offers no specific guidelines for the Student Information component but only states that "a section may be added at the beginning of the IEP format to include pertinent student information as determined necessary by the school district."[271] At the minimum the school should adopt the "personally identifiable" criterion which includes the child name, parents, address, personal identifier (e.g., social security number), or "a list of personal characteristics or other information that would make it possible to identify the child with reasonable certainty."[272]

Introductory Information

The first consideration which must be addressed when designing an IEP form is the extensiveness of introductory information. The information can vary from the most essential information (name, date of birth, grade/level)[273] to a detailed array of personal/family/school information (name, address, race, birth date, phone, parent data, case manager, IEP members, school district of residence, social security number, etc.).[274] What should be included in the IEP depends on State guidelines, the needs of the local educational agency, and the perceived importance of the various IEP elements. For this reason IEPs for different school districts and different States will vary widely. One school district might decide that a social security number is an important item to include in the IEP, while another school district might require more extensive parent information, or specific information concerning the determination of the disability by the evaluation team. The exact introductory information can vary but what information is included should not detract from either the educational plan or program of services.

Individualized Education Program					
1. Student Information					
Name:		Address:		City:	
Phone:		DOB:		School:	
Grade:		Parent		IEP Manager:	
IEP Meeting Date:			IEP Meeting Purpose:		
IEP Dates:	Beginning Date:		Ending Date:		

Essential Information

Student information should include basic student information such as name, address, telephone, gender, grade, school, date of birth, parent name,

IEP case manager, meeting type (e.g., initial, annual, amendment, transfer, declassification, etc.), and a comments section (e.g., important medical information). There is no need to include information that has no bearing on the implementation of the IEP such as checklists to show that parents have been given the various notices, funding information, etc. This information is certainly relevant but not in a child's IEP. If information involving funding agencies, parent history, etc. is needed, the person seeking this information will likely go to the child's file and not the IEP. The IEP is a plan and not a source for all information pertaining to the child's district, family (e.g., mode of communication of the parents).

Some information routinely included in IEPs is appropriate and necessary for tracking IEP Team business, but not necessary for the direct implementation of the IEP. Information should be available relating to parent notification, the last IEP meeting date, the next reevaluation or IEP meeting, and whether the parent has been given a copy of the IEP and has agreed to services. **But not all student information relating to an IEP must be included in the IEP**. Record-keeping is vital for addressing potential evaluation/IEP abuses and to ensure that all the due process provisions and regulatory guidelines are in compliance. However, including extensive record-keeping information and data in the IEP document is redundant (the local educational maintains this information elsewhere) and can distract from the focus on accommodations, goals and services. The task of developing an efficient and effective IEP is predicated on common sense and how IEPs are actually used. If information relating to medicaid was important, no one would consult the child's IEP to ascertain the exact information needed. When a child must be reevaluated, hopefully the school has a better tracking system for needed reevaluations than reviewing dates recorded on hundreds of IEPs.

The student information page should be flexible and not attempt to address every possible student need and contingency by a series of checkboxes and a recitation of State and federal codes. If there are family concerns that impact the implementation of the IEP, such as a guardian or surrogate parent, these should be addressed in the general summary of student needs (the next section of the IEP). If English is a child's second language, this factor is *considered* by the IEP Team when providing services, supports and accommodations. In other words, English as a second language is addressed by real services, programs and supports, and not by a checkmark on an IEP form. If ethnicity is an IEP category, there should be a reason for including this category in the IEP document other than to note that this information must be reported as part of IDEA requirements. This is not to say certain categories of information should not be included in the IEP, but that all information should have a bearing on the implementation of an appropriate educational program.

Certain data might be relevant to a child's IEP, but on a very individual basis. If a child has seizures, the IEP might include a statement in the special concerns section, a medial alert, or refer to an attached supplemental page for response guidelines. The IEP provides basic and invaluable preparatory information to assist service providers, but the IEP cannot anticipate every conceivable classroom need. A parent might need an interpreter or translator, but every IEP need not have a category indicating whether an interpreter was used in the conduct of the IEP meeting. This need to anticipate every circumstance, every contingency and to show that the IEP Team has considered every conceivable factor in the IEP document is one of the reasons why IEPs are confusing, excessive in detail and are not reasonable plans to provide children with appropriate educations.

An argument can be made for including a variety of data and information in the IEP, but there are several categories of data and information which should be carefully scrutinized. The information page should not show the educational placement, or list the continuum of services for every possible educational placement. Because the IEP form can dictate content, the educational placement (which is based on the IEP) should not be at the beginning of the IEP document, and not a part of the student information page. Placement decisions should be based on the IEP, and the presumption that the regular classroom will be the child's placement. If the placement decision is at the beginning of the IEP form, the IEP Team decision making might actually begin with the placement, or consider placement prior to the development of the IEP. The logical sequence of the IEP and the logical consideration of a child's needs should result in a placement that is the least restrictive and the most appropriate, and the IEP document should not compromise the development of the IEP by a misplaced emphasis on educational placement.

The IEP signature sheet has several purposes: signatures provide a record of attendance, indicate parental approval for the plan and services, and serve as a record for parents of agreed-upon services. As is the case with educational placement, the signature page should follow the last element developed by the IEP Team and not be part of the introductory page or first section of the IEP. The IEP Team members should consider each IEP element as it is developed, reach consensus for each element, and then sign the IEP. Signing the IEP before the IEP is developed suggests that IEP development is pro forma and not a real consideration of needs or services, and this is often exactly what happens. A teacher is assigned the task of writing IEPs, each case is quickly discussed by the Team with nary a change in the previously developed IEP, and then the IEP is signed . . . or signed while the IEP is being discussed . . . or signed with virtually no discussion at all. For parents the IEP should never be signed before services have been identified and the determination of educational placement. As with placement decisions the location of the signature page can affect the development of the IEP. The last order of business for the IEP Team should be to sign the IEP, and this page and this task should follow the development of the IEP.

There is flexibility as to what should be included in the information page but a general guideline is that this page should never be more than one page. A model of Student Information efficiency is the Alabama IEP which includes the following basic student information: name, date of birth, and school year. The Massachusetts IEP provides an excellent example of an IEP that minimizes introductory information and focuses attention in the substantive parts of the IEP:[275]

School District Name:
School District Address:
School District Contact Person/Phone #:
Individualized Education Program
IEP Dates: from to
Student Name: DOB: ID#: Grade/Level:

Finally, the IEP should not include data and information that is confusing such as special education funding codes, the various factors that the IEP Team must consider, ethnic codes, whether the child lives in a licensed home, the participation of other agencies (e.g., Department of Social Services, Department of Rehabilitation, etc.). There should not be a section on the document entitled "For Official Use Only," "For administrative use only," or "For School Reporting Purposes." If the IEP document becomes an administrative tracking device to show compliance, the original intent of the IEP is lost. Again, identification information should be information that is essential to identify a child. Information for Medicaid, serving district, anticipated high school graduation date, County Mental health services can be important information but not necessarily for a planning document that will be read and used by services providers, teachers and parents. The temptation might be great to include funding codes, IDEA reporting data and undecipherable acronyms, but this will not a planning document make. Team members must focus on the ultimate purpose of the IEP: a written statement for each child with a disability that is developed, reviewed, and revised in accordance with section 614(d) of IDEA.[276] Information that detracts from this purpose, the implementation of section 614(d) and the development and revision of an appropriate educational program, does not enhance the IEP. Admittedly, the temptation to include an abundance of data and information in the IEP is great but for purposes other than the need to identify a student, all IEP information should contribute an appropriate educational program.

After considering all the various district/school needs the group designing the IEP will include or exclude information depending on the needs of the school district. If a district has many children from other districts, or children placed in schools other than the school that would normally be attended, this information might be relevant. If information is sufficiently important to be included in the IEP, and the information impacts the implementation of the IEP, include this information in Student Summary, or as a supplemental report that is appended to the IEP.

More information can be administratively efficient so that the IEP document is not just for the child or service providers but for administrators to consolidate data, to accommodate administrative needs and to include an excess of detail that shows an attempt to produce an IEP that has complied with every conceivable recommendation, regulation and guideline. Is this important information to include in the IEP? Absolutely, but this is not information or data that should be included in the IEP document.

Introductory Information Guidelines

- **The IEP should focus on planned accommodations, goals and services.**

- **The IEP should minimize all unnecessary "office" information.**

- **The IEP form should be designed with one goal in mind: to provide a child with a logically developed, reasonably planned educational program**

- **The student information page should not replicate the child's complete record.**

- **The information page should focus on student identification.**

- **The information page should be as brief as possible.**

- **Don't clutter the student information page with bureaucratic codes.**

- **Don't indicate the child's placement on the student information page.**

- **Place the signature page at the end of the IEP document (but following attachments).**

- **If information is important for IEP implementation, add this information to those sections of the IEP that are impacted.**

Background, Disability and Concerns

2. Background, Disability and Concerns	
Student Summary:	(Reason for referral, description of educational and other needs, strengths and weaknesses, the child's disability and disability-related needs)
Parent and Teacher Input:	(Include specific concerns of parents and classroom teachers)
Special Concerns:	(Include specfial concerns, ESL needs, medical alerts, etc.)
Age of Majority:	

Student Summary

If available and for initial IEPs, the student summary should contain a brief description of the referral. This should include the reason for the referral, attempted classroom interventions and parent participation. This information provides the IEP Team with direction concerning needs, goals and possible services. For IEPs other than the initial IEP, the initial reason for referral may or may not be relevant but the IEP should indicate the child's current educational placement and/or special education and related services being provided.

The IEP should include a brief summary indicating the child's disability, how the disability impacts academic performance, and a brief description of regular classroom interventions and accommodations. If a child has been identified as having a specific learning disability in basic reading skill, the IEP Team should indicate in what area(s) the disability occurs. For example, a child never simply has a specific learning disability but rather a *specific learning disability in reading comprehension* or a *specific learning disability in written expression.* Whenever the type of disability can influence the type of service and accommodations, a brief statement of the disability should be provided. For a child with an Other Health Impairment, knowing that the disability is epilepsy or diabetes rather than attention deficit disorder is certainly an educationally important distinction. Likewise, indicating the extent of a child's visual loss or hearing acuity, the type of speech or language problem, or how autism is manifested is useful for identifying services and accommodations.

The summary should not repeat all the data and information contained in the evaluation report or information provided in the next section (Present Levels of Academic Achievement). A brief statement of the educational impact should follow the disability description. This might address how the disability affects participation in the classroom, the ability to do classroom work, grades, standardized test scores, etc. An IQ score might be included in the summary but not a detailed description of all the various IQ subtest scores (e.g., similarities, digit span, picture arrangement, etc.). Remember that an IQ score is not the same as "educational need." An IQ score of 55 indicates that a child is three standard deviations below the mean on a test; the child's educational needs might involve language, self-help skills, and adaptive behavior. An IQ score is nothing more than a standardized score and a determination of either disability or need is never based on measures "that are designed to provide a single general intelligence quotient."[277]

A summary of medical and disability-related assessments that help identify appropriate accommodations, goals and services should be included in the IEP. The extent of a child's hearing impairment, visual impairment, or medical needs is important when determining goals, services and needed modifications to the general curriculum. A child does not have a generic hearing or visual impairment, cerebral palsy or epilepsy but these labels are manifested by specific data and needs. A child with a mild hearing loss would probably not need the same services and accommodations as a child with a more severe hearing loss; a child who is able to use residual vision would probably not need Braille services; and cerebral palsy could require anything from a minimal accommodation (e.g., extended time to complete tasks) to extensive services involving assistive technology and highly individualized instruction.

Age of Majority

The age of majority component was included in IDEA–1997 because "current law is not clear on what is required when a child with a disability attains the age of majority. . . . The bill clarifies that when a child is considered incapable of making educational decisions, the State will develop procedures for appointing the parent or another individual to represent the interests of the child."[278] For the most States the age of majority is 18.[279] If rights do transfer to a student with a disability at age 18, all the rights listed under 615(m) are assigned to the student which include due process and procedural safeguard notices, as well as all matters relating to complaints, mediation, and due process procedures. Prior to the age of majority the student should understand their disability, their rights under IDEA and Section 504, and be able to advocate for these rights.

> **When a child with a disability reaches the age of majority under State law (except for a child with a disability who has been determined to be incompetent under State law) . . . all other rights accorded to parents under this part transfer to the child; and the agency shall notify the individual and the parents of the transfer of rights.**
>
> **–P.L. 108–446, 615(m)(1)**

In Illinois "when a student with a disability reaches the age of majority (18 years of age; see 755 ILCS 5/11–1) or becomes an emancipated minor pursuant to the Emancipation of Mature Minors Act [750 ILCS 5/Art. 11a] (except for a student with a disability who has been adjudged as a disabled person pursuant to 755 ILCS 5/Art. 11a–1): 1) The school district shall provide any notice required by this Part to both the individual and the parents, and all other rights accorded to parents under Part B of the Individuals with Disabilities Education Act, the implementing regulations at 34 CFR 300, and this Part shall transfer to the student."[280] In Virginia there are three ways for parents to make decisions for a student deemed incapacitated or unable to give informed consent) (1) the parent is appointed guardian, (2) the parent assists the adult student to appoint power of attorney to another adult, and (3) the parent is certified to be the "educational representative" of the student.[281] In New York "currently, under New York State law, no such transfer of rights is permissible. Since an amendment to current Education Law is required prior to allowing the transfer of rights to the student, the IEPs of students in New York State will not require the transfer of rights statement on the IEP."[282]

The Age of Majority is a part of the last substantive element cited in IDEA which relates to transition services (614(d)(1)(A)(i)(VIII)(cc) or

> **(cc) beginning not later than 1 year before the child reaches the age of majority under State law, a statement that the child has been informed of the child's rights under this title, if any, that will transfer to the child on reaching the age of majority under section 615(m).**

If the IEP includes a separate section relating to transition services, the statement indicating age of majority could certainly be included in this section (and it typically is). However, because the transfer of rights is so important, including this statement at the beginning of the IEP acknowledges the shift of rights (or not) from parent to student.

Chapter 10

PRESENT LEVELS OF ACADEMIC ACHIEVEMENT (PLAA)

How the child's disability affects the child's involvement and progress in the general education curriculum.

3. Present Levels of Academic Achievement and Functional Performance	
Summary of Levels of Academic Performance:	
Curriculum and Functional Performance Needs:	

For over 25 years the first substantive component of IEPs was the statement of Present Levels of Educational Performance (PLEP). As noted in the Senate report for IDEA–2004 the IEP must include a statement of the child's present levels of "achievement and functional performance," rather than simply "educational performance" as required by the 1997 law. The change from Educational Performance to Academic Achievement was enacted to emphasize academic achievement in a manner consistent with NCLB (No Child Left Behind) act (P.L. 107–10, Title I - Improving The Academic Achievement of The Disadvantaged), and to recognize that functional performance should be measured for some children. The intent of IDEA is for the IEP to highlight academic measurable goals and, when appropriate, functional goals.[283]

For IDEA–1997 the purpose of using a variety of assessment techniques (e.g., criterion-referenced tests, standard achievement tests, diagnostic tests, other tests, or any combination) "is to determine the child's **present levels of educational performance (PLEP)** and areas of need arising from the child's disability so that approaches for ensuring the child's involvement and progress in the general curriculum and any needed adaptations or modifications to that curriculum can be identified."[284] For IDEA–2004 PLEP was changed to **Present Levels of Academic Achievement (PLAA) and functional performance** "to emphasize academic achievement, consistent with NCLB, and recognizes that for some children, functional performance is also a critical element that should be measured. The committee intends that the statement of measurable annual goals should include academic goals, and, where appropriate, functional goals."[285]

The statement Present Levels of Academic Achievement (PLAA) and functional performance requires

> **(aa) how the child's disability affects the child's involvement and progress in the general education curriculum;**
>
> **(bb) for preschool children, as appropriate, how the disability affects the child's participation in appropriate activities; and**
>
> **(cc) for children with disabilities who take alternate assessments aligned to alternate achievement standards, a description of benchmarks or short-term objectives.**[286]

The information contained in the statement of PLAA has a threefold purpose: (1) to provide focus on how the child's disability affects academic progress, (2) to show that specially designed instruction is needed because the child's disability significantly affects educational performance, and (3) to provide a foundation for the statement of measurable annual goals.

The PLAA statement provides the basis for accommodations, measurable annual goals, services and supports that follow. If there is no basis in fact (*fact* being the individual evaluation) for an area of need, the PLAA is not the place to include unessential data and information. If behavior is not a concern in the individual evaluation, there is no basis for including a note in the PLAA referring to "poor classroom behavior," (unless, of course, the individual evaluation is in error). The needs identified in the PLAA must be addressed by accommodations, goals, or services. To this end, the integrity of the IEP can be evaluated by the degree that the PLAA articulates with all other IEP components.

The statement for present levels of performance is the foundation measurable annual goals, and the link between the full and individual evaluation and providing an appropriate educational program. Regardless of whether "educational performance," "academic achievement," or "functional performance" is described, the statement of *present levels* is often lacking in specificity. The problem of identifying appropriate levels of performance was not helped by the 1990 regulations which reasoned that the statement "should reflect the impact of the disability on the child's performance. Thus, raw scores would not usually be sufficient."[287] The fact is that many Statewide assessments and curriculum-based assessments rely heavily on raw scores. For example, a State might use a raw score cutoff to indicate acceptable performance to meet a State standard. In that these tests are often right on point with respect to the general curriculum, this data becomes essential for understanding how a child's disability affects progress in the general curriculum. In a similar manner the results of curriculum-based assessments are reported in one form of a raw score or another (e.g., percentage, summated rating). A raw score of 30 sight words identified will probably be more insightful for understanding specific levels of performance than a percentile rank of 1 on a standardized reading test.

The 1990 note was interpreted by many to mean that standardized scores were not only the basis of the statement but that raw scores, and thus most curriculum-based measures, were of trivial importance or not to be used at all. The regulations for IDEA–1997 clarified the purpose of present levels of educational performance by stating that levels of educational performance can be assessed by "criterion-referenced tests, standard achievement tests, diagnostic tests, other tests, or any combination of the above. The purpose of using these assessments is to determine the child's present levels of educational performance and areas of need arising from the child's disability so that approaches for ensuring the child's involvement and progress in the general curriculum and any needed adaptations or modifications to that curriculum can be identified."[288]

Standardized scores, curriculum-based measures and disability-related measures all must be used when appropriate to determine the need for special education, and specifically how the child's disability affects progress in the general education curriculum. Standardized scores often provide a normative base for determining the need for special education, and for determining relative areas of strengths and weaknesses. A child who is low (e.g., each score is more than one standard deviation below the mean) in all areas on a standardized test provides prima facie data that *something* is affecting educational performance. If this child is determined to have a disability, and all available data suggests that this disability is *the something* affecting educational performance, one element of the *present levels* statement has been established: **how the child's disability affects the child's involvement and progress in the general education curriculum**.

If areas of educational achievement performance are all within the "normal" range, the disability could affect and thereby limit progress in the general education curriculum even though progress appears to be in the normal range. For example, disruptive classroom behavior, screaming, yelling, temper tantrums, etc. might affect classroom work and productivity, the ability to participate in classroom activities, the ability to participate in nonacademic activities and the ability to be educated with nondisabled children.

The usefulness of a standardized test in assessing the curriculum is completely dependent on the degree that the test assesses what is taught in the curriculum. District-wide achievement tests, although often superior in terms of psychometric characteristics and overall standardization, are certainly not developed with a specific curriculum in mind. Most district-wide and nationally used tests were developed based on a cross-section of educational theory, common sense, curriculum theory, abstract curriculum goals, and a variety of other factors (ranging from political correctness to theoretical orientation of the test and item developers).

The actual inclusion of levels of educational performance in IEPs has caused some confusion in IEP development. Some IEPs stress standardized scores, others cite ratings of educational performance (e.g., always completes assignments, usually completes assignments, etc), and some IEPs suggest that the PLAA statement is yet another list of *considerations* which can include academic skills, vocational skills, language, motor performance, independent living skills. When in doubt, the IEP simply might say Present Levels of _____ with absolutely no guidance or comment how this statement articulates with the individual evaluation or measurable annual goals. In that measurable annual goals are often not measured, and thus no attempt is made to link goals with levels of performance, a statement that does not explicate educational and academic needs is consistent with the development of an IEP that is intended to show compliance rather than providing an appropriate and individualized education program.

The PLAA should include relevant data and information, summarizing data and reports so that information contained in students reports/files and the individual evaluation are not repeated, and by focusing on both standardized and nonstandardized measures that show how the disability affects performance.

The information contained in the statement of PLAA will include a "variety of assessment tools and strategies to gather relevant functional, developmental, and academic information, including information provided by the parent," and "the relative contribution of cognitive and behavioral factors, in addition to physical or developmental factors."[289] The variety of assessments cited in the PLAA can include standardized tests, grades, classroom tests and quizzes, curriculum-based assessments, behavior assessments, functional assessments, reports and ratings, observational data.

The goal is not to identify every assessment ever used with a child but to paint a portrait of the child's abilities and skills that affect educational performance. The task is not paperwork but to provide a link between the individual evaluation and goals, services and accommodations that follow. The PLAA statement should include information that identifies areas of need and strengths, provides the basis for the modifications, measurable annual goals, and services that follow.

Summary of Levels of Academic Performance

A summary of relevant standardized test information, including Statewide tests and assessments, should be included in the summary of levels of academic performance. Standardized test data provides an important dimension of academic achievement, although not the only or necessarily the definitive measure of academic achievement. When including test information in the individual evaluation report a variety of scores should be available for interpretation for district-wide tests, including raw scores, standardized scores (e.g., stanines, IQ-types scores having a mean of 100 and standard deviation of 15), grade equivalents, and percentile ranks.

The summary of standardized test performance need not include every subtest and every type of standardized score available (e.g., grade equivalents, age equivalents, percentile ranks) but should focus on what best explains academic achievement. There should be a close relationship between PLAA and other components of the IEP (viz., measurable annual goals and services). Devoting attention to isolated standardized subtests or esoteric subtests (e.g., digit span or whatever), when these data have no bearing on real educational needs detracts from the meaningfulness of the IEP. Simple rule: identify important data where "important data" is defined to mean data that must be addressed by modifications, goals or services.

The IEP Team must be parsimonious in the selection of relevant data. If a child's disability is a specific learning disability in basic reading skills or reading comprehension, overall scores in basic reading or reading comprehension would be more useful than to list every subtest score from the district-wide tests. Subtest such as *Sounds and Letters, vocabulary,* and *language mechanics* might be important information for the individual evaluation but specific subtests should only be listed in the IEP if they help direct the determination of disability or curriculum needs.

Standardized tests are extremely important for understanding academic achievement, but standardized test scores must be supplemented by curriculum-based measures of academic performance. Although standardized test scores provide a good indication of general academic need, these scores are often inadequate as a basis for creating measurable annual goals. In addition to the inability to repeat testing, standardized test scores provide very little guidance for modifying and measuring progress toward the goal. If a child is in the fourth grade and receives a grade equivalent of 2.5 on a standardized test in reading comprehension (or a standard score of 75 or a percentile rank of 7, etc.), a goal to achieve a score of 4.0 is obvious but this has little meaning in terms of curriculum intervention or monitoring progress. The solution is to use curriculum-based assessments that integrate tasks and items (but certainly not the same items) used in the standardized assessment to monitor progress over the course of the year.

For all standardized assessments the task is not to identify low test scores, and then provide interventions to improve these specific scores, but to intervene in order to improve academic achievement relating to the general education curriculum or the same curriculum used by nondisabled children. The general education curriculum is the focus and tests are only relevant to the extent that the general education curriculum is sampled and measured (by the test items).

The IEP Team must be aware that the general curriculum, and what the child does in the general curriculum, is the determining factor in the assessment of curriculum needs and not subtest names. In other words, subtests (especially subtests from an IQ test battery) do not signify curriculum needs. The subtest might be relevant, or simply might be a task unique to the test battery. Thus, performance on a *block design* task or *digit recall* task might be totally irrelevant to what a child needs to do to be successful in the general curriculum.

Curriculum and Functional Performance Needs

The key is not to rely solely on standardized scores but to use other indices of educational progress in the general curriculum. These include grades, teacher reports, teacher ratings, observational, data, classroom quizzes and tests, assignments, attendance, measures of classroom behavior (if available), and curriculum-based measures which show specifically how progress in the general curriculum is affected. Standardized test scores are useful for understanding academic needs, but to rely solely on standardized score performance undermines the need to enable classroom and curriculum participation. The various indices that can be used to support a determination of educational need include:

- **Test scores less than one standard deviation below the mean**

- **Test scores less than a percentile rank less than 15**

- **At least one grade level below current grade level**

- **State competency tests**

- **Grades**

- **Teacher reports and ratings**

- **Classroom participation**

- **Classroom behavior**

- **Homework**

- **Test and quizzes**

- **Classroom assignments**

- **Books and related activities**

- **Language arts (viz., reading, spelling, oral language, writing)**

- **Mathematics**

- **Workbook assignments**

- **Attendance**

- **Content area performance (e.g., science, social studies).**

The general curriculum is dynamic and includes all academic and nonacademic school programs, classes and activities. The IEP Team must not reduce the general curriculum to a test score or to a series of subtest scores. Identify important curriculum needs, provide modifications, goals and services for these needs, and standardized test performance will likely improve. The IEP Team focus modifications and interventions solely on standardized test performance to the extent that specific curriculum needs are ignored.

Functional Performance

Public Law 108–446 makes several references to *functional* activities such as functional assessment, functional performance, functional outcomes, functional goals and functional achievement standards. Whereas a functional behavioral assessment refers to an understanding of the function of a behavior, generic functional assessment denotes skills and abilities that are necessary to function in an environment and in the community rather than a predetermined set of skills and abilities (e.g., academic tasks). Functional assessment is used in reference to assistive technology to indicate the need for "a functional evaluation of the child in the child's customary environment,"[290] and assessments to obtain relevant functional developmental and academic information.[291] The definition of transition services in IDEA–2004 refers to the "acquisition of daily living skills and functional vocational evaluation."[292] For all students receiving IDEA services functional needs must be considered in the development of transition services. Last, the Senate report for IDEA–2004 refers to "functional performance skills" to facilitate the in IEP of independent living and instructional skills needed by blind or visually impaired students.

Most children will not need a functional assessment relating to basic communication skills, sensory-motor performance, self-help skills, daily living skills, and socialization. However, some children will need to develop functional skills to develop independence in the school and community. For children with developmental disabilities functional skills will include basic areas to improve basic social, motor, communication, and daily living skills.

Although IDEA only requires a *functional behavioral assessment* (FBA) pursuant to removing a child with a disability because of a behavior violation,[293] whenever behavior affects participation in the regular classroom or general curriculum a FBA should be conducted. The central theme of a functional behavioral assessment is an attempt to understand the function, cause or purpose of the behavior. The FBA should identify the specific behavior, what precedes the behavior, when the behavior occurs, and the function or purpose of the behavior (i.e., why does the child engage in the behavior) all must be considered. This assessment should highlight specific behaviors that affect academic performance. The key is specificity. If a specific behavior (or series of behaviors) prevents participation in the general curriculum, the goal is not to segregate the child from nondisabled children but to develop a plan and measurable annual goals that will allow for participation in the mainstream.

There are several ways in which functional performance can be included in the IEP. The simplest method for addressing functional performance is to include functional performance needs as part of the general curriculum. South Dakota describes functional assessments "as a 'step beyond' standardized testing to determine the educational strengths and needs of the student to progress in the general curriculum. Functional assessments help to identify specific skills the student can and cannot perform in relationship to his or her disability." And

> **if the student has a qualifying score in reading, and that is the area of concern, what is it the student can and cannot do when reading? Does the student have phonetic or sight word skills? Can the student read words in context? Can the student answer questions about a passage he or she has just read? Data is "functional" if it is skill based and identifies the student's present levels of performance to determine where to begin instruction with the student.**[294]

The South Dakota approach to functional assessment is to identify specific skills that the child can and cannot do in the classroom. A different interpretation of functional skills is to identify more basic life skills that children with more severe disabilities might need. These skills include communication and functional language skills, self-care and independent living, functional academics, vocational, mobility and motor skills, social and emotional skills, and recreation and leisure skills. The majority of children receiving services under IDEA will be able to participate in the general curriculum and regular classroom, but a relatively small percentage will require a very unique curriculum designed to meet very specific learning and independent living needs. By including functional skills and PLAA in the same section the IEP Team can focus on classroom participation for children able to participate in the general curriculum, and also meet the more functional or independent living needs for children with more disabilities and extensive needs.

Acceptable classroom behavior is an integral part of the curriculum. For children with disabilities no other factor will prevent participation in the classroom and general curriculum more than an inability to conform to classroom and school behavior expectations and standards. If behavior is an issue, a Functional Behavioral Assessment and Behavioral Intervention Plan might be appended to the IEP. Whether or not to append an FBA or BIP to the IEP or to incorporate the assessment and plan within the IEP depends on the extensiveness of the assessment and/or plan.

Grades can be extremely relevant in the development of a child's IEP. As a matter of fact, the grades a child receives in school provides first-hand data concerning teacher input as to the child's ability to participate with nondisabled children in the general education curriculum. Not only is this information usually ignored in a child's IEP, but the individual evaluation will often highlight nationally normed IQ and achievement measures but completely disregard a child classroom performance as determined by school grades. The task is not to report every grade but to show how grades are affected by the child's disability.

When appropriate, classroom grades and evaluations of classroom grades and quizzes should be included in the PLAA. This information can be overwhelming so this data should be carefully considered before inclusion in the PLAA. Several scores might exemplify a need, or a grade given for a report, or a reason for a low score or grade. Standardized assessments generally do not afford an opportunity to probe why a student received a low score. However, a teacher might have first-hand information why a low grade was given, or what specifically is needed to improve performance. A student might have received a low grade because not all assignments were completed, but the assignments that were completed were average or even above average.

An important function of the group of qualified professional and parent during the individual evaluation is to consider "the content of the child's individualized education program, including information related to enabling the child to be involved in and progress in the general curriculum, or for preschool children, to participate in appropriate activities."[295] The PLAA must expand the needs identified by standardized testing to show what specific skills the IEP must be address. To this end curriculum-based information provides a link between standardized assessments and the measurable annual goals which follow the PLAA statement.

Observational Data

Of all the data that is essential for understanding and enabling regular classroom performance, none is more important than observational data. The regulations for IDEA–1997 required a consideration of evaluations and information provided by the parents, current classroom-based assessments, and observations by teachers and related services providers.[296] For the determination of a specific learning disability at least one team member (other than the child's regular teacher) was required to "observe the child's academic performance in the regular classroom setting."[297]

Although there are many assessment protocols for collecting observational data (e.g., interval, duration or event recording), most regular classroom teachers have neither the time nor the inclination to collect exact behavioral information. A consultant teacher or an aide might be available to collect specific observational data, or the classroom teacher could be interviewed by a member of the evaluation team to identify important behaviors or skills that detract from regular classroom participation. If possible, the regular classroom teacher might spend several minutes each day identifying (e.g., using a daily log, rating scale) significant behaviors or events that impact classroom performance.

State Standards

State tests are extremely useful for determining the extent a child is able to participate in the general education because these tests are generally based on the documented curriculum required by the State for public schools. Unfortunately, these tests are often given infrequently and there is virtually no opportunity for repeated testing. A State assessment might be a legitimate goal, but steps must be defined that will enable this goal to be achieved. Assume that a score of 65 is required to pass a State assessment and a student has not been able to achieve this score. A measurable annual goal to achieve a score of 65 is far too general although the goal itself is clearly measurable. In order to achieve a score of 65 on the State assessments specific skills must be identified that can be measured and the progress periodically assessed that when achieved will result in a passing grade on the State assessment.

If a child is not able to participate in the general education curriculum because of the difficulty of the content, and accommodations do not mitigate the effects of the disability, State standards should be used to develop curriculum-based assessments to determine specific educational needs. For children not able to participate in State and district-wide assessments the IEP must include an explanation as to why the child cannot participate in the assessment and "the particular alternate assessment selected is appropriate for the child."[298] State standards should provide the frame of reference for aligning the assessment to State standards. When a child is not able to participate in regular assessments State standards provide a guide for developing the alternate assessment. The task for aligning the alternate assessment to standards entails a consideration of the standard content and the sequence of that content, and then creating an "appropriate" alternate assessment with modified content and sequence. This can rarely be accomplished using districtwide assessments. Districtwide achievement tests, although often far superior in terms of psychometric characteristics and overall standardization, are usually not developed with a specific curriculum in mind. Most districtwide and nationally used tests are developed based on a cross-section of educational theory, common-sense, curriculum theory, abstract curriculum goals, and a variety of other factors (ranging from political correctness to theoretical orientation of the test and item developers).

The individual evaluation provides data and information for establishing present levels of academic achievement, provide the basis for measurable annual goals; and measurable annual goals "enable the child to be involved in and make progress in the general education curriculum." State standards can be achieved for many students with disabilities when basic underlying skills, abilities or performance levels are developed or accommodations provided. However, for children with intensive needs who are not able to achieve State Standards, the individual evaluation must consider what standards can be achieved and, if necessary, how standards must be modified (i.e., the use of alternate State standards).

Statewide assessments provide the primary means to evaluate State standards in that these assessments provide the most direct link to the actual general education curriculum (in contrast to district-wide tests which sample a "national" curriculum). If available, data for Statewide assessments should provide specific data concerning the ability to participate in the general education curriculum. Unfortunately, these tests are infrequently given so that Statewide test data might not be available for consideration by the IEP Team. If passing a Statewide test is a goal, a practice test or practice questions relating to the Statewide test might be available to consider the child's probable level of performance on the test. At the very least, if a Statewide test is on the horizon for a child with a disability, a practice test or a curriculum-based assessment should be developed to provide some insight as to the child's level of performance. A child's ability to participate in statewide assessments is especially important to determine needed accommodations and the effectiveness of these accommodations and modifications to mitigate the effects of the child's disability.

Alternate Assessment Needs

For some students, and this is a small percentage of students with disabilities, participation in State and district-wide assessments will not be possible and alternative assessments will be required. Much of what is now required in IDEA–2004 stems from the regulations for NCLB act.[299] Thus, "regardless of where students receive instruction, all students with disabilities should have access to, participate in, and make progress in, the general curriculum. Thus, all students with disabilities must be included in the measurement of AYP toward meeting the State's standards" determination as either **proficient** or **nonproficient**[300] For students with disabilities the NCLB requires academic content standards, academic achievement standards, and assessments aligned to standards. For children with the most significant cognitive disabilities States can use alternative achievement standards. Nonetheless, "when students with disabilities are part of the accountability system, educators' expectations for these students are more likely to increase" (p. 68698). The guidelines in the Notice of Proposed Rulemaking (NPRM) note that "the Secretary proposed that the number of proficient and advanced scores based on alternate achievement standards included in AYP calculations at the State and LEA levels, separately, could not exceed 1.0 percent of all students in the grades assessed at the State and the LEA levels, respectively. One percent of all students is approximately 9.0 percent of students with disabilities."[301] For the small percentage of students using alternate standards States must "give equal weight to proficient and advanced performance based on the alternate standards in calculating school, district, and State AYP" provided that these scores do not exceed 1 percent of the children tested at the respective grade level (p. 68699).

For the majority of students with disabilities, State and district-wide assessments provide a benchmark for participation in the regular curriculum. This participation is important for enabling children with disabilities to participate in the general education curriculum. The Senate report for IDEA–2004 "reaffirms the existing Federal law requirement that children with disabilities participate in State and district-wide assessments. This will assist parents in judging if their child is improving with regard to his or her academic achievement, just as the parents of nondisabled children do."

When participation in the general education curriculum is very limited, a portfolio of the students work can be used to collect and align activities and work products with State standards. Kentucky uses an alternate portfolio assessment and has developed fairly rigorous criteria for evaluating content. Portfolios are scored by three teachers other than the students teacher(s) using a Rubric comprised of six dimensions:

- **Standards (linkage to KY Learner Goals and Academic Expectations)**

- **Performance (student progress on embedded IEP objectives in age appropriate products)**

- **Settings (number of integrated settings in which the student learns or applies skills)**

- **Support (degree of peer support and use of adaptations, modifications, and /or assistive technology)**

- **Social Relationships (opportunities for the student to develop relationships with peers)**

- **Self-Determination (opportunities for student choice and control over his/her own learning).**[302]

The availability of alternative assessment should not be an opportunity to prevent children from participating in the general education curriculum. The Kentucky alternative assessment portfolio is not only uncharacteristically detailed in terms of content and scoring, but the children for whom this option is available is intentionally limited: "The Alternate Assessment is specifically designed for the 1 percent of the student population for whom traditional assessments, even with modifications, would be an inappropriate measure of progress. In Kentucky, this number has stayed consistently at approximately .6 percent of the total school population over the last several years. That translates into between 900–1000 students in each accountability year."[303]

Alternate Assessment Progress

In Mississippi a student's goal progress is rated by members of the Alternate Assessment Review Committee (at least three members including the parent). Evidence is collected by teachers, service providers, parents etc. that substantiates progress and can include work samples, assessments, curriculum-based assessments, observational data, and other appropriate assessments. A scannable form is used to rate each goal according to the following scale: 0=No Progress, 1=Little Progress, 2=Progress, but Objective not Met, 3=Objective Met.[304] In Mississippi, an average rating between 1.5 and 3.0 is considered passing and below 1.5 failing. Georgia also uses a scannable form to generate an Alternate Assessment Report.[305] The Georgia form considers seven domains (daily/living personal management, motor, cognitive/functional academic, social emotional, community, vocational, recreation/leisure. Each domain is rated according to the following scale: initial, emerging, progressing, and functional.

The alternate assessment should be summarized in a manner similar to that of a standardized assessment. If the alternate assessment contains benchmarks and short-term objectives, the PLAA would contain a summary of the assessment and the measurable annual goal component would list the actual goals, benchmarks and/or short-term objectives. Another possibility is to provide a summary of the alternate assessment in the PLAA component, list the measurable annual and other goals in the measurable annual goal section, and then append a list of each goal and corresponding benchmarks and short-term objectives to the IEP as an Alternate Assessment Report or use the Alternate Assessment Report in conjunction with the IEP.

Goal		Rater	
1	#1	#3	#3
2			
3			
4			
n			

The Kentucky Alternate Portfolio is a very thoughtful variation of the above format for linking IEP to standards and scoring the alternate assessment. The Kentucky alternate assessment "measures student progress towards achievement of the 6 Learning Goals and the 54 Academic Expectations" (p. 2) and "research-based, effective practice instructional strategies" (e.g., the development of social relationships) "deemed important for students with disabilities." The portfolio is scored three times by individual teachers using a 6 dimension rubric which includes: standards lined to Kentucky goals and expectations, performance, integrated settings, degree of support (e.g., modifications), social relationships, and self-determination.[306]

PLAA Benchmarks

The use "benchmarks and short-term objectives" in the PLAA statement is not the same as the benchmarks and short-term objectives required in IDEA–1997 measurable annual goals statement. When an alternate assessment is used for a child with a severe disability (less than 1% of all children with and without disabilities tested[307]) the **benchmarks and short-term objectives *is the assessment* that is aligned to State standards and benchmarks**. This allows a child with a severe disability to participate in a curriculum that is aligned to State standards. These benchmarks and short-term objectives have the primary purpose of defining the alternate standards aligned to State standards, and are not measurable annual goals in which each goal is broken down into discrete components (short-term objectives) or anticipated levels of progress (benchmarks).[308]

The IDEA–2004 requires that "for children with disabilities who take alternate assessments aligned to alternate achievement standards, a description of benchmarks or short-term objectives."[309] The original version of this reads "until the beginning of the 2005–2006 school year, a description of benchmarks or short-term objectives, except in the case of children with disabilities who take alternate assessments aligned to alternate achievement standards, a description of benchmarks or short-term objectives shall continue to be included."[310] The intent suggests that benchmarks and short-term objectives are to help define PLAA (this is where the statement is included) and to be used in explicating measurable annual goals. However, because an NCLB report card for children with disabilities who take alternate assessments might not be sufficient, "benchmarks or short-term objectives may still be appropriate, and the bill requires these elements to be included in IEPs for these children even after the 2005–2006 school year."[310]

Chapter 11

MODIFICATIONS AND ACCOMMODATIONS

4. Modifications	
Classroom Accommodations:	(Describe the effective accommodations currently being used in the classroom.)
Assistive Technology and Aids:	(Describe any tiems, piece of equipment, or product system used to increase, maintain, or improve functional capabilities.)
Test Accommodations:	(Describe the reasonable and State and local test accommodations permitted.)
Alternate Assessment Needs:	(If standardized tests are not appropriate, describe the alternate test being used.)

LEAST RESTRICTIVE ACCOMMODATIONS

The need of children with disabilities participating in the classroom, the curriculum and assessments has underscored the importance of providing every child with the least restrictive accommodations. The IDEA does not require that a child with a disability have test accommodations and most students will be able to participate in assessments with no or minimally invasive accommodations; that is, accommodations that minimally affect test validity (e.g., test location, special furniture, large print). Many accommodations are disability-specific (e.g., Braille format, extended time, using a scribe) but the intent of these accommodations is not to change the test validity (although this will occur to a limited degree) but to allow the student to participate in the assessment on an equal footing with nondisabled children.

Each local educational agency shall ensure that assessments and other evaluation materials used to assess a child are used for purposes for which the assessments or measures are valid and reliable; are administered by trained and knowledgeable personnel; and are administered in accordance with any instructions provided by the producer of such assessments.

–P.L. 108–446, 614(b)(3)(A)(iii)–(v)

Not all accommodations are easily classified in terms of restrictiveness. Reading a social studies test to a child might be a legitimate accommodation that enables the child to demonstrate social studies knowledge, but this accommodation certainly impacts the test's validity to some extent. Depending on whether a test is primarily designed to measure content (a **power test**) or whether the time given to answer questions is a factor (a **speed test**), extended time could impact test validity. Finally, for both adaptations (e.g., test location, seating, large print) and test modifications (e.g., extended time, Braille, oral reading, scribe, ASL), one guiding rule is not to reduce the difficulty level of the test so as to create an out-of-level test (i.e., a test that is actually at a lower difficulty or grade level). This, however, is easier said than done. A Braille assessment might not include all the graphics associated with the regular assessment, or the graphics might be interpreted differently. Likewise, transcribing a test into American sign language might have a substantial impact on test validity so that for a child who is deaf and has a serious reading problem, assessing progress in the general curriculum becomes a very difficult task.

The No Child Left Behind act has added considerable force to the need for schools to enable children with disabilities to participate in assessments.

- ☞ **Test accommodations should be based on every-day classroom accommodations.**

- ☞ **Not every child will require either classroom or test accommodations.**

- ☞ **The IEP Teams are not required to indicate classroom or test accommodations unless necessary.**

- ☞ **Accommodations should be as least restrictive as possible.**

☞ **Children requiring alternate assessments should be confined to a small percentage <1%) of all children being tested.**

☞ **Test accommodations should be "reasonable."**

Classroom Accommodations

In many ways classroom and test accommodations are a direct extension of the child's present levels of academic achievement. Because of a child's disability one or more factors prevents the child from participating in the curriculum or educational testing. Classroom accommodations often represent the first attempt to address a child's needs in the classroom. The Massachusetts IEP identifies two major components of Present Levels of Educational Performance: General Curriculum (e.g., language arts, social sciences, mathematics, etc.) and Other Educational Needs (e.g., behavior, Braille, adapted physical education, AT, nonacademic, vocational, etc.). When making accommodations three questions are asked:[312]

How does the disability affect progress in the curriculum area(s)?

What type(s) of accommodation, *if any*, is necessary for the student to make effective progress?

What type(s) of specially designed instruction, *if any*, is necessary for the student to make effective progress?

In Vermont, the IEP Team IEP considers three categories of accommodations and modifications: (1) the accommodations, modifications, or supplementary aids and supports needed for the student; (2) the accommodations, modifications and supplementary aids and supports needed to participate in national, districtwide and school assessments; and (3) program modifications or supports that will be provided for school personnel to implement the IEP. Wisconsin allows accommodations in four areas: (1) Time Accommodations (e.g., administer the test in shorter sessions with more breaks or rest periods, space testing over several days), (2) Environment Accommodations (e.g., administer the test to a small group or in an individual session, allow the student to work in a study carrel), (3) Format Accommodations (e.g., use an enlarger or enlarged copy of the test for students with visual impairments, use a Braille edition of the test for students with visual impairments), and (4) Recording Accommodations (e.g., have someone record the student's responses, use a computer board, communication board, tape recorder).

Classroom and test accommodations are often considered by the IEP Team after the determination of services and supports. However, IDEA is not entirely clear where to place accommodations in the IEP. The statement of services includes "special education and related services, and supplementary aids and services . . . and a statement of the program modifications or supports for school personnel." However, many States include accommodations in the statement of "any individual appropriate accommodations that are necessary to measure the academic achievement and functional performance of the child on State and district-wide assessments."[313]

NCLB and the Assessment of Children with Disabilities

"Provide for the participation in assessments of all students and the reasonable adaptations and accommodations for students with disabilities (as defined under section 602(3) of the Individuals with Disabilities Education Act) necessary to measure the academic achievement of such students relative to State academic content and State student academic achievement standards."

–NCLB, SEC. 1111(b)(3)(ix)

There are, however, several reasons why both general classroom accommodations and test accommodations should be considered before determining measurable annual goals and services. First, test accommodations are based on accommodations, if the child is in the regular classroom, currently being used. This provides a direct link to the regular classroom and immediately addresses the IEP Team's obligation to provide aids, services, and other supports in the regular classroom (viz., supplementary aids and services). Second, certain classroom accommodations might require corresponding services or supports, and the extent of these services and supports will vary depending on disability and the extent of the child's needs. If the child requires an aide to serve as a scribe or reader, or help provide/program an assistive technology device, these accommodations should be identified first. The following sections of the IEP can then consider the goals, services and supports necessary to implement these accommodations.

Third, because general classroom accommodations guide the selection of test accommodations, classroom accommodations often provide the basis for identifying appropriate test accommodations that are consistent with State regulations. The instructions for the Alabama IEP require that "the accommodations specified below are in keeping with what has been practiced regularly in the classroom when the student receives instruction and takes classroom tests."[314] The guidelines for Alabama test accommodations further state that

> **When determining appropriate accommodations for an assessment, the IEP Team must look at accommodations regularly being made on the student's classroom tests over time in that particular subject area. Accommodations must be reasonable, proven successful for the student, and be part of the student's instructional program. The IEP Team must work within the framework of the approved accommodations for special education students on the accommodations checklists in Appendix A. An accommodation cannot supplant the skill the test is designed to measure. Accommodations that change the nature, content, or integrity of the test, such as reading of a reading test designed to assess the skill of reading, are not allowed.**[315]

What is noteworthy in Alabama's use of accommodations is the threefold requirement for accommodations: (1) accommodations must be reasonable, (2) accommodations must be based on data (proven successful), and (3) accommodations must be useful (part of the student's instructional program). Thus, if a child requires a test reader, this accommodation should be data-based.

Although classroom accommodations generally guide the selection of test accommodations, this is not always the case. If a child has a reading problem, the child might be able to participate successfully in the regular classroom without a reader. Indeed, the vast majority of reading problems cannot be approached by eliminating the need to reading, and thus literacy, as a goal. Because of reading needs a child might be at a disadvantage in the regular classroom, but specialized instruction and other supports will not only improve reading but also regular classroom participation.

Classroom tests provide an ideal opportunity to determine the need and effectiveness of accommodations. Reading a social studies test aloud might seem like an obvious accommodation for a child with a reading disability, but this is not necessarily the case. A consultant teacher or other trained individual who reads the social studies, mathematics, or science test might find that reading the test does not overcome attentional, vocabulary, or problem-solving needs. Reading a test aloud to a student requires very specific guidelines so that the reader does not answer the questions, define terms, or otherwise solve or unintentionally give the answer to the test question. When a test is read orally and if a copy of the test is also available, the extra time required to read items, verbal recall and other factors can severely impact a test's validity.

By first identifying general classroom accommodations before test accommodations the IEP Team can identify those accommodations and strategies that have been found effective for meeting a child's needs. When identifying accommodations the IEP Team must focus on accommodations that are necessary to enable a child to participate in the classroom, and not select accommodations to give a child an advantage or to provide extra assistance because a child has a disability. Providing every child with a disability a reader would not only be restrictive but discriminatory. For many children a reader, when not necessary, would prevent participation in the general curriculum (viz., learning to read). Likewise, indicating that a child should have a scribe when a child is able to function independently might be altruistic in motive but highly restrictive and inappropriate.

All classroom and test accommodations are not one and the same. The IEP Team might indicate that activities and classroom assessments should be no longer than 15 minutes, but this could an impermissible accommodation a Statewide assessment and an accommodation that could potentially have a negative impact on the child's standardized performance. For example, allowing a child to complete 15 minutes of a test and then providing a break before continuing with more difficult items might actually be a disadvantage.

Identifying Classroom Accommodations

An important source for determining classroom modifications and supports is the regular classroom teacher who is expected to help identify "appropriate positive behavioral interventions and supports, and other strategies, and the determination of supplementary aids and services, program modifications, and support for school personnel."[316] If behavior is a factor that affects classroom participation, input from the classroom teacher concerning specific behaviors and strategies for dealing with real needs is absolutely essential for the development of an effective IEP. This type of input from the classroom teacher is often ignored when IEPs are developed before the IEP meeting, or when IEPs are computer generated.

REQUIREMENT WITH RESPECT TO REGULAR EDUCATION TEACHER.–A regular education teacher of the child, as a member of the IEP Team, shall, to the extent appropriate, participate in the development of the IEP of the child, including the determination of appropriate positive behavioral interventions and supports, and other strategies, and the determination of supplementary aids and services, program modifications, and support for school personnel consistent with paragraph (1)(A)(i)(IV).

–P.L. 108–446, 614(d)(3)(C)

The IEP Team should identify all accommodations used in the classroom and use this as a basis for identifying test accommodations. The IEP Team must base State and district-wide assessment accommodations on those used in the regular classroom, while at the same time taking into account State guidelines concerning permissible accommodations, and "are administered in accordance with any instructions provided by the producer of such assessments."[317]

Frequency of Accommodations

The IDEA–2004 requires "the projected date for the beginning of the services and modifications described . . . and the anticipated frequency, location, and duration of those services and **modifications**." For many accommodations and modifications the frequency will be whenever the activity is engaged (e.g., extended time for test), the duration will be the length of the activity (which will obviously vary), and the location will be in all settings. Using the traditional table for specifying services will not only be awkward but often difficult to interpret. If a child requires Braille text, the frequency and duration of this service occurs whenever traditional reading material is used with children who are not disabled. If a child needs enhanced lighting, a special desk, or a dehumidifier, this is not indicated by frequency, duration, or even location. In all likelihood if a child needs these accommodations in one classroom or setting, the same accommodations will be needed in all classroom settings.

The one exception for including frequency, location and duration data is when an accommodation requires a corresponding service. If a child requires a scribe to write, a reader, or an individual aide to participate in assessments, the frequency, location and duration of these services should be specified as part of Services–Supports for School Personnel section.

AT Classroom Accommodations

Assistive technology (AT) is an extremely inclusive term in that it can very from a simple device (e.g., pen holder, desk) to services requiring specialized expertise. For all children with disabilities the IEP Team must "consider whether the child requires assistive technology devices and services."[318] Many children with disabilities can be successful in the regular classroom with appropriate AT devices and services. According to IDEA–2004 the assistive technology needs of a child are met by considering AT devices which include "any item, piece of equipment, or product system, whether acquired commercially off the shelf, modified, or customized, that is used to increase, maintain, or improve functional capabilities of a child with a disability." In addition, the IEP Team should consider a broad ranges of services such as evaluation services, acquisition of assistive technology devices, "electing, designing, fitting, customizing, adapting, applying, maintaining, repairing, or replacing of assistive technology devices," coordinating services, training.[319]

There is obvious overlap between classroom accommodations, test accommodations and assistive technology. If an AT device is described in the section on classroom accommodations (e.g., special chair), there is no need to repeat the item under a different IEP section. Many low-technology accommodations will be listed under classroom accommodations, while high-technology accommodations will be listed under AT accommodations. Many high-technology AT accommodations will require a service component, and these services should be listed in the Service section.

Good Teaching and Accommodations

The list of general classroom accommodations that can be selected by the IEP Team is virtually endless. For the IEP form to list every conceivable accommodation is not only unrealistic but will result in the selection of unnecessary accommodations from a list or checklist simply because they appear on the IEP form. The IEP Team should also avoid the selection of accommodations that suggest good teaching rather than a necessary accommodation. Enhanced instructions or more practice items might be sound advice for a teacher, and useful for all students, but the task of the IEP Team is not to dictate good teaching but to identify those accommodations that are necessary for a child to receive an appropriate education.

Indicating in a child's IEP that periodic positive reinforcement, using manipulatives, giving extra cues, or reviewing material are certainly good teaching strategies but to routinely cite these in every child's IEP can trivialize the importance of specific modifications necessary to receive an appro-

A Sampling of Assistive Technology Devices

Abacus	Magnification aids
Adjustable keyboard	Mouse adaptations
Adjustable workstations	Optical scanner
Alternate computer keyboard	Page turner
Alternative communication	Paper holder
Amplification aids	Perkins Brailler
Bold-lined paper	Placemarkers
Bookstand	Reading stand
Braille	Reading windows
Bubble format	Screen enlarger
Calculator	Scripted tests
Cassette tapes	Sound buffer
Closed circuit television	Special chair, desk, table
Color transparency	Speech synthesizer
Communication board	Talking calculator
Computer notebook	Tape recorder
Dehumidifier	Telescope
Felt-tip pens	Test environment
Headphones	Test location
Keyboard guards	Text-to-speech software
Kurzweil reader	Transcriber
Language master	Vaporizer
Large display calculator	Variable intensity lamp
Large print	Visor cap
Letter board	Voice activated systems
Letter/language board	

priate education. If the service provider responsible for implementing an IEP must be told to provide periodic reinforcement, the qualifications of the service provider are probably an even greater concern.

If preferential seating is necessary, this should be based on a specific need and there should be evidence that the accommodation will mitigate the effects of the disability. If there is no evidence that a child needs or has ever used large print, indicating the need for a large print accommodation in the IEP would be inappropriate and probably not even implemented. Accommodations that are not based on need or are unlikely to be implemented diminish the currency of the IEP. Stating in the IEP that all questions for tests should be written on one line to facilitate reading might be impossible to implement on most tests, even if there was someone available to make such an accommodation.

Test Accommodations

There are there three general categories of test accommodations that the IEP Team must consider: (1) classroom assessments, (2) districtwide assessments, and (3) State assessments. State assessments are usually the most restrictive with respect to allowable accommodations, followed by district-wide assessments or standardized achievement tests (e.g., Stanford Achievement Test, Metropolitan Achievement Test). Accommodations for classroom assessments should be linked to needed general classroom accommodations. More importantly, classroom test accommodations provide useful feedback for determining the need and probable effectiveness of State and district-wide test accommodations.

District-wide assessments are usually accompanied by publisher guidelines for permissible test accommodations, although the availability of different district-wide test formats is usually limited. For example, the American Printing House for the Blind (APH) has developed large print and Braille versions for Stanford Achievement Test (9th Edition, Form S),[320] a Braille version of the Brigance Diagnostic Comprehensive Inventory of Basic Skills (Revised 1999, Student Braille Edition),[321] and the KeyMath (1988 Revised: A Diagnostic Inventory of Essential Mathematics: Braille Edition, Form A).[322] However, for many district-wide tests different formats for the tests are either not available or the norms are dated (e.g., the KeyMath cited above is for 1988).

Statewide assessments are usually available in several formats such as a large print version, Braille, audiotape or in conjunction with a reader. Unlike district-wide test State assessments usually have very strict guidelines. In Tennessee, the Tennessee Comprehensive Assessment Program (TCAP) warns that "test validity is seriously threatened by modifications that change the nature of the task being tested." The TCAP assessment accommodations include large print and Braille versions. The Braille version of the TCAP can be used in conjunction with an audiotape, "students using "Readers" must have the Visual Impairment verified on the IEP. Extended time for students using Large-Print editions is not permitted unless required conditions for Special Accommodation B are met.[323] In Texas, the Texas Assessment of Knowledge and Skills allows for large print and Braille versions, oral or taped recorded responses when appropriate. However, "an examinee may not receive any reading assistance on the writing, reading, and English language arts tests. Examinees who are identified as having dyslexia or a related disorder may qualify for an oral administration of the mathematics, social studies, and/or science tests."[324]

State and District-wide Accommodations

Participation in State and district-wide assessments is achieved by designing measurable annual goals that address skills and content to enable participation, and by providing "reasonable adaptations and accommodations for students with disabilities (as defined under section 602(3) of the Individuals with Disabilities Education Act) necessary to measure the academic achievement of such students relative to State academic content and State student academic achievement standards."[325] Public Law 108–446 has been aligned with the No Child Left Behind act by requiring

1. **A statement of any individual appropriate accommodations that are necessary to measure the academic achievement and functional performance of the child on State and district-wide assessments consistent with section 612(a)(16)(A); and**

2. **If the IEP Team determines that the child shall take an alternate assessment on a particular State or district-wide assessment of student achievement, a statement of why–**

    a. **the child cannot participate in the regular assessment; and**

    b. **the particular alternate assessment selected is appropriate for the child.**[326]

The need for accommodations is often a basic requirement for accommodations provided in conjunction with State standards. The underlying principle is to have high expectations for children with disabilities and that this is not achieved by providing accommodations that circumvent both disability needs and the need to progress in the general curriculum. This, of course, is the underlying principle of the No Child Left Behind act and the emphasis on all children participating in evaluations and assessments. North Dakota considers the following for accommodations provided to achieve standards and benchmarks:

- **Can the performance specified in the standards and benchmarks be achieved without accommodations or modifications?**

- **If the specified performance cannot be met without supports, what accommodations, modifications, or supplementary aids** and services are necessary for the student to achieve the performance level specified in the standards and benchmarks?

- Can the performance specified in the standards and benchmarks be met if the content difficulty is altered or expanded OR if specially designed instruction that focuses on prerequisite skills is provided?

- Can the performance specified in the standards and benchmarks be met if supportive training related to the disability is provided?[327]

Allowable Test Accommodations

The IEP Team must consider **allowable test accommodations** that conform to State requirements and do not invalidate the test. There is considerable flexibility in the use of accommodations in the classroom so that for a classroom test or quiz a variety of formats could be used to determine the most effective accommodation. For the majority of students with disabilities standardized, Statewide and other "high-stakes" tests provide a benchmark for degree of successful curriculum participation as well as entry into courses, advanced courses, and diploma programs.

Test accommodations should be a part of the section detailing regular classroom accommodation in that regular classroom accommodations often provide the basis for allowable State and district-wide test accommodations. For the Louisiana Educational Assessment Program, "test accommodations should not be different from or in addition to the accommodations provided in the classroom during instruction and assessment as indicated on the student's IEP or Section 504 plan."[328] In other words, test accommodations cannot be made apart from accommodations already being used in the classroom but rather test accommodations are based on and therefore must follow the designation of classroom accommodations and "if an accommodation is not provided in regular instruction or assessment, even though it is an indicated accommodation, it would be inappropriate to provide that accommodation during testing; even though it might improve the student's score on the assessment."[329] In Wisconsin, "when considering accommodations for students with disabilities, IEP Teams should consider the supplemental aids and accommodations the student currently uses in the classroom. These teachers/teams should consider all accommodations that have been successful in assisting the student to access the general education curriculum, except those that would invalidate the assessment by changing the content measured by the test or the intent of the test."[330] Providing help with syntax and vocabulary when measuring writing, reading test questions designed to measure reading, or using a calculator when measuring primary facts would be examples of test invalidation.

For Statewide and district-wide assessments validity is an extremely important concern; that is, the test must measure what it purports to measure. Reading a reading test to a child would no longer measure reading; allowing a child to use a spellcheck device as part of a spelling assessment would invalidate the spelling test. Content difficulty can be considered on a child's IEP (e.g., reducing the language difficulty of assignments) but this would invariably invalidate most tests. Pre-teaching, providing verbal reinforcement, and emphasizing important information are important teaching strategies but these strategies may be inappropriate or explicitly disallowed for Statewide assessments. The IDEA–2004 specifically requires that tests are

☛ **are used for purposes for which the assessments or measures are valid and reliable;**

☛ **are administered by trained and knowledgeable personnel; and**

☛ **are administered in accordance with any instructions provided by the producer of such assessments.**[331]

When tests are not administered in accordance with the test instructions provided by the test producer, when validity has not been considered or even undermined, and when a test has been changed beyond recognition, the disability needs of a child have not been served.

The IEP Team must be aware of test validity when making accommodations, know what modifications are used in the regular classroom, and what accommodations are permitted for State and district-wide tests. What the IEP Team should not do is select accommodations that *seem appropriate* or *appear to be useful* from a long list of possible test accommodations. Not only can this invalidate a test, but often the selection of test accommodations by this method is not based on actual need, the accommodation may or may not be used, or the accommodation may or may not be permitted by the test publisher. The IEP Team must base all accommodations on demonstrated need, and take into consideration State and/or test publisher guidelines concerning allowable accommodations.

IEP Team Accommodations

An OSEP/OSERS memorandum emphatically directs that "neither the SEA nor the LEA can limit the authority of the IEP Team to select individual accommodations and modifications in administration needed for a child with a disability to participate in State and district-wide assessments of student achievement." On the other hand, the SEA or LEA must ensure that assessments are reliable and valid. The need to select reliable and valid accommodations requires that the IEP Team "base all decisions regarding accommodations or modifications on a full understanding of the consequences for reporting and accountability."

State and local educational agencies cannot dictate or otherwise "constrain the IEP Team's decisions about accommodations and modifications" but agencies "can provide guidelines and training to assist IEP Teams in making informed decisions:"

> **Such guidelines should delineate instructions and conditions for the appropriate administration of a selected accommodation. For example, these guidelines can define the role of the scribe when the IEP Team has selected dictation of answers as an accommodation, or prescribe conditions for reading test items aloud if the IEP Team has selected reading test items as an accommodation. Accommodations guidelines should also clearly inform IEP Teams of any implications for how scores will be reported or any consequences for students or schools resulting from the selected accommodations.**[332]

Out-of-level Testing

Out-of-level testing and alternate assessments are unique assessments that measure and meet unique student needs. The National Center on Educational Outcomes (NCEO) defines out-of-level testing to mean "that a student who is in one grade is assessed using a level of a test developed for students in another grade. Below-grade-level testing is almost universally what is meant when the terms "out-of-level," "instructional-level," "off-level," or "functional-level" are used.[333] The NCEO explains that advocates of out-of-level testing believe this approach is a better measure of actual student instruction, is more accurate and is less stressful. Those critical of out-of-level testing believe that "out-of-level testing information does not show whether students meet enrolled-grade proficiency requirements, and harms students by institutionalizing below grade-level expectations."

Test Accommodations Guidelines

The following are several general guidelines that the IEP Team should consider when identifying test accommodations:

Consider accommodations being used in the classroom. Accommodations used in the classroom provide a frame of reference for additional classroom accommodations that might be necessary, and also provides the foundation for identifying test accommodations. Many accommodations used in the classroom might be permissible for use with State assessments but, for the most part, test accommodations are generally more restrictive than classroom accommodations; that is, an accommodation may be used in the classroom but not necessarily used in testing. The goal of both classroom and test accommodations is to mitigate the affects of the disability and to either evaluate content (e.g., assessment) or allow the student to participate in the content, but classroom accommodations also provide the opportunity to evaluate the need for the accommodation. Consistent with the LRE mandate, unnecessary accommodations should be avoided as much as possible. During formal or standardized testing accommodations should not be used that invalidate the test (e.g., eliminating difficult items, *reading* reading-test items), are not permitted (e.g., multiday testing might not be allowed), not necessary (e.g., individual testing), or not available (e.g., an individualized administered standardized test might not be available in large print or Braille).

Accommodation	Used in Classroom	Used for Testing
Yes	Assessment	Assessment
No	Not necessary Participation	Invalidates test Not permitted Not necessary Not available

"Test" classroom accommodations. The classroom is where the need for test accommodations should be "tested" and not during more formal or standardized test situations. Whether the accommodation is a special desk, extended time or sign language, the effectiveness of the accommodation and training personnel for the implementation of the accommodation should be determined. If the IEP Team is asked to consider accommodations that have never been tried either during the individual evaluation or in the classroom, the evaluation data is insufficient for the IEP Team to consider the accommodation needs of the student.

Provide the least restrictive accommodations. If a child can participate with extended time rather than having the test read aloud, provide extended time. If an individual administration is permissible and effective, provide this accommodation rather than one that will change the format (e.g., reading a test aloud) or the time requirements (tests must be administered in accordance with any instructions provided by the producer of such assessments).

The Virginia Department of Education's Sample IEP Form requires that "accommodations/modifications provided as part of the instructional and testing/assessment process will allow the student equal opportunity to access the curriculum and demonstrate achievement. Accommodations and modifications also provide access to nonacademic and extracurricular activities and educationally related settings. Accommodations/modification based solely on the potential to enhance performance beyond providing equal access are inappropriate."[334] An accommodation that is not useful or does not meet a need is an overly-restrictive accommodation.

Accommodations should be based on need. One of the dangers of using a list of accommodations on an IEP form or IEP checklist is a tendency to indicate accommodations that certainly might be useful but ones that are not based on need or at least demonstrated need. The checklist might indicate that noise buffers (earphones) or that a carrel is permitted, but the IEP Team should not select these accommodations simply because they are listed on the IEP form and they might be beneficial. If a child does just as well without noise buffers, a carrel, or extended time, the use of these accommodations would be overly restrictive and therefore inappropriate. For extended time, the amount of extended time needed to perform on an equal basis with nondisabled students should be determined. The simple guideline for all accommodations is that every classroom or test accommodation should be based on data or observation.

Select accommodations because of need and not disability. Not all children with disabilities need **extended time** or **directions given in a variety of ways**; not all children with specific learning disabilities **modified tests**; not all children with ADHD (Other Health Impairments) need **shortened assignments** or **frequent breaks**. Almost invariably when an accommodation is given to all, however *all* is defined, the accommodations is based on disability rather than need and is likely discriminatory.

Accommodations should be "individualized." The list of accommodations that could be cited in every child's IEP (or for every child in the general population) is infinite. Providing "positive feedback" or "clarifying instructions" are undeniably good ideas, but the IEP is not a list of teaching strategies that should be a part of every teacher's repertoire. Accommodations that warrant inclusion in a child's IEP are those that are necessary to mitigate the effects of the child's disability and to allow participation in the classroom or general curriculum (especially tests).

Always consider State guidelines. Not all accommodations are permissible within State guidelines. Also, certain accommodations might have very specific requirements such as the responsibility or interpreters, readers or scribes (e.g., exact reading and/or recording of student responses).

Accommodations are not intended to give the student an advantage. Just as a scribe or reader should never provide help by making corrections or giving answers, all accommodations should be provided with the intent to allow a student to participate on a comparable basis with nondisabled children.

Don't "fish" for accommodations. "Fishing" occurs when the IEP Team selects accommodations that are unrelated to data or student need on the chance that the accommodation might be useful. Indeed, many accommodations that are not needed to mitigate the effects of a disability might be useful, but these accommodations are inappropriate if they are not necessary. There is no rule or regulation that requires every child with a disability to have accommodations. However, there is a rule (the LRE requirement) that accommodations should enable participation in the classroom and curriculum.

Don't pad the IEP with accommodations. Because the IEP includes a section for accommodations does not mean that the IEP must include accommodations. Accommodations and other elements of an IEP that are not needed detract from the overall validity of the IEP. This occurs because the IEP "padding" will never be implemented, were never intended to be implemented but were included to make the IEP more like, well, someone's vision of an IEP.

Chapter 12

MEASURABLE ANNUAL GOALS

*Measurable annual goals designed to meet the child's
needs that result from the child's disability.*

5. Measurable Annual Goals (Each Measurable Annual Goal must include a **measured beginning level of performance** and a corresponding **measurable annual goal** to meet academic, functional needs and postsecondary needs.)		
Describe how progress is reported to parents:		
MAG (Include a description of the assessment used to measure each goal)	**Measured Beginning Level of Performance**	**Measured Annual Level of Performance**

The primary criticism of measurable annual goals, and why IEP goals are often woefully ineffective for meeting individual learning needs, is not the concept of measurement but the reality of measurement. Everyone who has worked with IEPs has come upon empty goals such as "to improve reading as determined by teacher observation to the 85 percent level." In *Evans v. Rhinebeck* the IEP goals were derisively said to repeatedly incant the phrases "teacher observation," and "80 percent success," but little indication is given of the beginning level of success "when the IEP was written."[335]

Measurable annual goals link the individual evaluation to the plan for specially designed instruction. If needs are correctly identified, and data is available to substantiate these needs, the measurable annual goals identified by the IEP Team provide the essence of the individualized planning document.

The Essence of an IEP

Measurable annual goals provide the best and most straightforward index of an IEPs appropriateness as to whether the IEP has been developed to meet a child's needs or to facially comply with IDEA and the regulations. First, evaluate whether the goal is measurable or likely to be measured. A goal such as "improve classroom behavior to 80 percent as determined by teacher observation" is typical of goals that have no intention of being measured and therefore will have no impact on classroom performance. However, even a goal as trite and vague as this has a "kernel" of truth. A teacher could simply indicate a percentage on a rating form next to "classroom" behavior so this goal, for what it's worth, could actually be measured. And this is the problem: many goals could be measured but never are . . . and are not intended to be measured. Of course, some goals are so vague (e.g., improve reading, self-concept) that the sheer lack of specificity makes the measurable annual goal meaningless.

Every measurable must address an important need. Every goal should be based on measurable behavior. Every goal should have a beginning level of performance. If this is lacking, serious doubt must be given to how the goal was conceptualized. If the goal is to improve sight word recognition to 100, there must be data showing the current number of sight words known. If the goal is to reduce classroom screaming to three incidents a week, data should be available indicating the number of screaming incidents that occur on a daily or weekly basis. Every measurable annual goal should provide a clear

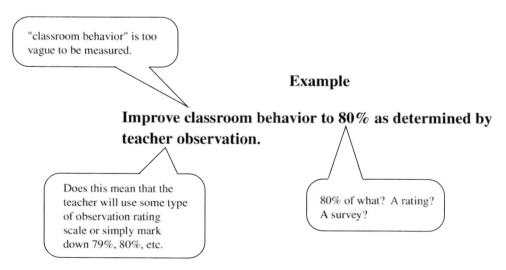

Figure 12.1. Evaluating Measurable Annual Goals.

link between an important and measured need (i.e., someone actually measured the trait, skill or ability) and the goal.

A clear sign of an inappropriate IEP are goals carried over from year to year, often verbatim, but there is never a measurement as to whether the goal has been achieved or not. Often the content and/or difficulty for these goals are entirely inappropriate. One might suppose that a goal for a child to comprehend 80 percent of grade-level material read would be a "legally" measurable goal. However, a "legally" measurable annual goal (and comprehending 80% of what is read is potentially measurable) is far different than actually determining the percentage of grade level material a child is able to comprehend. In this regard the law is less than clear.

Finally, there should be an obvious relationship between goals and services. If the program goal for a child is to develop beginning reading skills and the service to meet this need is to simply assign the child to a self-contained classroom, something is amiss. If a child is to receive speech, physical therapy or occupational therapy but there are no goals for these areas, the IEP is incomplete. If a child has serious classroom behavioral problems, but specific goals and services are not provided to address these problems, there is a serious discrepancy between needs and services. Measurable annual goals are an extension of the individual evaluation and statement of needs; services are an extension of the goals cited to meet these needs. Specific goals should be reflected by services to achieve annual goals. As noted in IDEA–1997 measurable annual goals are part of the strategic planning process and that "once the IEP Team has developed measurable annual goals for a child, the team can . . . develop strategies that will be most effective in realizing those goals."[336]

 A real educational plan must contain real goals, that are really measured and that really address a child's needs. Goals should focus on areas affected by the child's disability rather than all educational goals. If a child is able to achieve satisfactorily in mathematics but the IEP includes mathematics goals, the IEP might actually prevent participation in the regular curriculum in that specialized instruction would be provided in an area that was unnecessary. Even more important, the goal might detract from time in which the child should be participating in the general curriculum and with nondisabled children. If a student has an orthopedic impairment, one goal might relate to using an augmentative communication device to participate in regular classroom social studies assessments. If the student's cognitive ability to deal with the regular classroom social studies content was unaffected, there would be no need to develop or list separate social studies goals. Obviously, if this were done, especially in a separate location, this could result in the creation of a separate and unique social studies curriculum when, in fact, the child is able to participate in regular curriculum.

Measurable annual goals "should focus on offsetting or reducing the problems resulting from the child's disability that interfere with learning and educational performance in school." As indicated in IDEA–1997 regulations "a public agency is not required to include in an IEP annual goals that relate to areas of the general curriculum in which the child's disability does not affect the child's ability to be involved in and progress in the general curriculum. If a child with a disability needs only modifications or accommodations in order to progress in an area of the general curriculum, the IEP does not need to include a goal for that area; however, the IEP would need to specify those modifications or accommodations" (Question #4). IDEA–2004 requires

> **(II) a statement of measurable annual goals designed to—**
>> **(aa) meet the child's needs that result from the child's disability to enable the child to be involved in and make progress in the general education curriculum; and**
>> **(bb) meet the child's other educational needs that result from the child's disability.**[337]

The IEP must address how the child will be involved in the general curriculum but that some children have other educational needs that are not directly linked to the curriculum. "For example, if the IEP Team determines that in order for a child who is deaf to participate in the general curriculum he or she needs sign language and materials which reflect his or her language development, those needs (relating to the child's participation in the general curriculum) must be addressed in the child's IEP. In addition, if the team determines that the child also needs to expand his or her vocabulary in sign language that service must also be addressed in the applicable components of the child's IEP."[338]

Data-based Needs

The purpose of IEP measurable annual goals is to create independence and not dependence. This is accomplished by identifying important data-based needs. The difficulty for achieving a goal should not dissuade the incorporation of a goal in a child's IEP. If attendance is the reason why a child with a disability is not achieving academically, a goal (increasing school attendance) or accommodations (increased home instruction, parent participation) might be appropriate. Likewise, pre-determined goals do not guide goal selection. Basing measurable annual goals on State goals, or a predetermined bank of computer-generated goals, incorrectly places a preconceived notion of need before the multiplicity of actual student need. A data-based need indicates that there is specific information or data showing a level of performance that should be improved. This is the essence of an appropriate education which centers about finding those areas that, unless otherwise improved, will prevent a child from receiving an appropriate education.

A data-based need indicates that the beginning level of performance (e.g., the behavior, grade, score) is below expectations and that a goal, if successfully achieved, will bridge the gap between the beginning level of performance and the level of performance anticipated by the annual goal. Regardless whether the data is a behavior such as not teasing other children or a score on a test or classroom grades, whatever the child exhibits is an indication of a strength. If a child is able to write a composition with 20 errors per 100 words, the 20 errors indicate a weakness but being able to write a composition is a strength. The task and the goal should be to bridge the gap between what the child currently does (the strength) to what the child can reasonable be expected to do at the end of the year (potential strength).

The goal itself could involve specific behaviors such as on-task behavior, excessive talking, limited written language, poor syntax, minimizing word reading, or increasing reading vocabulary from 5 to 50 words, or oral language from one to 10 words. The metric for a goal can be based on a test score, percentage, frequency, rating, grade, etc. In every instance the behavior, score or frequency should focus on important classroom needs and skills, and should be sensitive to changes in improved performance.

The specificity in identifying data-based levels of performance should not be confused with the specificity of the goal itself. A measurable annual goal might indicate that the child will perform all primary fact operations up and through single division facts with minuends 0 though 9 and subtrahends equal to or less than minuends. The goal is specific enough but without a data-based beginning level of performance, the achievability of the goal cannot be ascertained. Obviously, for a child with intensive cognitive needs, limited communication and academic skills, the impracticality of this goal is obvious. For a child not having these math skills the achievability of the goal depends on the beginning level of performance. For a child who is able to perform addition and subtraction facts, this goal might be feasible; for a child able to perform some multiplication facts, this would be very attainable; but for a child in the process of developing number concept and learning basic addition facts, the probability of achieving this goal might be very small. A goal to know 80 percent division facts or comprehend 80 percent of grade-level reading material is only feasible when compared to the beginning level of performance. The importance of this becomes readily apparent when reviewing IEPs which have not been updated (because goals are never really measured). Without actually measuring performance neither need nor progress can be measured because need is defined as the difference between the beginning level of performance and the desired ending (annual) level of performance.

The format for measurable annual goals in the IEP should be simplified so that two elements are stressed: a brief description of the relevant data at the beginning of the school year, and the anticipated data at the end of the year. If the goal is to decrease classroom outbursts to 0 at the end of the year, the number of classroom outbursts at the beginning of the year must be known. If the goal is to improve reading comprehension to 70 percent at the end of the year, the degree of reading comprehension at the beginning of the year must be determined. Beginning levels of performance require that skills, abilities and behaviors are actually measured and not stated in a "will be measured" format.

There is no need to create IEP forms that attempt to codify every combination of elements comprising measurable annual goals. This not only requires considerable effort **considering what will be done** rather than actually **measuring what is done** but recording this information in the IEP form becomes the priority task. Each measurable annual goal should be self-contained, self-explanatory, based on actual measurement, and directly related to a needed identified in the statement of PLAA.

Measured Beginning Levels of Performance

The fictionalization of goals is often enabled by creating elaborate criteria that have no bearing on the actual measurement of the goal or goal progress. This is achieved by listing in the IEP what appears to be a very detailed list of goal properties such as Evaluation Criteria (e.g., test score, teacher-made tests, % accuracy, frequency, etc.), Evaluation Procedures (e.g., tests, observation, etc.), and Evaluation Schedules (e.g., daily, weekly, etc.). If a beginning level of performance exists, there is no need to indicate whether a test observation was used in that this will be included in a description of the skill or behavior. For example, assume that an evaluation indicates that a child is able to identify 32 sight words from a list of 220 most frequently occurring words so that the beginning level of performance is "able to identify 32 of 220 sight words when presented individually." This not only indicates that a measure (e.g., test, observational protocol) actually exists but that **the measure** was actually used **to measure** performance. Similarly, by saying that "the child is able to solve 75 percent of grade-level word problems" there is no doubt how the skill is measured or how progress will be assessed at the end of the year. Compare this to what is usually done: no beginning level of performance, no real measure to ascertain the level of performance other than the ubiquitous "teacher observation," an equally ubiquitous, albeit cryptic, an anticipated level of progress of "85 percent" by the end of the year.

EVANS v. Rhinebeck Central School District
930 F.Supp. 83 (S.D. NY, 1996)

Catherine Evans, the plaintiff, initiated this action on behalf of her son. Frank, the a fifteen year old student with above average IQ, was identified as dyslexic. Apparently, the school district classified Frank as having a specific learning disability in spelling (which is no longer a SLD subcategory). Evans was displeased with procedural timelines (conducting an impartial hearing within 45 days), an appropriate IEP, a statement of present levels of performance, and the process for determining a specific learning disability (viz., not including the classroom teacher, not writing a specific SLD report, not conducting a classroom observation). In the end the court opined that "In light of the foregoing, Evans is entitled to a declaratory judgment, and this matter is remanded to the District's CSE with instructions to develop an IEP for Frank that will address his particular needs, consistent with this decision."

And about those IEP goals . . . "The IEPs include only broad, generic objectives and vague, subjective methods for monitoring Frank's progress. For example, the first goal in Frank's October 1994 IEP provided that he would be evaluated on the listed objectives by reference to "teacher observation" and "80 percent accuracy." With reference to the second goal, the October 1994 IEP provided that Frank would be evaluated by "teacher observation" and "80 percent success." Although the IEP repeatedly incants these phrases–"teacher observation," "80 percent success"–because there is little indication of what Frank's level of success was when the IEP was written, it fails to specify strategies for adequately evaluating Frank's academic progress and determining which teaching methods are effective and which need to be revised. Again, Zeisler conceded, with regard to the June 1994 IEP, which used the same mantra to a large extent, that it did not set forth measurable criteria to assess progress." "_____ testimony is also enlightening on this issue. She had not met Frank when she wrote the goals and objectives that appear on the October 1994 and January 1995 IEPs, but based them on information that she acquired from Bloomer, Smith and Zeisler at the June CSE meeting. _____ wrote a goal that Frank would increase computation skills in math at the eighth grade level, but testified that she had no idea why he had failed seventh grade math. She wrote a goal for eighth grade physical science, but testified that she did not know whether he had passed seventh grade science or what his functioning level was in physical science. She wrote a goal for spelling, but testified that she did not know what his functioning level in spelling was. She testified that she did not know why there were no goals for the individual instruction in social studies that she was to provide Frank. Finally, she testified that she did not know why the IEP did not reflect the other scores obtained from testing by _____, the fact that Frank failed every subject his seventh grade year, or teacher information."

Measurable Annual Goal Guidelines

Specificity and Need: Identify specific and significant areas of need that will enable participation in the regular classroom or general curriculum. One of the primary tasks of the individual evaluation is to specify present levels of academic achievement. This includes observable and measurable levels of all skills, and behaviors that might limit participation in the classroom or curriculum.

Select Meaningful Goals: This is the essence of the individual learning plan. Without meaningful goals, or ignoring real goals, the plan is irreparably flawed. If the IEP Team is unable to identify meaningful goals, the individual evaluation is incomplete, or the data from the individual evaluation is either not understood or is being ignored.

Measurable Goals: Whether the area of need is study skills, socialization, reading, mathematics or mastery of content area, the overriding factor is measurability. "To improve study skills" might be right on the mark, but if the IEP Team is unable to specify how study skills will be measured, there is a good likelihood that study skills (or whatever is being considered) has never been measured, and will never be measured at the end of the year. The essential characteristic of measurable annual goals is not that a behavior, ability or skill *can* be measured, but that the behavior, ability or skill has been measured (beginning level of performance) and will be measured again at the end of the year to determine the extent of annual progress.

Beginning Levels of Performance: If a goal does not have a beginning level of performance, or a valid estimate of performance, the IEP Team does not have sufficient information or data to develop a meaningful measurable annual goal.

Annual Progress: Based on the child's current level of performance consider the level of performance expected by the end of the year.

Frivolous Goals: Frivolous goals are often those that are not measurable and will be utterly ignored during and at the end of school year. Sheer number does not increase the overall worth of goals. Three, four, or five pages of computer generated goals might not only be frivolous but mask the inherent meaninglessness of goals, and cause real goals to be ignored. This often occurs when the IEP attempts to define daily objectives or activities (e.g., initial consonants, blends, etc.), but the very detail masks the development of a meaningful annual plan for providing an appropriate education.

Nonmeasurable Goals: A real measurable annual goal cannot be developed without a clear understanding of the beginning level of performance. When this information is not available the IEP will incant the meaningless phrase to comprehend "with 85 percent accuracy as determined by teacher observation." In that no effort was made to determine the current level of reading comprehension (or whatever trait or ability is being considered), even by the vague and overused criterion "teacher observation" (which is generally never used to yield an actual measurement of performance), there is no way to determine whether the goal has been achieved or to what extent the goal has been achieved.

Regular Classroom Participation: Identify goals that enable regular classroom and curriculum participation. If a child requires a more restrictive placement, identify goals that will enable eventual or gradual participation in the classroom.

Measuring Annual Performance

Describing Progress

The statement of progress toward achieving goals in P.L. 94–142 required the IEP to include "appropriate objective criteria and evaluation procedures and schedules for determining, on at least an annual basis, whether instructional objectives are being achieved."[339] The IDEA–1997 expanded this statement to emphasize regular measurement periods ("regular" being the frequency of reports of progress for nondisabled children), the extent of current progress toward achieving goals, and the likelihood that current progress is sufficient to achieve annual goal.

IDEA–1997 IEP Statement of Progress Requirements

(I) how the child's progress toward the annual goals described in clause (ii) will be measured; and

(II) how the child's parents will be regularly informed (by such means as periodic report cards), at least as often as parents are informed of their nondisabled children's progress, of–

(aa) their child's progress toward the annual goals described in clause (ii); and

(bb) the extent to which that progress is sufficient to enable the child to achieve the goals by the end of the year.

–IDEA–1997, 614(d)(1)(A)(viii)

Public Law 108–446 has repositioned the IEP statement of progress from the last element of IEP content to immediately follow the statement of measurable annual goals. The intent of this is to show the close relationship between goals and the statement of progress, and that common sense indicates that this statement should either follow or be included with the statement of measurable annual goals. In addition, the frequency of reports to parents must be "concurrent with the issuance of report cards." The IDEA–2004 has simplified IEP content to simply require **how progress will be measured** and **when period reports will be provided**:

> **a description of how the child's progress toward meeting the annual goals described in subclause (II[340]) will be measured and when periodic reports on the progress the child is making toward meeting the annual goals (such as through the use of quarterly or other periodic reports, concurrent with the issuance of report cards) will be provided.**[341]

There are several methods that are used to report progress to parents such as report cards, subjective qualitative reports, IEP report card, periodic measurements (teacher-made tests, ratings, standardized tests), conferences or conference calls, written reports, holistic or analytic rating scales, and benchmarks and short-term objectives.

Adequate Yearly Progress

The No Child Left Behind Act stipulates that adequate yearly progress' shall be defined by the State in a manner that

(i) applies the same high standards of academic achievement to all public elementary school and secondary school students in the State;

(ii) is statistically valid and reliable;

(iii) results in continuous and substantial academic improvement for all students;

(iv) measures the progress of public elementary schools, secondary schools and local educational agencies and the State based primarily on the academic assessments described in paragraph (3);

(v) includes separate measurable annual objectives for continuous and substantial improvement for each of the following:
(I) The achievement of all public elementary school and secondary school students.
(II) The achievement of—
(aa) economically disadvantaged students;
(bb) students from major racial and ethnic groups;
(cc) students with disabilities; and
(dd) students with limited English proficiency.

–P.L. 107–10, Title I, 1111(b)(2)(C)

Benchmarks Revisited

The IDEA–1997 required "a statement of measurable annual goals, including benchmarks or short-term objectives, related to . . ." while IDEA–2004 has been simplified to a "statement of measurable annual goals designed to. . . ." The rationale for this change is the belief that by "eliminating the requirements for benchmarks and short-term objectives will reduce unproductive paperwork and allow greater attention to be focused on the child's annual IEP goals and on the methods of measuring progress and reporting that progress to parents in a meaningful way."[342]

One of the advantages of benchmarks and short-term objectives is that each benchmark or short-term objective, when measured, provides an indication of goal progress, and this data can be used to provide a forthright evaluation of progress that can be reported to parents. Because the NCLB act requires report cards "the duplicative use of benchmarks and short-term objectives is eliminated for most children with disabilities beginning in the

2005–2006 school year."[343]

Benchmarks were originally intended to "establish expected performance levels that allow for regular checks of progress that coincide with the reporting periods for informing parents of their child's progress toward achieving the annual goals." Short-term objectives were intended to facilitate instruction by breaking down skills into smaller discrete instructional components. For children with severe disabilities the benchmark and short-term objective requirement has a twofold purpose: benchmarks and short-term objectives are clearly intended to provide a reporting framework for **alternate assessments** aligned to **alternative achievement standards**. This assessment function is the reason why benchmarks and short-term objectives are now included in the PLAA statement.

The purpose of benchmarks and short-term objectives was a thoughtful solution to the problem of measuring progress over the year and periodically measuring performance. The usefulness of benchmarks and short-term objectives "to help track the child's progress," was thought to be offset by contributing "greatly to the paperwork burden on educators and parents, and often bears no relationship to the non-linear reality of a child's development."[344] In that many IEP goals are never based on real measurements and are included in the IEP to show compliance, benchmarks and short-term objectives certainly did contributed to paperwork. However, the problem of excessive paperwork is not alleviated by eliminating benchmarks or short-term objectives, but by actually measuring beginning and annual levels of performance, and creating meaningful benchmarks and short-term objectives.

IF an IEP is comprised of goals that are void of meaning, paperwork will certainly be reduced by eliminating benchmarks and short-term objectives. But goals will be no more meaningful and meaningless goals beget a meaningless IEP. The quality and efficiency of goals will only be improved when they are based on measured levels of performance; if measurable annual goals are not measured, IEPs will entail less paperwork but with no improvement in quality or effectiveness. Although short-term objectives are no longer required, there are situations when the incorporation of short-term objectives or benchmarks in the IEP might be required or beneficial such as when parents request a report of progress, when the behavior or skill requires periodic measurement; or when addressing State standards that have been modified. A parent or teacher might appreciate a plan that charts the expected progress for a skill or behavior over the course of the year. The intent is not to add paperwork to the IEP but rather, when needed or requested, providing a yearly plan by means of short-term objectives or benchmarks. For children requiring alternative assessments the added paperwork required by benchmarks or short-term objectives is necessary to ensure educational programming that is aligned to the general curriculum.

Benchmarks and Goal Development

Eliminating benchmarks or short-term objectives does focus attention of measurable annual goals and overall annual progress. If the IEP Team is uncertain how to gauge the level of annual progress, or the team or parents request a careful and periodic accounting of the level of behavior or ability, benchmarks or short-term objectives might be very useful. When the IEP Team has a clear or reasonable idea how to gauge annual progress, a **top-down approach** to goal specification is appropriate (i.e., first identify annual goals). If there is concern for estimating annual progress and/or a careful and periodic accounting of progress is required, a **bottom-up approach** to goal writing in the form of benchmarks or short-term objectives might be appropriate (e.g., i.e., first identify the benchmarks where the last benchmark is the annual goal). This approach can result in extra work, and admittedly extra paperwork, but the meaningfulness and achievability of the goal might be greatly improved.

State Standards and Benchmarks

For State standards benchmarks or short-term objectives are often incorporated in the Standards. For example, the Illinois science standard for *applying concepts, principles,* and *processes of scientific inquiry* includes the following: describing an observed event, developing questions, collecting data, recording and storing data, arranging data, and comparing observations.[345] If science is an area impacted by the child's disability, the IEP would need to include a measurable annual goal for assessing progress in science. One method for doing this would be to simply have the teacher rate progress in science based on a subjective scale with no empirical basis (e.g., satisfactory progress in science, unsatisfactory progress, etc.). An alternative method for evaluating progress toward achieving this goal would be to collect data for each of the areas specified (e.g., describing an observed event, developing questions, etc.). For children taking alternative assessments a benchmark approach provides a method for aligning the individualized education to State standards.

The potential use of benchmarks was recognized in an early version of IDEA (April 30, 2003) that stipulated "until the beginning of the 2004–2006 school year, a description of benchmarks or short-term objectives, except in the case of children with disabilities who take alternate assessments aligned to alternate achievement standards, a description of benchmarks or short-term objectives shall continue to be included."[346] Although benchmarks or short-term objectives are no longer required, this does not mean that they cannot be included as a means to report progress or to estimate and measure progress over the course of the year. If measurable annual goals are not defined by benchmarks or short-term objectives, there is even a greater need to ensure that every measurable annual goal has a beginning measured level of performance and an annual measured level of performance. Again, the key here is the word "measured" as in actually measure a skill or performance and not the intent to measure or, even more disingenuous, a statement that is so vague that there is no pretense of actual measurement.

Benchmarks are Expected Levels of Performance

The purpose of both is to enable a child's teacher(s), parents, and others involved in developing and implementing the child's IEP, to gauge, at intermediate times during the year, how well the child is progressing toward achievement of the annual goal. IEP teams may continue to develop short-term instructional objectives, that generally break the skills described in the annual goal down into discrete components. The revised statute and regulations also provide that, as an alternative, IEP teams may develop benchmarks, which can be thought of as describing the amount of progress the child is expected to make within specified segments of the year. Generally, benchmarks establish expected performance levels that allow for regular checks of progress that coincide with the reporting periods for informing parents of their child's progress toward achieving the annual goals. An IEP team may use either short term objectives or benchmarks or a combination of the two depending on the nature of the annual goals and the needs of the child.

–IDEA–1997, 34 CFR 300, Appendix A, #1

Direct and Indirect Measurement

Many IEPs rely on **indirect measurements** of goal progress. Whether the goal is to decrease behavior from 10 to 0 incidents (e.g., kicking, hitting, spitting), to improve expressive vocabulary from 0 to 10, or to increase reading comprehension from 40% to 65%, **direct measurement** usually provides the most unambiguous estimation of goal progress. On the other hand, an indirect measurement is generally easier to obtain although the usefulness for evaluating goal progress is far less clear. An indirect measurement of progress can be a rating of goal progress, a subjective estimation of goal progress (e.g., "The goal is being achieved"), or a holistic estimation of goal progress (e.g., "I believe that _____ has achieved 85% of the goal."). Many IEPs tacitly encourage indirect measurements by listing subjective progress indicators for each goal (e.g., goal in progress, mastered, completed, discontinued), evaluation criteria (e.g., % accuracy, frequency, # of attempts), or evaluation methods (e.g., teacher observation, student conferences, unit tests, portfolios, work samples, tests, grades, charts).

A check or code might be entered to show that the goal is "in progress," "some progress" is being made, or the goal has been "completed." An even more indirect measurement is a subjective evaluation of performance. If the goal is to increase reading comprehension to 85 percent, a teacher could subjectively estimate the amount of progress achieved. This subjective evaluation of reading comprehension is not really a percentage but a holistic evaluation of performance.

The IEP format often requires detailed data entry but the amount of paperwork does not conceal the fact that goals are not or never will be measured. The following example illustrates the variety of categories that could be included in the IEP. Notice, however, that there is no actual beginning data, no inkling as to what "observation" means.

Measurable Annual Goal	Evaluation Procedure	Evaluation Criteria	Evaluation Schedule	Location of Services	Service Provider	Progress
Improve reading comprehension	Observation	Percentage	Weekly	Regular Classroom	Mr. Smith	Making Progress

The IEP format is further obfuscated by means of computer-generated goals so that reading comprehension might be goal R06, and the "observation" evaluation procedure codified as 3 (where 1=tests, 2=work samples, 3=observation, etc.). On a similar basis, other categories are also coded, including progress toward goal achievement (1=no progress, 2=progress, 3=mastery). The IEP data takes on the appearance of quantitative acceptability when all the coding is completed but the lack of real measurement has not been overcome.

Measurable Annual Goal	Evaluation Procedure	Evaluation Criteria	Evaluation Schedule	Location of Services	Service Provider	Progress
R06	3	2	2	1	Mr. Smith	2

What makes the above misleading is the use of computer-generated IEP goals that allows for the creation of a huge number of goals, all acceptably codified, but providing no evidence whatsoever that the skill or ability is measured or ever used as a gauge of progress from the beginning to the end of the year.

Many IEPs use the progress report to parents as the measurement of the goal. This might include an "IEP report" card or some other device which indicates the child's progress. For example, the Senate report (SR 105–17, p. 22) offers the following format:

Ted will demonstrate effective literal comprehension:

No Progress   Some Progress   Good Progress   Almost Complete   Complete

The above method for showing progress is often codified as illustrated by the following five formats:

a)   1=completed, 2=in progress
b)   1=no progress, 2=some progress, 3=considerable progress, 4=goal achieved.
c)   1=no progress, 2=in progress, 3=completed
d)   1=continue, 2=discontinue, 3=mastered, 4=not started
e)   C=continue, M=mastered

Subjective evaluations of progress are sometimes (but not always) less meaningful than data-based evaluations. If the goal is to decrease teacher prompts for off-task behavior from 30 per day to 0, indicating that a child is making progress toward the goal is certainly less meaningful than providing observational data that shows the number of prompts has been reduced to 28 or 10, etc. The problem of goal meaningfulness (or lack thereof) is not solved by having yet another code for *making sufficient progress to achieve the goal by the end of the year.* Using the IEP form the teacher quickly enters a code for progress, including the end-of-the year progress evaluation. The measurable annual goal could be absolutely meaningless but a coded entry for progress would suggest that the goal was actually measured. However, during the year these progress estimates are simply poor indicators of actual performance.

If the goal is to increase spoken language from two words to 50 words by the end of the year, and the child's performance for this goal is reported as *in progress* (or even more cryptically as a code of 2), actual progress could be 1 percent or 99 percent. The best indication of progress is to provide actual data. Just as a goal rating of in progress is imprecise, indicating no progress can be just as cryptic in that there is usually no indication as to the cause or reason for lack of progress. The North Dakota IEP is an exception in that an explanation is also required to explain lack of progress (lack of prerequisite skills, more time needed, inadequate assessment, excessive absences/tardiness).[347]

If the child's spoken language increases from two to eight words, indicate this and not engage in IEP paperwork by filling in repetitive codes. If the goal is to improve performance on classroom quizzes, attendance, or decrease classroom outbursts, aggressive behavior or self-injurious behavior, indicating actual performance is much more powerful than recording that progress is being made. This is especially important when the annual goal is evaluated. There should be some empirical evidence that the goal has been achieved, and not that progress is continuing (and the same stodgy, paperwork driven goal is carried over to the next year).

The intent of the requirement that "parents will be regularly informed . . . at least as often as parents are informed of their nondisabled children's progress, of the sufficiency of their child's progress toward the annual goals" also indicates an obligation to make a serious attempt to evaluate progress, an attempt that is commensurate with progress reports for nondisabled children. Nondisabled children are periodically evaluated, and the quarterly grading period might be comprised of numerous grades, assignments and conclude with a major examination. The period reports for nondisabled children are based on actual work and evaluations of that work. Likewise, the periodic reports to parents regarding their child's progress toward meeting goals and the likelihood that annual goals will be achieved should be based on objective data. Parents of nondisabled children are entitled to more than a statement of progress based entirely on a subjective evaluation of student work, and such an approach provide no accountability to ensure the accuracy of reported progress or objective data for a child to improve performance. For nondisabled children, when the whole purpose of special education is a plan for progress (i.e., the IEP), progress reports based on objective data is even more important.

For children with disabilities requiring alternative assessments, ratings of work, portfolios, ratings of portfolios and checklists are all useful for evaluating progress. If the overused *teacher observation* is cited in an IEP goal, at the very least the teacher observations should be based on a specific scale comprised of specific items. If the measurable annual goal is improvement in written expression, rather than simply saying that writing will be improved "to the 80% level as determined by teacher observation," a beginning level of writing performance, as well as periodic evaluations, could be determined by a simple teacher rating scale:

Area	Low	Below Average	Average	Above Average	High
Vocabulary		✔			
Sentence Use		✔			
Punctuation		✔			
Handwriting	✔				
Spelling	✔				
Mechanics	✔				
Ideation			✔		

The regular classroom teacher could rate the child based on teacher observation of actual work samples. Not only does the above rating scale provide data for measuring performance, but the items within the scale offer an opportunity to consider both strengths and weaknesses. For the above scale where low is a 1, below average a 2, etc., the summated rating is 2+2+2+1+1+1+3 or 12. This is equal to an average rating of 12/7 or 1.71. Even that elusive "80 percent" level of performance often cited in IEPs, which is rarely measured, can be determined from the above rating scale. If the maximum rating for the seven items is seven items times a maximum rating of five or $(7)(5) = 35$, then a summated rating of 12 is equal to 12/35(100) or 34 percent. By adjusting the number of items in the rating scale or the content of the items, everything from progress in science, behavior (e.g., self-concept, peer relationships, motivation), reading (e.g., word reading, phonics, etc.) can be assessed by that infrequently defined "teacher observation."

Best Practice

The best practice for reporting progress is to undertake periodic measurements of actual performance. If the measurable annual goal for a child is to be on task for a 20-minute period by the end of the year, and nondisabled children are evaluated four times a year, the on-task behavior for this student should be reported four times a year. Obviously, a direct measurement of the ability, skill or behavior is the best index of annual goal progress. For on-task behavior an estimation of the amount of on-task behavior at each evaluation point is far more meaningful than simply stating either *no progress* or *progress* is being made.

OBERTI v. BOARD OF EDUC.

Rafael is an eight-year-old child with Down's syndrome. "The Individualized Education Plan (IEP) developed by the School District for Rafael for the 1989–90 school year assigned all of Rafael's academic goals to the afternoon special education class. In contrast, the only goals for Rafael in the morning kindergarten class were to observe, model and socialize with nondisabled children. Rafael's IEP for the 1989–90 school year included no provisions for supplementary aids and services in the kindergarten class aside from stating that there will be "modification of regular class expectations" to reflect Rafael's disability. The only goal provided for the regular kindergarten teacher was to facilitate Rafael's adjustment to the kindergarten classroom.

"In sum, in determining whether a child with disabilities can be educated satisfactorily in a regular class with supplemental aids and services (the first prong of the two-part mainstreaming test we adopt today), the court should consider several factors, including: (1) whether the school district has made reasonable efforts to accommodate the child in a regular classroom; (2) the educational benefits available to the child in a regular class, with appropriate supplementary aids and services, as compared to the benefits provided in a special education class; and (3) the possible negative effects of the inclusion of the child on the education of the other students in the class. Thus, the IDEA requires school systems to supplement and realign their resources to move beyond those systems, structures, and practices that tend to result in unnecessary segregation of children with disabilities.

"Finally, in affirming the district court's order that the School District develop a more inclusive program for Rafael in compliance with IDEA for the upcoming school year, we emphasize that neither this court nor the district court is mandating a specific IEP for Rafael. The development of Rafael's IEP, and the specific nature of his placement, is, of course, the job of the Child Study Team."

Before Rafael entered kindergarten the school district wanted to place Rafael in a segregated self-contained special education class. The parents disagreed and an administrative hearing affirmed the school district's placement. . . . the IEP indicated that Rafael had behavioral problems and needed help with toileting, the IEP did not spell out a plan for managing these problems. "If Rafael was as difficult as defendants claim he was, provision of a personal aide in March (instigated by a request from the parents), without any definite plan with respect to her functions, and irregular, *ad hoc,* assistance from another teacher and the school psychologist, were wholly insufficient efforts to meet Rafael's special needs. Moreover, children placed in segregated or partially segregated settings must be simultaneously included in mainstream components to the maximum extent appropriate. Finally, in accordance with the purposes and practices expressed by Congress in Public Law 108–446, the goal for every child should be directed toward moving up on the continuum in the direction of full inclusion."

"We note that these experts challenged the School District's view that readiness for the mainstreaming or inclusion could successfully be developed within a segregated setting and argued that it is illusory, and perhaps even pretextual, to contend that segregation can breed readiness for inclusion."
–789 F.Supp. 1322 (D.N.J. 1992) and 995 F.2d 1204 (3rd Cir. 1993)

Standardized Score Goals

Standardized test scores (viz., district-wide assessments) and State assessments generally lack the measurable specificity to be used as measurable annual goals. To say that a child should achieve at grade level is obvious. What must be included in the IEP is a plan for achieving at grade level, and this plan is defined by measurable annual goals. Likewise, achieving passing grades is an obvious goal that we want for all children, but if a grade in a course is used as a measurable annual goal for a child with a disability, the goal should delineate specific areas which can be measured and will result in a passing grade (e.g., completing homework assignments, passing weekly quizzes or course-related curriculum-based assessments).

Standardized scores are useful for determining general educational need, but these scores are often inappropriate as benchmarks for measurable annual goals. Whether an overall standardized score is used (e.g., overall reading performance) or subtest scores (e.g., word usage, reading vocabulary, reading comprehension), there are several reasons why standardized scores are difficult to use as measurable annual goals. First, a child with reading needs might be below average on a district-wide achievement test or subtests (e.g., sounds and letters, language mechanics, etc.), but this does not mean that the score or scores on this particular test are the cause of this child's reading problems. Indeed, there are probably a large number of tests and subtests, and an equally large number of different test names that also correlate with low reading performance. Second, standardized scores are not easily interpreted. For example, the difference between a percentile rank of 50 and a percentile rank of 16 (one standard deviation) is equivalent to a difference between percentile ranks of 16 and 2 (also one standard deviation). Third, standardized measures, especially wide-range assessments, are not sensitive to instructional levels of growth. A child might make important gains during the year but these gains may or may not correspond to standardized test score gains. One of the difficulties with using standardized achievement scores from district-wide tests is that these measures are not sensitive for measuring small increments of improvement. A child might have received a percentile rank of 16 on a standardized reading test, but to say that the goal is to improve performance to a percentile rank of 50 is neither specific nor likely sensitive to actual improvements in reading performance. On a standardized achievement test, a goal of average performance is obvious but this hardly provides insight as to what should be done or what tasks should be used. Finally, standardized tests are difficult to use on a repeated basis because the repeated use of the same tests and the same items (sometimes for years on end) confounds test performance.

Classroom-based Goals

Classroom-based goals includes observed behavior, ratings of behavior, on-task behavior, completion of assignments, homework completion, classroom participation, workbook assignments, successful classroom participation, quizzes, weekly tests, classroom activities, etc. The task is not to select classroom-based goals from a list because these are thought to be important areas, but to select goals that will enable a child to successfully participate in the classroom. Inexplicitly, although regular classroom participation is underlying purpose of special education, identifying what a child needs to participate in the regular classroom is often given little consideration. Standardized tests are indirect measures of the general curriculum and indices of regular classroom participation. An IEP that does not consider specific classroom needs is deficient and will likely not enable regular classroom and curriculum participation.

When considering the need to create classroom-based goals, the importance of the IDEA requirement that a regular education teacher participates in the development of the IEP and the determination of strategies and supplementary aids and services becomes readily apparent.[348] At the IEP meeting, the regular classroom teacher must help identify classroom activities and skills that promote success in the classroom and in the general curriculum. Participation in the general curriculum begins with a thoughtful consideration of what the child can and cannot do in the regular classroom. In part, a classroom observation can be used to provide some idea of classroom needs, but the primary source for classroom-based goals should be the classroom teacher.

Measured Annual Level of Performance

The actual measurement of annual goals requires a re-measurement of the initial benchmark. Because many IEP goals have no beginning level of performance, and a beginning measurement, final goal progress is often never measured. Whenever a goal has no beginning level of performance, and the key phrase "teacher observation" appears, the goal is probably a pretend goal that has no purpose other than to give the illusion of IDEA compliance.

The task is not to simply have a goal that might be measurable, but identify goals that have been (beginning level of performance) and will be measured (final or annual level of performance). If the goal is to improve the ability to write a paragraph by the end of the year as determined by *teacher observation*, data from teacher observations should be available to determine the level of beginning performance. The following illustrates various metrics that can be used as the basis for measuring goal performance. Whatever metric is used, the essential element is the beginning level of performance. By merely stating that the goal is to improve reading comprehension to 85 percent does not suggest how this 85 percent is measured regardless of whether a code is also provided that suggests that reading comprehension will be measured by a teacher-made test. However, when a beginning measurement is required, somehow, someway reading comprehension must be actually measured. In the below table the annual goal indicates how the beginning level of performance is measured. For example, the goal could be to improve reading comprehension based on a 20 question teacher-made evaluation of grade-level reading material. The use of this assessment during the individual evaluation reveals that the child is able to answer seven of the 20 questions (35%), and the IEP Team decides that a reasonable annual goal would be 75 percent.

Measurable Annual Goal (topic)	Measured Beginning Level of Performance	Measured Annual Level of Performance
Identify sight words	20	50
Decrease classroom interruptions	50 per day	5 per day
Increase classroom responses	0 per day	5 per day
Improve writing skills	75 errors per 100 words	10 errors per 100 words
Increase attendance	10 absences per month	1 absence per month
Increase reading comprehension	35%	75%
Improve classroom grad average	45%	70%
Improve homework assignments	0 completed	90% completed

The General Curriculum and Goals

The importance of the general curriculum in developing appropriate educational programs for children with disabilities has been given added emphasis by NCLB. This act requires that each State has "statewide annual measurable objectives"[349] for assessing mathematics and reading or language arts to ensure that "all students will meet or exceed the State's proficient level of academic achievement on the State assessments within the State's timeline."

David D. v. Dartmouth School Committee
775 F.2d 411 (1985)

This case involved a 17-year-old adolescent with Down's Syndrome. The student was enrolled in "a special day program with some supplementary services in the local school district" (p. 415). Unfortunately, David had "repeatedly and unrelentingly engaged in sexual and aggressive behavior." David's parents believed that David had not been taught the necessary self-control "rendering the IER the Town proposed for him fatally deficient." The parent's believed that unless David was able to exhibit appropriate behavior he would not be able to participate in a community-based program, and this had already been identified as an appropriate IEP objective. Although there were academic benefits to mainstreaming, David D. v. Dartmouth indicates that an IEP cannot ignore critical needs.

The Senate report for IDEA–2004 reiterates the need for both curriculum-related and other needs created by a child disability by requiring "that the statement of measurable annual goals should include academic goals, and, where appropriate, functional goals." The report goes on to state that "for most students with disabilities, many of their IEP goals would likely conform to State and district-wide academic content standards and progress indicators consistent with standards based (on) reform within education and the new requirements of NCLB" and that "IEPs would also include other goals that the IEP Team deemed appropriate for the student, such as life skills, self-advocacy, social skills, and desired post-school activities."[350]

Standards and the General Curriculum

The IEP is not a restatement of State standards, especially those Standards which are not affected by the child's disability. The individual evaluation and present levels of academic achievement outlines a child's needs; State standards do not give legitimacy to these needs to the extent that a need without a corresponding State standard would be ignored. For needs such as on-task classroom behavior, specific reading or study skills, or disability-related skills involving Braille, sign language, assistive technology, etc., there is probably no State standard that would conform to these types of specific needs.

North Dakota makes a useful distinction between IEP goals that are designed to develop specific skills, abilities or behavior (e.g., behavior, reading, mathematics skills, etc.) to achieve standards, and IEPs which specifically reference State standards. If a student has difficulty with a specific standard, or the standard must be modified, the standard or modified standard is cited in the IEP. If a child requires an alternative placement because of behavioral needs but is able to progress in the general curriculum, there would be no need to select State standards for inclusion in the IEP if the ability to achieve standards is not affected by the child's disability. The task is not to "find" applicable State standards to include in the IEP but to identify needs that prevent participation in the general curriculum.

State standards are especially important when a child is in an alternative placement or when working with specialists, in resource rooms, or at a different instructional/content level within the general education curriculum. The IEP Team should not begin with a listing of State standards to determine goals but to select measurable annual goals that "enable the child to be involved in and progress in the general curriculum." The IEP is not based on standards but on the general curriculum, and the presumption that there is a connection between State standards and the general curriculum.

A report by Thompson, et al. (2001) suggests that one explanation why State standards are often not mentioned in IEPs "is that standards are often equated with the general curriculum. An assumption is made that if students have access to the general curriculum, they will be working toward standards," and add that "we hope this dream will come true."[351] There is no doubt that many IEP Teams do not consider or incorporate State standards IEPs. However, if the focus is on participation of the general curriculum, and the general curriculum is reflective of State standards, this is not a problem. As is the case for nondisabled children State standards are addressed in the general curriculum, and nondisabled children are (usually) not evaluated by their ability to achieve State standards other than the need to pass Statewide assessments which, along with the general curriculum, determine State standard competency. In other words, emphasis on the general curriculum should result in achieving State standards, and proficiency on Statewide assessments provide a further check on achieving State standards.

If an IEP Team focuses on State standards rather than participation in the general curriculum, the IEP Team might actually create a curriculum for children with disabilities that is different than the general curriculum. One of the deficiencies of alternative placements is the disregard for the general curriculum and the creation of a separate "special education" curriculum. As is now required by IDEA–2004 alternate assessments aligned to State assessments are intended to promote the general curriculum as a frame of reference for all students, especially for students with disabilities.

Consistent with the Senate report for IDEA–2004 the goals for most students with disabilities will "conform to State and district-wide academic content standards." This does not mean that IEP measurable annual goals are a list of State standards, but that goals enable participation in the general curriculum which, in turn, will allow children with disabilities to achieve State standards. For example, being on-task or mastering specific math or language arts content will allow participation in the general curriculum and thereby allow the achievement of State standards. For most children with disabilities curriculum goals will be the same as those used with nondisabled children. There is no need to repeat these goals in the IEP. If a child is able to achieve regular curriculum goals, but an alternative placement uses a curriculum unique to the placement, the placement is inappropriate. A child with a disability is entitled to participate in the general education curriculum regardless of the placement. Furthermore, State standards are not intended to be behavioral objectives so that listing fairly complex standards in a child's IEP goes far beyond what is necessary. The above mentioned goal for "a student should be able to speak and write well for a variety of purposes and audiences" is intended to be an integrated and real-life achievement but this should not be listed in the IEP for every child with a disability regarding language arts.

The confusion between services and placement is never more apparent than when a child's placement limits or prevents access to the general curriculum. Children in residential settings or self-contained classrooms might be able to participate in the general curriculum but the public school curriculum, textbooks and related materials are abandoned for a scattered, unstructured curriculum that is not standards-based and, should the child be mainstreamed in the regular classroom, detracts from eventual classroom participation. Because of this the use of State standards and goals as guideposts are especially important for children placed in alternative and residential settings, for children in resource rooms and receiving pull-out services relating to the general curriculum, and for children requiring modifications to State standards.

For some children accommodations and modifications are incorporated to allow participation in the general curriculum either in the regular classroom or in an alternative placement. For a child using Braille the general curriculum might require some degree of modifications but, by and large, most children using Braille will be able to conform to State and district-wide standards.

Curriculum Goals

Every State has (or should have) specific standards, goals, and/or benchmarks indicating what students should acquire over the course of a year or for grade levels (elementary, middle (or junior high) and high school, or grade ranges (e.g., 9–12). Nelson states that promoting K–12 curriculum coherence is one of the many benefits of State benchmarks and standards and that "research tells us that learning requires making connections between ideas and creating linkages that make sense in a larger context. Unfortunately, as the data from TIMSS indicate, the U.S. curriculum is too often a series of disjointed ideas and experiences, lacking both focus and coherence."[352] For special education a lack of curriculum focus is one of the main obstacles that prevent FAPE. The curriculum provided to students with disabilities is often disjointed and represents little more than a hodgepodge of activities that vary from placement to placement and from provider to provider. Even in the regular classroom a child with a disability might be engaged in a curriculum other than that provided to nondisabled children.

The benchmarks and standards indicate specific content standards (e.g., algebra skills) and corresponding benchmarks or guideposts (e.g., simplify algebraic equations). For children with disabilities the presumption is that every child will be educated in the regular classroom; a corollary for this presumption is that children in the regular classroom are responsible for achieving regular curriculum goals or the same goals that are provided for nondisabled children. For children who require modified standards, these standards should be cited in the IEP. A child might not be able to master algebra skills for a middle school mathematics standard involving inequalities and complex algebraic equations, but the standard might be modified to enable an understanding of more basic mathematical skills. Disability should not dictate curriculum. A child's disability should not prevent participation in the general curriculum or participation with nondisabled children because of disability-required modifications to the curriculum. This was emphasized in the regulations for IDEA–1997 which cautioned that "a child with a disability is not removed from education in age-appropriate regular classrooms solely because of needed modifications in the general curriculum."[353] If a student uses Braille, **available** Braille materials should not be the basis of the child's education curriculum. The same curriculum used by nondisabled children should guide the development or acquisition of Braille materials. On a similar basis, an aide or interpreter does not determine the child's curriculum; an aide, interpreter, assistant teacher must be appropriately supervised to ensure that general curriculum goals and standards are achieved.

Classroom Participation Goals

If a child requires services outside of the regular classroom or an alternative placement, the IEP Team should consider the extent of classroom participation so that these restrictive services promote independence and inclusion in the regular education environment as much as possible. In addition, service providers outside of the regular classroom must recognize that the goal for children in more restrictive settings is to develop inclusive skills that will generalize to independent daily living and regular classroom participation. The IEP can include specific goals that promote the inclusion of children with disabilities in the regular classroom and general curriculum. Possible areas that can be considered by the IEP Team for increasing classroom participation include increasing participation in classroom assignments and activities, time spent in the regular classroom, and participation in nonacademic activities.

Alternative Assessment Goals

For alternative assessments, and when standards must be modified, State standards often provide excellent measurement and instructional content guidelines. The third grade content standard in Alaska is "a student should be able to apply mathematical concepts and processes to situations within and outside of school." The alternate performance standard for this content standard is "respond to and use patterns. *[May also include numbers, calculations and measurement]*."[354] In California, a Mathematics Content Standard[355] includes the following standard relating to number sense (understanding relationships between numbers, quantities, and place value in whole numbers up to 1,000) to be achieved by the end of Grade two:

> **1.1 Count, read, and write whole numbers to 1,000 and identify the place value for each digit.**
>
> **1.2 Use words, models, and expanded forms (e.g., 45 = 4 tens + 5) to represent numbers (to 1,000).**
>
> **1.3 Order and compare whole numbers to 1,000 by using the symbols <, =, >.**

For a student with a disability that affects achievement in mathematics the Standard 1.1 shown above might be modified to "count, read, and write whole numbers to 30." This provides a clear link to a relevant State standard and also indicates a measurable task for this standard. If this standard were listed in a child's IEP, the ability to "count, read, and write whole numbers" would have been measured and the beginning level might have indicated that the child is able to "count numbers to 5." Based on this beginning level of 5, an annual goal of 30 (or whatever is thought to be feasible) might be considered achievable.

There are a variety of reasons why a child might not be able to participate in the general curriculum, other than ability (i.e., the relative difficulty of curriculum standards or goals). A child might have the cognitive capacity to achieve a standard or goal, and thus participate with nondisabled children in the general curriculum, if disability-related skills are achieved or accommodations provided. For a child with a specific learning disability in basic reading skills, the inability to participate in the science, social studies or English general curriculum is not the difficulty of the content but the skill (basic reading) that prevents access to the content. A child with this disability might require goals to address the disability, and accommodations to access the curriculum (e.g., a reader). The same is true for a child with emotional needs who might have the ability to achieve general curriculum goals and standards were it not for the behavior or emotional needs that prevents curriculum participation. For this child specific behavior goals might be necessary, and adjustments to the learning environment to accommodate behavior needs (e.g., short instructional periods, breaks, small group instruction). What is extremely important for children with disabilities is that for those able to achieve State standards and goals that these standards and goals provide the framework for the curriculum. This is especially important for students placed in alternative settings where departures from the general curriculum will exacerbate the inability to eventually participate in the general curriculum.

Chapter 13

IEP SERVICES

. . . children placed in segregated or partially segregated settings must be simultaneously included in mainstream components "to the maximum extent appropriate."[356]

6. Services			
Beginning date of services:			
Service	(Describe the specific service provided.)	Frequency	Duration
Special Education:			
Related Services:			
Support for School Personnel:			
Nonacademic and Other Services			

DIFFERENTIATING SERVICES

The traditional format for IEPs has been to differentiate the service components cited in IDEA. For P.L. 94–142 in 1975 this consisted of two areas: "specific educational services," and the extent of participation in regular educational programs. For IDEA–1990 transition services was added to

198

required IEP content. The IDEA–1997 further expanded the service statement to include **supplementary aids and services, program modifications**, and **supports for school personnel**. The IDEA–2004 now requires "a statement of the special education and related services, and supplementary aids and services, **based on peer-reviewed research to the extent practicable**, to be provided to the child, or on behalf of the child, and a statement of the program modifications or supports for school personnel."[357]

Differentiating Services and Placement

A child might require two hours of indirect services a week, two hours of direct instruction daily, or 15 hours of specialized instruction each week to enable regular classroom participation and to meet other needs. After the IEP has been developed, the IEP Team might decide that services could be provided in the regular classroom, or that another placement is required on a part-time or full-time basis. In any case, the IEP team clearly differentiates between placement and services. This becomes difficult using a fixed form but if a word processing template is used, service entries could be added to the form as necessary.

The best practice for differentiating services and placement is not to include the location of services when first considering services. Location will only confound the service/placement differentiation. The location of services should be determined after the IEP has been developed.

Frequency, Location and Duration

". . . the projected date for the beginning of the services and modifications . . . and the anticipated frequency, location, and duration of those services and modifications."[358]

The statement for the frequency, location and duration of services defines the extent of the specially designed instruction needed to meet a child's needs and participate in the general curriculum. Because IDEA specifies "the anticipated frequency, location, and duration of those services and modifications" IEPs have traditionally included an IEP component comprised of five columns: Service, Date, Frequency, Location and Duration. Specifying the location of services often precludes the IEP team from considering what a child needs to participate in the general curriculum. If the IEP Team decides that a child requires services in a resource room or in a self-contained classroom, the Team might wrongly conclude that the resource room or the self-contained classroom is the service. The correct distinction between service and placement would be to first define the service (e.g., individualized help with reading comprehension in content areas), and then indicate the frequency and duration (e.g., three one-hour sessions a week). After all the services have been identified, where these services are provided is decided. Requiring the IEP Team to focus attention on services and not placement (i.e., location), and to decide placement after the IEP has been developed, is exactly what the IDEA requires.[359]

Service	Date	Frequency	Location	Duration

The determination of location of services could be made by a simple modification to the above table so that the last column (location) is made after all services have been decided.

*Location of services are decided after all services have been considered.				
Service	Date	Frequency	Location	Duration

Another approach is to eliminate the determination of location of services from the services section of the IEP and relocate this decision to a section devoted to placement.

Beginning date of service:		
Service	Frequency	Duration

Frequency and Duration

When specifying frequency and duration of services, frequency is usually stated as Time per Week (or Time per Month is sometimes indicated) and duration indicates the duration of each weekly period or session so that Frequency=5 hours and Duration=60 minutes (or 1 hour) is equivalent to five hours per week. If Duration indicates Total Weekly Hours receiving services, the duration of each weekly period is then (Total Weekly Hours)/Frequency. Indicating duration in minutes provides greater flexibility in identifying necessary services. However frequency and duration are recorded, the IEP provider should have a clear idea as to the extent of services envisioned by the IEP Team. The Team should be aware of the makeup of the regular school day. If school day periods are 44 minutes, indicating a period duration of 60 minutes could be disruptive to the child's regular classroom scheduling and participation.

Service	(Describe the specific service provided.)	Frequency	Duration
Special Education:			

Supplementary Aids and Services

Supplementary aids and services is the key to a successful IEP. By first considering the full range of services that a child needs to participate in the general curriculum and regular classroom, the IEP Team creates a standard for all children with disabilities. This standard is the general curriculum and regular classroom. Paradoxically, the IEP form does not necessarily require a separate Supplementary Aids and Services category. As discussed below, the consideration of supplementary aids and services for every child with a disability is actually the statutory method for meeting the least restrictive environment mandate: Children are only removed from the regular classroom when supplementary aids and services cannot be achieved satisfactorily.[360]

The term supplementary aids and services means "aids, services, and other supports that are provided in regular education classes or other education-related settings to enable children with disabilities to be educated with nondisabled children to the maximum extent appropriate in accordance with section 612(a)(5)."[361] The statement of the special education and related services and supplementary aids and services required in every IEP is confusing in that there is not only overlap between the terms special education, related services and supplementary aids and services, but the order in which the services listed should be reconsidered. If a child has a disability under IDEA, the child must receive special education (i.e., specialized instruction). If special education is provided in the regular classroom by an itinerant teacher, a consultant teacher, or mainstreaming special education specialist, this service is a supplementary aid and service. Likewise, if a related service is provided to enable regular classroom participation, or a classroom accommodation enables a child to be placed in a regular classroom by providing special furniture, lighting, sound amplification or environmental accommodations (e.g., a dehumidifier), these are all supplementary aids and services.

Supplementary aids and services are always the IEP Teams first consideration. Supplementary aids and services should not be treated as a separate and unique set of services and accommodations that exist apart from the special education related services, etc. There is not a unique category of supplementary aids and services. Supplementary aids and services include all special education, related services, accommodations and supports that enable a child with a disability to be educated with nondisabled children. There is nothing unique about these services other than each service or accommodation enables participation in the general curriculum or regular classroom. Of all the considerations which the IEP Team must entertain, supplementary aids and service are essential for the implementation of IDEA.

Public Law 108–446 begins with the Congressional direction that after "over 25 years of research and experience has demonstrated that the education of children with disabilities can be made more effective by providing appropriate special education and related services, and aids and supports in the regular classroom, to such children, whenever appropriate." The task is not to remove a child from the regular classroom because this is an administratively convenient thing to do but to "to ensure that all children with disabilities have available to them a free appropriate public education that emphasizes special education and related services designed to meet their unique needs and prepare them for further education, employment, and independent living."[362]

If there is one primary consideration that must guide the IEP Team it is the identification of accommodations, services and supports that enable participation in the regular classroom and in the general curriculum. For every child with a disability the focus is always the regular classroom and the regular classroom curriculum. Regular classroom participation is not only for children with mild disabilities, but for all children receiving services under IDEA. This does not mean that children with severe disabilities are included in all classroom activities, or that all children are capable of participating in all classroom and curriculum activities. What the emphasis on regular classroom participation means, and what the presumption for being educated in the regular classroom means, is that a child with disabilities is educated with nondisabled children to the maximum extent appropriate. If the goal of special education is to maximize a child's ability to function as an independent adult, **increasing** a child's ability to function independently and to participate with nondisabled children is a logical and essential mandate of IDEA.

The regular classroom is pivotal for understanding what services should be provided, how services are documented, and the order for considering services. The IEP Team must determine the extent the child can be educated satisfactorily in regular classes with the use of supplementary aids and services. However, the distinction between services and placement often becomes blurred; that is, educational placement is tantamount to the provision of educational services. This, of course, is contrary to the presumption of regular classroom participation to the maximum extent appropriate. An emotional disability might require intensive specialized instruction, teacher support (e.g., an aide) and a variety of accommodations in order to provide the child an appropriate education. However, to say that the appropriate services for a child with an emotional disability is to place the child in a separate classroom for children with emotional disabilities is contrary to IDEA in that a child must be placed because of specific educational needs and not because of the disability.

Supplementary Aids and Services is not a separate IEP component set apart from special education, related services and supports, but a **consideration** of all services that all regular classroom and curriculum participation. This is essentially the first test for mainstreaming in *Daniel v. State Board of Education*[363] which asks whether supplementary services were considered and "if not, if accommodations in the regular classroom have not been considered, the school district is in violation of the Act." In order to participate in the regular classroom one child might need an assistive technology device or alternative communication device to access the curriculum; a second child might need to acquire specific behaviors that will result in the child not affecting the learning of others; and a third child might need an interpreter or an alternate curriculum (e.g., in Braille). For each child this is what is necessary to function in the regular classroom as opposed to a placement which presumes that these needs will be addressed. The IEP Team should not begin by placing a child with assistive technology or behavioral needs in a special education class because this does not address the specific needs that a child has to function in the regular classroom. After services have been designated, the placement is considered where these services can be provided as least restrictively as possible. A child with behavioral needs might require a different placement, or a different placement for a part of the day.

Daniel provides a rather straightforward guideline for IEP Teams when considering supplementary aids and services. The IEP Team must ensure services are sufficient and entail the **full range of services**,[364] evaluate the academic benefits of these services, and consider the impact these services have on other children. Furthermore, "if the state is providing supplemental aids and services and is modifying its regular education program, we must examine whether its efforts are sufficient. The Act does not permit states to make mere token gestures to accommodate handicapped students; its requirement for modifying and supplementing regular education is broad."[365] The courts have been very clear (Oberti,[366] Daniel[367]) that the appearance of services or "mere token gestures" to enable a child to participate in the regular classroom is insufficient and not consistent with IDEA.

The IEP form does not require a unique category of Supplementary Aids and Services. This is redundant in that all services that constitute supplementary aids and services can be identified in the special education, related services, accommodations, etc. sections of the IEP. What the IEP Team must do is to first consider what is needed to succeed in the regular classroom. When the IEP Team does this, when the IEP Team considers the full range of services that will enable a child to be successful in the regular classroom, the obligation to provide supplementary aides and services will have been achieved.

IEP Decisions and Forms

The IEP form could be modified so that each service category has a specific number of rows thereby suggesting a specific number of services. This results in form dictating content. The IEP Team should develop the collective skill of identifying necessary services, and adjust the length of the IEP form accordingly.

In order to accommodate every possible combination of services, many IEP forms are cluttered with services that the IEP supposedly must consider but are rarely used. The IEP Team should have a supporting document available to ensure that all services are considered but the IEP document need not list every conceivable service. For example, the IEP Team must consider Braille instruction for children who are blind or visually impaired. Yet, children with visual impairments account for less than one-half of a percent (.44%) of children receiving services under IDEA (see Table 6-1, p. 76). Of this small percentage of children requiring Braille, even fewer will need instruction in Braille. Braille services are extremely important for developing literacy skills and thereby provide an appropriate education for children who are blind who have a definite need for Braille. However, the IEP should not include every service category that a child might need simply to show that the IEP Team is complying with the law. The IEP Team must consider all necessary services; the IEP Team must document all necessary services; but the services that must be considered need not appear as distinct IEP categories. When the emphasis changes from **showing compliance** to **providing children with an appropriate education**, the IEP document will be truly individualized and, hopefully, uncluttered by categories, checklists and verbatim quotes from regulations and state codes.

Least Restrictive Services and Supports

The least restrictive environment mandate applies not only to placements as indicated by the increasing restrictiveness of the continuum of placements (instruction in regular classes, special classes, special schools, etc.). *The* least restrictive special education service is indirect consultant teacher services (e.g., planning, program modifications, consultation, etc.). For each service specified in the IEP, there should be a need for the service, and the frequency and duration of the service should be based on need. Assigning all children with specific learning disabilities to one hour of direct daily instruction would be restrictive for some children, and probably insufficient for others. Only when services are considered to meet the unique needs of each child, and only when the amount of services is proportionate to meet these needs, will they be as least restrictive as possible.

Services for "All" Children

The Committee has heard from many parents and teachers regarding the special situations of children with a medical condition that is degenerative (i.e., a disease that results in negative progression and cannot be corrected or fully stabilized). For these children, services under the IEP can be provided to help maintain the child's present level of functioning for as long as possible in order for the child to fully benefit from special education services. In developing an IEP for these children, the IEP Team may consider recommendations from professional consultants familiar with the child and the medical condition in the development of the IEP. The IEP Team can include related services designed to provide therapeutic services prior to loss of original abilities to extend current skills and throughout the child's enrollment in school. These services may include occupational and physical therapy, self-help, mobility and communication, as appropriate.

–House report 108–77, IDEA–2003 (H.R. 1350), p. 112

Special Education

The IEP Team must identify special education services for every child; that is, services provided by a certified special Education teacher. If a child does not need special education, the child should not be receiving services under IDEA. The first special education service to be considered by the IEP Team should be specially designed instruction in the regular classroom.

Because support services are instrumental for supporting the regular classroom teacher and special education teacher, these services are considered next. The various supports for school personnel include direct and indirect consultant teacher services, aides, teacher assistants, related service consultation (e.g., social works, school psychologist), etc.

Special education is defined as "specially designed instruction, at no cost to parents, to meet the unique needs of a child with a disability, including instruction conducted in the classroom, in the home, in hospitals and institutions, and in other settings; and instruction in physical education."[368] Specially designed instruction means "means adapting, as appropriate to the needs of an eligible child under this part, the content, methodology, or delivery of instruction (i) To address the unique needs of the child that result from the child's disability; and (ii) To ensure access of the child to the general curriculum, so that he or she can meet the educational standards within the jurisdiction of the public agency that apply to all children."[369] Every child receiving services under IDEA must **need** and **receive** specially designed instruction.

After considering all factors that affect a child's educational performance, the IEP Team's next task is to define the specially designed instruction that a child needs. This specially designed instruction is defined by measurable annual goals and the services, accommodations and supports needed to achieve these goals. The special education and related services that are provided to meet a child's needs must adhere to the LRE principle so that the "removal of a child from the regular educational environment occurs only when the nature or severity of the disability of a child is such that education in regular classes with the use of supplementary aids and services cannot be achieved satisfactorily."[370] For example, providing a child with four hours of special education per day when one hour would suffice (i.e., suffice to the extent that education in regular education classes would be successful) would be restrictive. Thus, prior to placement, the IEP Team must determine the least amount of services necessary to function successfully in the regular classroom. The IEP Team must view services as comprising a **continuum of services** where the restrictiveness of services is defined by the extent which the service prevents participation with nondisabled children or participation in the general curriculum. This is not to say that a service that prevents such nonparticipation is not necessary but that services which do so are restrictive and must be minimized as per the LRE mandate.

After the least restrictive services have been identified, and the substance of the IEP has been completed, the IEP Team then considers placement. For every child the presumed placement is the regular classroom. If a child cannot be educated in the regular classroom satisfactorily, the concept of a **continuum of alternative placements** is used to select the least restrictive placement, or the mix of placements, where services can be provided. The IDEA defines points on the continuum of alternative placements as comprising instruction in regular classes, special classes, special schools, home instruction, and instruction in hospitals and institutions.[371]

The IEP Team must not confuse the continuum of services with the continuum of alternative placements as is done in New York where the continuum is referred to as a continuum of services which includes transitional support services, consultant teacher services, resource room services, special classes, and homebound and hospital instruction. This is really a variation of a continuum of placements and not a continuum of services where services is defined as a specific activity or specially designed instruction to meet a child's needs. Consultant teacher services are just that: direct and indirect services provided to enable a child to participate in regular classes. However, a special class is not a service but the place where specially designed instruction is provided. An assumption must not be made that simply designating a special class is the same as specifying needed services. A child might require extensive instruction in language development, basic academic skills and self-help skills. The placement where these services can be provided might be the regular classroom, a special class or a combination of the two. Assuming that the placement is the service automatically designates the regular classroom as inappropriate because this is not the service/placement.

Transition Services

The term 'transition services' means a coordinated set of activities for a child with a disability that:

> **A) is designed to be within a results-oriented process, that is focused on improving the academic and functional achievement of the child with a disability to facilitate the child's movement from school to post-school activities, including post-secondary education, vocational education, integrated employment (including supported employment), continuing and adult education, adult services, independent living, or community participation;**
>
> **B) is based on the individual child's needs, taking into account the child's strengths, preferences, and interests; and**

C) includes instruction, related services, community experiences, the development of employment and other post-school adult living objectives, and, when appropriate, acquisition of daily living skills and functional vocational evaluation.[372]

The IDEA requirement for including transitions services in a student's IEP no longer makes the distinction between services required by age 14 (a student's course of study) and 16 (transition services, interagency responsibilities, or linkages). The IDEA–2004 requires a statement of transition services

beginning not later than the first IEP to be in effect when the child is 16, and updated annually thereafter–

aa) appropriate measurable postsecondary goals based upon age appropriate transition assessments related to training, education, employment, and, where appropriate, independent living skills; bb) the transition services (including courses of study) needed to assist the child in reaching those goals.[373,374]

Many IEPs include a separate section for transition services as does IDEA at 614(d)(1)(A)(VIII) although these services could be included as part of special education services and related services. Schools have approached the task of meeting transitional IEP needs in widely varying ways. For all IEPs the IEP Team must consider transition services (**beginning not later than the first IEP to be in effect when the child is 16**). The IEP does not require a transition services section but rather for the IEP Team to meet the transition service needs of each student. Because of the importance of transitional services a separate IEP section devoted to vocational goals, relevant to transition services and supports and accommodations is often very appropriate. Thus, a student would have measurable annual goals, special education and related services, and/or post-secondary, employment and daily living goals, as well as transition services (e.g., job coach) and post-secondary linkages. Rhode Island includes a client-centered section relating to transition needs: "When I exit school, I would like to be doing the following (long-term goals): Employment, Post-Secondary Education and Training, Independent Living, Community Participation." The Arkansas IEP form lists a wide range of very specific transition services (e.g., identify personal values met through work, classify jobs into occupational categories). Other states include several general categories of transition services such as transition services for community experience, daily living, employment, post-school outcomes, and vocational needs. Because of the nature and importance of transition services, a separate IEP form category is often appropriate.

The following Table lists a sampling of the many transition services/needs that can be included in a student's IEP (see Burns, 2001, p. 212).

Table 13-1.

Transition Services	
Acquisition of daily living skills	Job application skills
Adult education	Job coach services
Adult foster care	Job Opportunities and Basic Skills
Adult goal identification	program (JOBS)
Applied technology education	Job placement assistance
Apprentice programs	Job retention skills
Assistive technology training	Job skill training
Career counseling	JTPA (Job Training Partnership Act)
Church participation	Junior college placement
Civic participation	Medical and dental needs
Club participation	Money management
College placement	Occupational licenses
College placement exam training	Plan for Achieving Self Support (PASS)
Communication skills training	Post-school objectives
Community based adult education	Post-secondary education
Programs	Pre-employment training
Community participation	Psychological services
Continuing adult education	Recreational enhancement
Counseling services	Regional occupational center programs
Department of Rehabilitation Services	Rehabilitation services
Determining adult outcomes	Related service needs
Development of interview skills	Residential care living
Development of job search skills	Semi-independent living
Draft registration	Sheltered workshop programs
Employment search	Special education needs
Employment training	Speech and language therapy
Family planning	Supplemental Security Income
Financial assistance	Supported employment
Food stamps	Training material
Functional vocational evaluation	Transportation services
GED preparation	Vehicle modification
Group home living	Vocational aptitude assessment
Health insurance	Vocational goal development
Household management skills	Vocational needs assessment
Identification of agencies	Vocational training
Independent living	Volunteer placement
In-home support services	Work activity programs
Integrated employment	Work/Transportation training
Intermediate care facility	

Extended School Year Services (ESYS)

The IEP form often contains a section for extended school year services or services beyond the normal 180-day school year. These services are not provided to all children and are not intended to serve as a summer program for all children with disabilities. Extended school year services are provided so that a child receives FAPE, and the deciding factor for these services is the extent of regression and recoupment during the summer months; that is, will a lack of services during the summer significantly increase the likelihood that the child will lose the skills acquired during the school year.[375]

Related Services

"based on peer-reviewed research to the extent practicable"

Extended School Year Services
(a) General.
    (1) Each public agency shall ensure that extended school year services are available as necessary to provide FAPE, consistent with paragraph (a)(2) of this section.
    (2) Extended school year services must be provided only if a child's IEP team determines, on an individual basis, in accordance with §§300.340–300.350, that the services are necessary for the provision of FAPE to the child.
    (3) In implementing the requirements of this section, a public agency may not (i) Limit extended school year services to particular categories of disability; or (ii) Unilaterally limit the type, amount, or duration of those services.
(b) Definition. As used in this section, the term extended school year services means special education and related services that
    (1) Are provided to a child with a disability (i) Beyond the normal school year of the public agency; (ii) In accordance with the child's IEP; and (iii) At no cost to the parents of the child; and
    (2) Meet the standards of the SEA.
                                    –IDEA–1997, 34 CFR 300.309

Related services (e.g., speech and language, physical therapy, etc.) enable a child to benefit from special education. If a child requires only a related service, the service should be provided under Section 504 and not IDEA in that IDEA requires the determination of a disability as defined by IDEA and the need for special education. If a related service is deemed necessary, the related service provider should be a member of the IEP Team. For a child whose primary disability is a speech and language impairment, the speech therapist would service on the IEP Team as the child's special education teacher. If the child has a disability other than speech and language, but the child receives speech and language pathology services, the speech therapist would attend IEP meetings when appropriate.

The House report for IDEA–2004 has made clear that "appropriateness" is the guiding factor for assigning services, especially related services. The task of the IEP Team is not to provide every conceivable service but services needed to meet a child's educational and other needs. For related services the requirement is very specific: a related service enables a child to benefit from special education:

> **The Committee is very concerned about the appropriateness of some of the activities that local educational agencies have been required to provide through the provision of related services. The Committee reminds local educational agencies that related services are required to assist a child with a disability to benefit from special education. Related services face the same requirements as do special educational services and local educational agencies are reminded that there is not a requirement to provide every possible related service, but they must provide those services that are appropriate.[376]**

The inclusion of the "based on peer-reviewed research to the extent practicable" clause concerns the provision of related services that actually help a child benefit from special education:

> **Local educational agencies are able to use their discretion to determine whether a requested service will actually enable the child to benefit from special education. To help local educational agencies determine what related services are appropriate to be provided at public expense, the bill encourages the IEP Team to include related services that have been peer-reviewed, to the extent practicable, to determine whether the service**

**is beneficial and related to the special educa-
tion services. The Committee also encourages
the Department to focus its research efforts to
help expand the level of research on related
services to ensure that all appropriate related
services have a solid foundation of research
and peer-review.**[377]

One of the reasons for the "based on peer-reviewed research to the extent
practicable" clause is the identification of related services that may not be
needed. In part this clause is a restatement of the LRE provision in that a
service of questionable need might actually result in removal from the regular classroom. The IEP Team must give careful consideration for every service in that assigning a service that is not needed can be restrictive and prevent a child from participation in the regular classroom or curriculum.
Providing special transportation for all children with disabilities, speech and
language services, or any other related service based on *disability* rather than
need is restrictive and discriminatory.

Related services are services provided to a child so that the child can benefit from special education. If a child requires a related service but not special education, the required services should be provided under Section 504
(if the child also has a disability under this section) and not IDEA. Related
services include the following:

- **Audiology Services**

- **Corrective Services**

- **Counseling Services**

- **Cued Language Transliteration Services (see Interpreting
  Services)**

- **Developmental Services**

- **Early Identification and Assessment Services**

- **Including Therapeutic Recreation**

- **Interpreting Services**

- **Medical Services (for diagnostic and evaluation purposes only)**

- **Orientation and Mobility Services**

- **Physical and Occupational Therapy**

- **Psychological Services**

- **Recreation Services**

- **Rehabilitation Counseling**

- **School Health Services**

- **Social Work Services**

- **Speech-Language Pathology**

- **Supportive Services**

- **Transliteration Services (see Interpreting Services)**

- **Transportation Services**

- **Travel Training Instruction**

Needed related services are not confined to a specific list but as already said, these services include all services that will enable a child to benefit from special education. Related services are not selected apart from special education but are provided so that a child can benefit from special education. To this end related services can include social work, counseling services, orientation and mobility services, speech and language school health services, travel training instruction, auditory training, language habilitation, parent and teacher counseling, guidance counseling, art therapy, leisure education, vocational rehabilitation services, career development services, and transportation services (where transportation includes travel to and from school, in and around school, etc.).

Although nonacademic in nature, transportation services fall within the purview of related services and includes travel to and from school, travel in and around school buildings and specialized equipment.[378] Some IEPs include a category for Transportation Services (e.g., **Special Transportation Services** ❑ **Yes** ❑ **No**) to be checked at the IEP meeting if special transportation needs are required. The presumption is that most students will not need special transportation so there is generally no need to clutter the IEP

with yet another item to check and consider. Of course, transportation services must be considered if a child is to benefit from special education (viz.,
by getting to school), but there is no need to prioritize this related service to
show that the IEP team has been diligent in its considerations.

When assigning services, licensure and certification in certain areas is
extremely important. The IDEA–2004 requires that the qualifications for
related service personnel "are consistent with any State-approved or State-
recognized certification, licensing, registration, or other comparable requirements that apply to the professional discipline in which those personnel are
providing special education or related services."[379]

Also, when identifying related services the services should be integrated in
the IEP rather than appended to the IEP as a separate report. The IEP
should represent an overall and coherent plan for providing an appropriate
education, and not a series of separate reports and unrelated goals. The problem of related services that are independent of the IEP occurs when related
service providers do not play an active role at the IEP meeting and in IEP
Team considerations.

To the maximum extent appropriate related services should be provided
in the regular classroom. Obviously, this is not always possible because of
equipment or the type of service being provided. For example, transportation can be a related service if a child's transportation needs require special
equipment or services. If a child requires an instructional goal relating to
transportation (e.g., behavior, mobility training), this goal might be achieved
outside of the regular classroom.

Program Modifications

Curriculum and classroom modifications are required in the IEP as part
of the services section for the child "or on behalf of the child." Previously
program modifications should be part of the section relating to classroom
and test accommodations. If a program modification has a specific service
component (e.g., an aide, interpreter), the frequency and duration of services should be identified in the service section of the IEP. In order to reduce
content redundancy in the IEP, and not treat simple accommodations as
services (e.g., indicating frequency and duration for an augmentative communication device), a simple rule to follow is this: If a program modification
is assumed to entail all aspects of the curriculum, include the accommodations in the classroom and test accommodation section; if the program modification warrants consideration of specific frequency and duration information, or entails a service component, include this accommodation under services.

Supports for School Personnel

Often program accommodations and supports for school personnel are grouped together no doubt because of the wording of IDEA: a statement of the program modifications *or* supports for school personnel. The Tennessee IEP form has a section entitled PROGRAM MODIFICATIONS/SUPPORTS FOR SCHOOL PERSONNEL.[380] The instructions for this section state that "this is not a place to indicate additional personnel" but to indicate the need for in-service training, consultation, workshops, specific teaching strategies, "instruction on how to use equipment or how to utilize a program." Florida has a similar interpretation of supports for school personnel as training or in-service workshops,[381] "The purpose of the training should be targeted directly toward assisting the teacher to meet a unique and specific need of the student" but "the training cannot be participation in a general in-service training program provided by the school district to a group of individuals." Examples of support include specific training or specific staff development, training in level system for behavior management "consultant services, collaborative teaching, or assistance from a paraprofessional or teacher aide."

As is the case with all services, supports for school personnel can overlap with special education and related services. A teacher might require two hours of indirect help via a special education consultant teacher (a special education service) or by weekly meetings with the school psychologist, social worker, or occupational therapist (related services). In addition to special education and related services, school-wide supports can be extremely effective sources for providing regular classroom support. The regular classroom teacher might meet with the Child Study Team or Instructional Support Team on a scheduled albeit periodic basis, or have similar meetings with a master/lead teacher.

Many IEPs provide little direction for program modifications and supports other than paraphrasing IDEA that "program modifications or supports for school personnel are provided for the child to advance appropriately toward attaining the annual goals, to be involved in and make progress in the general education curriculum, participate in extracurricular and other nonacademic activities; and to be educated and participate with other children with disabilities and nondisabled children in the activities described in this subparagraph." Unlike program modifications that apply to all or most classroom activities, supports for school personnel require specification of frequency, duration and location. The following are examples of supports that can be provided to the regular or special education teacher:

- Aides (viz., part-time, full-time, shared)

- Assistive Technology Services

- Child Study Team assistance

- Consultant Teacher Services

- Consultation from specialists

- In-service (e.g., developing Functional Behavioral Assessments or Behavioral Intervention Plans)

- Lead teacher assistance

- Parent support

- Personnel with special expertise (e.g., AT specialist)

- Related service support (e.g., training by a related service provider)

- Remedial support (e.g., assistance from a remedial reading teacher, speech therapist)

- School health services

- Social work services

- Staff development (focusing on special education)

- Training (e.g., behavior management, using AT devices)

- Transition Services (e.g., job coach assistance)

- Volunteer support

- Workshops

Supports for school personnel include the use of direct and indirect consultant teacher services, teaching assistants, aides, volunteer services, resource room services and remedial services. Supports for school personnel can include training for aides, indirect supports, or providing direct instruction to disabled and nondisabled children. A consultant teacher might assist or lead a classroom instructional activity so that the classroom teacher is able to work directly with a child that has a disability. The ultimate purpose of this instruction is to provide FAPE by enabling the child to successfully participate in general curriculum.

The focus of these supports is not to remove a child from the classroom but to provide services that enable a child to participate in the curriculum and/or classroom. Most important, supports are not intended to be separate from the regular classroom and especially not separate from the regular curriculum. Every aide should have very specific responsibilities for enabling participation in the classroom. Aides do not determine the curriculum; aides are not responsible for developing curricular activities; and aides are always supervised and trained. This was the problem in *Oberti v. Board of Education* where a personal aide was provided "without any definite plan with respect to her functions, and irregular, *ad hoc,* assistance from another teacher and the school psychologist, were wholly insufficient efforts to meet Rafael's special needs."[382]

A classroom aide can be an essential classroom support but the IEP Team must follow basic guidelines when providing this type of classroom support:

> ☛ **Aides must be trained.**

> ☛ **Aides must be supervised by qualified personnel.**

> ☛ **Aides must provide the least restrictive services.**

> ☛ **Aides must understand the fundamental goal to include children with disabilities in the regular education classroom and in the general curriculum.**

> ☛ **Aides must be periodically evaluated.**

As is the case with all classroom supports, the resource room as a support resource for the regular classroom should provide support for regular classroom participation. Resource room support for the regular classroom teacher can be provided directly in the classroom or in a remedial format. The resource room could provide a curriculum different from the general curriculum, and this could be a legitimate IEP service, but the resource room is no longer a support vehicle for the regular classroom. In most instances, the degree of support between the regular classroom and the resource room can be determined by the degree of communication between the regular classroom teacher and the resource room teacher regarding progress in the classroom and the curriculum.

Nonacademic and Other Services

The IEP Team must always keep in mind the statement of special education and other services is intended to enable a child to advance appropriately toward attaining the annual goals, to be involved and make progress in the general curriculum, "and to participate in extracurricular and other nonacademic activities." Therefore, the full range of services that a child might require to participate in the regular classroom and other environments is far-reaching. These services are not restricted to meeting a child's academic needs but includes all areas of the curriculum and ways to access the curriculum. The IDEA–1997 regulations specifically identified nonacademic services and physical education so that "in providing or arranging for the provision of nonacademic and extracurricular services and activities, including meals, recess periods, and the services and activities set forth in §300.306, each public agency shall ensure that each child with a disability participates with nondisabled children in those services and activities to the maximum extent appropriate to the needs of that child."[383] Public Law 108–446 also acknowledges the importance of nonacademic and extracurricular activities as an essential part of the school curriculum by requiring services and supports to allow a child not only "to be involved in and make progress in the general curriculum" but "to participate in extracurricular and other nonacademic activities."[384]

Special education must not be used to limit a child's ability to participate in programs available to nondisabled children, and the IEP itself must not be written with a segregative intent that disability and not ability determines program participation. If a child requires special services involving other program options such as special physical education services, these should be specified in the IEP. If the IEP Team decides that a more restrictive environment is necessary to meet a child's needs, the school is nonetheless responsible for ensuring that the services specified in the IEP are provided. Examples of blatant discrimination include restricting access to courses in the sciences, mathematics and foreign languages, not because of an inability to participate but because the child has a disability. If appropriate, a child with a disability should participate in art, consumer and homemaking education, industrial arts, music, physical education and vocational education.[385]

Most children will not need every conceivable service and there is no need to list each of these services in the form of a checklist in the IEP to show that every possible service has been considered. The IEP Team should focus on including in the IEP all services, supports, and accommodations necessary to enable regular classroom participation rather than glancing over a list of possible services. There is certainly no harm in a checklist to indicate extended school year services, regular or special transportation, or regular/adaptive/no physical education. However, the IEP Team must make a decision based on IDEA, state policy, and individual need. As is the case with physical education and other program options, the vast majority of nondisabled children participate in regular education, regular school transportation, and the regular school year. If at all possible, and consistent with a child's needs, this same participation should be the goal for a child with a disability.

Chapter 14

PLACEMENT (LOCATION)

*The appropriate mix will vary from child to child and, it may be
hoped, from school year to school year as the child develops.*[386]

			(Extent child will not participate with nondisabled children in the regular class.)			
7. Location of Services (Indicate the **frequency**, **location**, and **duration** of each service.)						
Statement of Nonparticipation:						
Time	**Monday**	**Tuesday**	**Wednesday**	**Thursday**	**Friday**	
1						
2						
3						
4						
5						

Placement is not a discrete decision such that a child is either in the regular classroom or in a special education setting or alternative placement (residential setting, etc.). The first placement task of the IEP Team is not to select a placement but to determine what supplementary aids and services are needed for a child to perform satisfactorily in the regular classroom. If a child is not able to achieve satisfactorily in the regular classroom with supplementary aids and services, the next task of the IEP Team is to determine the extent a child can participate in the regular classroom and general curriculum. After the consideration of supplementary aids and services, and after the determination of the extent of regular classroom participation, the

IEP then considers necessary albeit least restrictive alternative placements. The IEP Team must not begin this process backwards so that the first placement, and often the presumed placement, is the alternative placement.

Maximum Classroom Participation

If a child is not able to participate in the regular classroom satisfactorily, the IEP Team must determine the extent a child is able to participate. One child might be able to participate in the regular classroom 95 percent of the day, a second child is able to participate 50 percent and a third child is able to participate only 5 percent of the day. This is what is meant by "the appropriate mix" cited in *Daniel*.[387] Placement is not a series of discrete settings (e.g., the regular classroom, resource room, alternative setting) but a mix of placements that begins with the regular classroom. When the maximum amount of time a child is able to participate in the regular classroom has been determined, the maximum amount of time in the least restrictive environment is determined.

The amount of time a child is able to participate in the regular classroom and in regular classroom activities is an extremely important benchmark. For children in more restrictive placements regular classroom participation is often static in that once a child has been assigned a placement there is no attempt to increase regular classroom participation. A child might receive five hours of resource room services a week for years with no consideration that fewer (or more hours) might be needed. The IEP Team must consider the maximum amount of time a child can participate with nondisabled children whenever a child's IEP is being considered or being reevaluated. This applies to children requiring resource room services, children assigned to special classrooms, and especially for children residential placements.

Public Law 108–446 is very clear that the presumed placement for every child is the regular classroom. A child with a disability is not *placed* in the regular classroom; the regular classroom is the presumed placement, and a child is removed from the regular classroom "only when the nature or severity of the disability of a child is such that education in regular classes with the use of supplementary aids and services cannot be achieved satisfactorily."

Location

Public Law 94–142 in 1975 required a statement for the projected date for the initiation of services and the anticipated duration of services. This statement was modified by P.L. 105–17 in 1997 to include, in addition to the projected initiation date of services and the duration of each service, anticipated frequency and location of services and modifications. This statement has added a level of accountability to IEPs in that when, where, and how frequently each service is provided must be stated in the IEP. The rationale for adding the *location* of services was that where services are provided "influences decisions about the nature and amount of these services and when they should be provided to a child. For example, the appropriate place for the related service may be the regular classroom, so that the child does not have to choose between a needed service and the regular educational program."[388]

The last substantive decision for the IEP Team is to determine the location of services. If the frequency and duration of services has been determined in the Service component of the IEP, this information is then combined with location to indicate the educational placement. The determination of a placement map for all services which combines the frequency, duration and location of each service allows the IEP team to focus on the maximization of time in regular classes, and to consider the effect of services on regular classroom participation.

The Placement Decision

The frequency and duration of services identifies services and modifications necessary to enable a child to participate in the general classroom and other needs. The actual placement where these services and modifications are provided (i.e., location of services) requires the consideration of two factors: time and setting. If the school day is comprised of 43-minute periods, each period indicates the duration and time or when and where the service can be provided. If the IEP Team decides that a child requires two hours of individualized help with reading in the content area three times a week, the frequency and duration of this service would have been specified when identifying IEP services. During the placement phase of the IEP development the IEP Team then determines when and where this three-hour service of individualized help should be provided. For a child in second grade, the IEP Team might decide that this service should be provided in the regular classroom; or for a student in the sixth grade a resource room might be a more appropriate location.

Service	(Describe the specific service provided.)	Frequency	Duration
Special Education:	Individualized content area reading help	3	43 Min

The first consideration for the location of service is always the regular classroom. If regular classroom participation is not possible for a particular service, the Team then selects the **least restrictive time and place** where the service should be provided. The selection of the least restrictive placement is guided, in part, by the continuum of alternative placements. The regular classroom is less restrictive than a separate classroom; a separate classroom is less restrictive than a special school, etc. When considering the least restrictive educational placement, setting must be considered in relation to when services are provided (i.e., the time of the service). If a child requires individualized instruction in reading, providing this instruction during regular classroom reading might be counterproductive. If a child requires resource room services three days a week, this service should be provided so that the impact of the service on regular classroom participation is minimized.

In the chart below, the time period indicates the duration of the service, the frequency is denoted by the day, and the service is designated within the school time frame by a service code (CT = Consultant Teacher, SP = Speech), a location code (RR = Resource Room) or a combination of service and location (e.g., speech can be provided in the regular classroom or on a pull-out basis). This indicates that the IEP Team has determined that the child needs five periods of special education services a week. The Team then decided that this can be accomplished by two hours of consultant teacher services and three hours of resource room services a week. If the child also needed two hours of occupational therapy a week, this could be indicated by OT (Occupational Therapy in the regular classroom) or a pull-out service (OT-P).

Time	Monday	Tuesday	Wednesday	Thursday	Friday
1. 8:00 - 8:42		CT		CT	
2. 8:45 - 9:27	RR				RR
3. 9:30 - 10:12			RR		
4. 10:15 - 11:17		OT-P		OT-P	
10. 2:45 - 3:27					

For children in more restrictive settings extensive special education pull-out services might be required. Nonetheless, for all children, the determination of placement begins with identifying the extent of regular classroom participation, and then providing necessary pull-out services in the least restrictive setting at the least restrictive time. For children requiring separate school or residential placements, the determination of regular classroom participation is extremely important in that a placement cannot preclude participation with nondisabled children or participation in the general curriculum. This occurs when providing educational experiences with nondisabled children is inconvenient; or when the separate placement facility uses a curriculum completely remote from the general curriculum. A child might legitimately require services in a separate setting, but transportation and other factors make participation in regular classes difficult. Likewise, providing the general curriculum in a separate placement is certainly not an easy task. However, these are real problems but not really relevant factors. The mandate for the IEP Team is to provide the *least restrictive environment* and not *first an environment* and then allow that environment to impose restrictions on the extent a child is able to participate with nondisabled children. Many of the problems associated with placements, especially placements in alternative settings, can be dealt with by first considering the extent of regular classroom participation, whether it be one hour a week or one day, and then selecting the least restrictive placement for meeting a child's needs.

Regular Classroom Placement

Providing the least restrictive placement can only be achieved if the IEP Team considers the maximum amount of time a child is able to participate in the regular classroom. Whenever possible, the IEP Team should provide services in the regular classroom or provide services that enable a **regular classroom placement**. The Office of Special Education Programs has established criteria for regular classroom, resource room and separate settings. A regular placement is defined as less than 21 percent time outside the regular classroom. A resource room setting is from 21 percent to 60 percent of the time in the regular classroom, and a separate classroom placement is more than 60 percent of the day outside of the regular classroom.

Office of Special Education Programs (OSEP) Placements		
Placement	Time Outside Regular Classroom	Time Inside Regular Classroom
Regular Classroom	<21%	>79%
Resource Room	21% to 60%	79% to 40%
Separate	>60%	<40%

Between 1990 and 1994 there was a general increase in regular classroom placements and a corresponding decrease in resource room placements. Although the increase in regular classroom placements has been less pronounced in recent years the regular classroom is the placement for almost 50 percent of children receiving services. For the IEP team the OSEP regular classroom placement percentage (<21%) provides excellent guidelines when

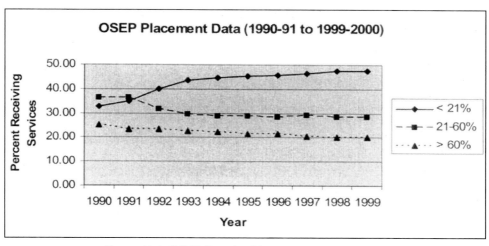

Figure 14-1. OSEP Regular Classroom Placement Data

considering the amount of services provided outside of the regular classroom.

The placement decision is always based on the child's IEP. For the IEP Team this means that placement should never be determined (or assumed) prior to the development of the IEP, or made at the beginning of the IEP process. In addition, the placement decision must be determined at least annually; the decision is as close as possible to the child's home and the child is educated in the school that he or she would attend if nondisabled; and "in selecting the LRE, consideration is given to any potential harmful effect on the child or on the quality of services that he or she needs."[389]

Services and Placement

Actual services must drive the placement decision and not vice versa. A child's behavior and learning needs might be such that even with a full-time aide and extensive one-to-one consultant teacher services, the child would gain little from the regular classroom curriculum, and disrupt the learning of others. Mainstreaming and inclusion are **not mandated by IDEA**, but ignoring factors (e.g., the continuum of services) that prevent the selection of the least restrictive environment is discriminatory and contrary to IDEA.[390]

If a child's behavior impedes or clearly prevents regular classroom participation, the IEP Team might determine that the regular classroom is not the least restrictive environment. However, in order to determine that a child would not receive educational benefit in the regular classroom, the IEP Team must first determine what services are necessary to succeed in the regular classroom, compare the benefits in the regular classroom and more restrictive setting, and then consider the impact of the child's regular classroom placement on other children. If services cannot be provided in the regular classroom, the degree of regular classroom participation must then be considered. A fundamental tenet of the IEP process is that the child's placement is based on the child's IEP.[391] This means that the IEP is developed before the placement is made. The IEP is not a license to remove a child from the regular classroom. Unfortunately, this is exactly what occurs when the placement decision is made prior to the development of the IEP or when the IEP lacks substance and does not address a child's individual needs.

Four Essential Placement Considerations

☛ **First, determine what is necessary for a child to function successfully in the regular classroom.**

☛ **Second, consider the regular classroom as placement for services. In other words, consider the full range of supplementary aids and services.**

☛ **Third, consider the least restrictive alternative placement from a continuum of placements.**

☛ **Fourth, if an alternative placement is necessary, consider the degree the child is able to participate in the regular classroom while in the more restrictive placement.**

Special education is not tantamount to removal from the regular classroom; the purpose of special education is to design an individualized education program meet the child's needs that result from the child's disability to enable the child to be involved in and make progress in the general curriculum.[392] Mainstreaming is not a right that is earned but the regular classroom is a right to which every child is entitled, and the presumed placement for every (with or without disabilities).

Statement of Nonparticipation

The statement of nonparticipation is "a statutory requirement and cannot be deleted."[393] The reason for requiring a statement of nonparticipation in the

IEP is to ensure that the IEP Team "carefully considers the extent to which a child can be educated with his or her nondisabled peers." If a child is not able to participate full-time in the regular classroom and in the general curriculum, the statement must explain why "full participation is not possible." The Office of Special Education and Rehabilitative Services OSERS) interpretation of the statement of nonparticipation is a statement that explains the reason or reasons why "full-time" participation is not possible:

> **If (for example) a child needs speech-language pathology services in a separate setting two or three times a week, but will otherwise spend full time with nondisabled children in the activities described in 300.347(a)(4), the "explanation" would require only the statement described in the preceding sentence. A similar explanation would be required for any other child with a disability who, in the judgment of the IEP team, will not participate on a full time basis with nondisabled children in the regular class. Thus, while the IEP needs to clearly address this situation, the required explanation does not have to be burdensome.[394]**

Vermont's considerable success involving mainstreaming and including children with disabilities in the general curriculum can be traced, in part, to the emphasis on the regular classroom in the development of the IEP. For the section in the IEP requiring a statement of the extent of nonparticipation Vermont cites the basic regulation (The IEP shall also include an explanation of the extent, if any, to which the child will not participate with non-disabled children in the regular classroom, general curriculum, extracurricular and other nonacademic activities) but also requires annual goals to reintegrate children into regular classes. Not only does Vermont place a high degree of emphasis on regular classroom participation but regular classroom participation must be viewed as a goal for children requiring more restrictive placements. For children in Vermont requiring residential placements "the student's IEP shall contain annual goals and short-term objectives or benchmarks designed to reintegrate the student into a local school district placement, and a description of how they will lead to reintegration." For children who require removal from the regular classroom in excess of 50 percent of the school week placements in excess of 50 percent of the school week "the IEP shall contain annual goals and short-term objectives or benchmarks designed to reintegrate the student into the regular education environment at the earliest appropriate opportunity."[395]

A Continuum of Participation

Daniel v. State Board of Education provides one guideline for the IEP Team when determining placements: "First, we ask whether education in the regular classroom, with the use of supplementary aids and services, can be achieved satisfactorily for a given child." Second, "if it cannot and the school intends to provide special education or to remove the child from regular education, we ask, second, whether the school has mainstreamed the child to the maximum extent appropriate."[396]

> **". . . it is illusory, and perhaps even pretextual, to contend that segregation can breed readiness for inclusion."[397]**
> –Oberti, 789 F.Supp. 1322 (D.N.J. 1992)

The placement decision is not a choice between regular education and special education. The first task is not a placement decision but a determination of the extent of possible regular classroom participation, and then to determine the least restrictive placement for all other alternate environments. As stated in *Daniel* "the school must take intermediate steps where appropriate, such as placing the child in regular education for some academic classes and in special education for others, mainstreaming the child for nonacademic classes only, or providing interaction with nonhandicapped children during lunch and recess. The appropriate mix will vary from child to child and, it may be hoped, from school year to school year as the child develops."[398] This last statement is indeed most insightful and captures the real meaning of the continuum of services; that is a continuum in which the task is not to select discrete placements but the appropriate mix of services, a mix that will vary from child to child and a mix that is predicated on a **continuum of participation** rather than a series of discrete services or placements.

In *Hartmann v. Loudoun County Board of Education*, the parents of an eleven-year-old child with autism were dissatisfied with the IEP Teams decision to change their child's placement from a regular education classroom with supplementary aids and services to "a class specifically structured for autistic children." The reasons for the change included behaviors such as hitting, pinching, kicking, biting, removing shoes and clothing, and distracting vocalizations. The District Court agreed with the parents but the Court of Appeals of Eastern Virginia chided the District Court for ignoring previous appellate and Supreme Court (*Hudson v. Rowley*) rulings. The Court of Appeals reprimanded the District Court for ignoring school, professionals and the Court noted that "one Loudoun official was dismissed outright as 'a philosophical opponent of inclusion' for daring to state that he saw no evidence that Mark had progressed in the regular classroom." The Court of Appeals cited their ruling in *DeVries v. Fairfax County School Board* (882 F.2d 876 (4th Cir. 1989)) which stated that mainstreaming is not required when (1) the child does not receive educational benefit from mainstreaming, (2) the marginal benefits of mainstreaming are outweighed by the benefits in a separate education setting, and (3) the child is a disruptive force in the regular classroom.

The Loudoun decision makes an important distinction between social and academic benefits in that the mainstreaming "provision only creates a presumption" which "reflects a congressional judgment that receipt of such social benefits is ultimately a goal subordinate to the requirement that disabled children receive educational benefit."[399] This emphasis on educational benefit only reinforces the importance of regular classroom placements because it is in the regular classroom where the highest degree of educational benefit can be attained.

Many of the due process conflicts involve placement decisions, and many of these decisions result from a lack of communication. Parents must be very clear when communicating with the IEP Team. As per IDEA–2004 (612`10[B][ii & iii]) a court or a hearing officer may require the agency to reimburse the parents for the cost of that enrollment if the court or hearing officer finds that the agency had not made a free appropriate public education available to the child in a timely manner prior to that enrollment.

> **The cost of reimbursement described in clause (ii) may be reduced or denied–if–at the most recent IEP meeting that the parents attended prior to removal of the child from the public school, the parents did not inform the IEP Team that they were rejecting the placement proposed by the public agency to provide a free appropriate public education to their child, including stating their concerns and their intent to enroll their child in a private school at public expense.**

Meeting the LRE Mandate

The least restrictive environment provision is the essence of IDEA. What is sometimes forgotten in the placement process is the need to educate children, "including children in public or private institutions or other care facilities," to the maximum extent appropriate with children who are not disabled. The LRE provision is not for only children with disabilities in regular classes but for all children with disabilities in all educational environments. There should be no distinction between a child in a resource room, self-contained classroom, or in a residential setting. Every child with a disability should be educated with nondisabled children to the maximum extent appropriate. If a child is in a separate school setting and the child is able to participate five hours a week with nondisabled children, the LRE placement is 5 percent with nondisabled children and 95 percent in the separate classroom. If a child is in a resource room 50 percent of the day but is able to participate with nondisabled children 75 percent of the day, the appropriate placement is 25 percent resource room and 75 percent regular classroom. When making the LRE determination the appropriate placement must not be undermined by bureaucratic convenience, or the selection of a placement that precludes regular classroom or general curriculum participation.

IEP Team LRE Guidelines

☞ **For the IEP Team the LRE provision requires consideration of supplementary aids and services to achieve a satisfactory education in regular classes.**

☞ **If a child requires a placement other than the regular classroom, the IEP Team must then determine the extent the child can participate in regular classes.**[400]

☞ **After the extent of regular classroom participation has been determined, the IEP Team then selects the least restrictive environment from the continuum of alternate placements.**

☞ **The maximum amount of participation for each placement on the continuum is determined before a more restrictive placement is considered. This is the "mix" of placements that results in the least restrictive placement.**

☛ **The IEP Team must ensure that a child with a disability is able to participate in the general education curriculum to the maximum extent appropriate. A child's placement must not prevent participation in the general curriculum.**

☛ **Necessary modifications to the general curriculum must be the reason for selecting an alternate placement.**

☛ **The LRE provision applies to all modifications and services in that all modifications and services can restrict access to the general curriculum or participation with nondisabled children.**

The LRE mandate is twofold: first, the "removal of children with disabilities from the regular educational environment occurs only when the nature or severity of the disability of a child is such that education in regular classes with the use of supplementary aids and services cannot be achieved satisfactorily." Second, "to the maximum extent appropriate, children with disabilities, including children in public or private institutions or other care facilities, are educated with children who are not disabled.[401] The first provision refers to the need to include children in regular classroom environments to the maximum extent appropriate. The second provision stipulates that children with disabilities are educated with nondisabled children to the maximum extent appropriate. This means that children with disabilities should be involved in the general curriculum and regular classroom in a manner similar, as much as possible, to that of nondisabled children.

The consideration of supplementary aids and services goes hand-in-hand with the presumption of a regular classroom placement. By considering all services and modifications (in other words *supplementary aids and services*) that will enable a child to be successful in the regular classroom for all children, priority is given to this "presumed" placement rather than to an otherwise "assumed" alternate placement.

Continuum of Alternate Placements

The IEP Team is required to select services that are the least restrictive by utilizing a continuum of services. Services provided in the classroom are least restrictive when the maximum of time a child is able to participate in one setting is determined before considering the maximum extent of participation in the next setting. The services provided are not discrete and can draw upon a variety of services from the continuum. For example, one child with a severe disability might receive 90 percent of all services in the regular classroom or 100 percent or services; another child with a severe disability might require 90 percent of services in a special classroom or school; and for five children receiving resource room each might have a different mix or regular classroom and pull-out services. The only rule that the IEP Team must follow is that services are as least restrictive as possible and not based on disability. For example, if all children with a disability received instruction in special classes, regardless of need or restrictiveness, this would be discriminatory and contrary to the LRE mandate.

The requirement that children with disabilities in all educational settings are educated with nondisabled children to the maximum extent appropriate clearly creates a continuum of services. The percent of time a child could be educated with nondisabled children could be 100 percent or in rare instances (in terms of the number of children with disabilities) zero percent. The types of placements in the continuum often cited (i.e., instruction in regular classes, special classes, special schools, home instruction, and instruction in hospitals and institutions) exemplify the continuum of environments but not the continuum for an individual child's placement.[402] A resource room is more restrictive than the regular classroom, a self-contained-classroom more restrictive than a resource room, and a special school more restrictive than a self-contained classroom. However, this must not be interpreted to mean that a child is placed in a regular classroom, resource room, self-contained classroom, or special school.

If an alternative placement is necessary, the placement should be as least restrictive as possible. The choice is not simply the regular classroom or a special education classroom, but first determining the amount of time that a child is able to benefit from the least restrictive environment. Although each State can specify a continuum of placements that is reflective of the special education services available, the continuum must include "instruction in regular classes, special classes, special schools, home instruction, and instruction in hospitals and institutions," and "make provision for supplementary services (such as resource room or itinerant instruction) to be provided in conjunction with regular class placement."[403]

LRE and Funding

IN GENERAL–A State funding mechanism shall not result in placements that violate the requirements of subparagraph (A), and a State shall not use a funding mechanism by which the State distributes funds on the basis of the type of setting in which a child is served that will result in the failure to provide a child with a disability a free appropriate public education according to the unique needs of the child as described in the child's IEP.

ASSURANCE–If the State does not have policies and procedures to ensure compliance with clause (i), the State shall provide the Secretary an assurance that the State will revise the funding mechanism as soon as feasible to ensure that such mechanism does not result in such placements.

–P.L. 108–446, 612(5)(B)

Location and Services

Consultant Teacher Services

Just as the first placement considered for every child with a disability is the regular classroom, the first special education service should invariably be consultant teacher services which include all direct and indirect services that enable a child with a disability to participate in the regular classroom and progress in the general curriculum. Consultant teacher services are direct and indirect services provided by a qualified special education teacher to enable a child with a disability to participate in the regular classroom and general education curriculum. The Conference Committee for IDEA clarified that,

> a special education teacher who provides only consultative services to a highly qualified teacher (as such term is defined in section 9101 (23) of the Elementary and Secondary Education Act of 1965) should be considered a highly qualified special education teacher if such teacher meets the requirements of section 602(10)(A) of this legislation. Such consultative services do not include instruction in core academic subjects, but may include

> **adjustments to the learning environment, modifications of instructional methods, adaptation of curricula, the use of positive behavioral supports and interventions, or the use of appropriate accommodations to meet the needs of individual children.**[404]

Direct consultant teacher services entail instructional activities in the regular classroom that may also benefit nondisabled children. Public Law 108–446 stipulates that "for the costs of special education and related services and supplementary aids and services provided in a regular class or other education-related setting to a child with a disability in accordance with the individualized education program of the child, even if one or more nondisabled children benefit from such services."[405] Direct teaching services might be in the form of one-to-one, small or large group instruction. The availability of a consultant teacher in the classroom will also provide the regular classroom teacher with instructional support to become an integral part of the specialized education program that will enable a child to participate in the classroom.

Indirect consultant teacher services include consultation with the regular classroom teacher and other personnel, and modifying and adapting curriculum materials, designing and implementing test accommodations and modifications, and providing necessary training and supervision for classroom support personnel (e.g., aides).

For direct and indirect consultant teacher services the frequency and duration of services should be specified in the IEP. The extent of direct and indirect services is important for defining the consultant teacher's schedule and the extensiveness of a child's instructional needs. A child who requires two hours or of direct services a day to participate in the regular classroom would likely have very extensive needs, while a high school student who received two or three hours of indirect services a week should be functioning at a fairly independent level with minimal direct instructional needs. Because of the unique needs of children receiving consultant teacher services (e.g., providing less direct services over the course of a year), a range of services might be appropriate "only if the IEP team determines that stating the amount of services as a range is necessary to meet the unique needs of the child."[406] However, a range of services may not be used to compensate for teacher shortages or the likelihood of personnel availability of shortages.[407]

The need to specify the amount of services should not be used to provide unnecessary services, and therefore more restrictive services. For example, requiring all children identified as having specific learning disabilities to receive one hour of resource room services a week would be basing the amount of services on disability rather than need.

Resource Room

Resource Room services can be either an alternative placement or a supplement to the regular classroom. The original concept of the resource room to provide a "small amount" of assistance, and a supplementary service "to be provided in conjunction with regular classroom placement"[408] has often evolved into a *resource room placement.* The OSEP guideline that a resource room placement is between 21 percent and 60 percent outside of the regular classroom indicates that a placement which requires this amount of time outside the regular classroom is, indeed, an alternative placement. Of course, there is certainly a difference between a child who spends 21 percent of the day outside the classroom and a child who spends 60 percent of the day outside of the regular classroom. Yet, each child, regardless whether that separate setting is called a resource room or special education class, is considered a resource room placement. The IEP Team must first attempt to use resource room services to supplement the regular classroom, and use the resource room as a separate placement (21% to 60%) only when absolutely necessary.

When first considering resource room services, the initial goal should be to determine what is necessary to supplement the regular classroom and not arbitrarily assign a child to the resource room for a fixed amount of time. For example, if all children identified as having a specific learning disability are assigned to a resource room for a minimum of one hour a day, two hours a week, etc., the placements are clearly based on disability rather than need. The IEP Team would be well served to follow the original "little bit of help" philosophy for providing resource room service and not automatically regard the resource room as a placement, and definitely not assign all children who receive resource room help to a fixed amount of time.

Separate Placements

Special school, residential school, or homebound settings do not preclude the need to consider what services are required for regular classroom participation. A major area for noncompliance involves providing children with the least restrictive environment when the alternative placement is a special school or residential placement (see National Council on Disability, p. 95). After the IEP is developed, and so that the placement decision can be based on the IEP, an alternative placement might be necessary to provide an appropriate education. This, however, does not absolve the IEP Team from considering what services a child might need to participate in the regular classroom. This determination of participation with nondisabled children in restrictive placements will provide a benchmark for whatever placement a child might eventually require, and also is an important guideline for the alternative placement to meet the least restrictive requirement mandate. For example, if a child is placed in a special school or residential setting, the IEP might reason that the child is able to participate in regular education classes one hour a day, or 30 minutes a day, or a half-day a week. If this is the IEP Team's determination, then the separate placement must abide by the child's IEP. What personnel from the separate placement must not do is to ignore the child's IEP or, even worse, to create a new IEP. Every child who receives services under IDEA has one IEP and one IEP Team, and these are provided under the auspices of the local educational agency. When a second IEP is created, even though not called an IEP but the plan documents specific goals and services, parents often are not invited to participate and regular classroom needs are not considered.

IEP Implementation and Placement

Before services are provided to a child with a disability, the IEP must be completed and consent provided by the parents. Following consent the IEP is implemented as soon as possible, and must be in effect at the beginning of the school year. The IEP must be available to the classroom teacher and other service providers who have IEP-designated responsibilities.

Placement Guidelines

The basic requirementsxxiv for determining a child's placement are general yet exceedingly important:

- **The regular classroom is the presumed placement for all children.**

- **"The placement decision is made by a group of persons, including the parents, and other persons knowledgeable about the child, the meaning of the evaluation data, and the placement option."**

I.   **The placement is the least restrictive environment possible.**

II. **The placement is based on a continuum of alternate placements.**

III. The placement is determined at least annually.

IV. The placement is based on the child's IEP.

V. The placement is as close to the child's home as possible.

VI. The child is educated in the school that he or she would attend if nondisabled.

VII. In selecting the LRE, consideration is given to any potential harmful effect on the child or on the quality of services that he or she needs.

VIII. A child with a disability is not removed from education in age-appropriate regular classrooms solely because of needed modifications in the general curriculum.

Chapter 15

SIGNATURES, REPORTS
AND/OR APPENDICES

8. IEP Team Members		
Member	**Name** (print or type)	**Signature**
Parent(s):		
Regular Ed. Teacher:		
Special Ed. Teacher:		
Qualified Special Ed. Supervisor:		
Individual-Special Expertise:		
Student:		
Other:		
Other:		

IEP TEAM SIGNATURE PAGE

The IEP should include a list of participants but this should be the concluding section of the IEP. The signature for the participation page indicates that the member participated in the process but does not mean agreement with any or all of the services indicated. Public Law 108–446 does not require parents to sign the IEP, but a signature page is useful for recording IEP attendance and provides the parent with a signed record of services.

If certain conditions are met, a signed IEP by the parent can be used to indicate parent approval of the IEP.[410] If the parent IEP signature is used as consent for services three conditions must be met: (1) the parent understands all of the elements of the IEP; (2) the parent understands all of the services that will be provided; and (3) that "consent is voluntary on the part of the parent and may be revoked at any time" although revocation of consent is not retroactive.[411] For IDEA–1990 Appendix C suggested that a signed IEP was a way to document meeting attendance, provides parents with a signed record of services, and "an IEP signed by the parents is one way to indicate that the parents approved the child's special education program." If a parent signature is used to indicate IEP approval, this must be a separate signature and the conditions for approval should be cited. For the above signature page, the parent signature is not parental consent for the IEP in that the meaning of the parent signature would be decidedly different than that for other Team members (i.e., a signature cannot mean consent for one Team member and simply evidence of Team participation for another).

Because parents have routinely been given a period of time in which to consider the IEP, consent given for services at the IEP meeting is usually premature and does not afford parents a real opportunity to review the IEP or seek help to better understand IEP content. If a signed IEP indicates only participation, parents should be told that they will receive a copy of the IEP and a request for consent for services following the meeting. Most important, if the parent does not agree with any of the services or accommodations in the IEP, this should be indicated in the IEP document (and initialed or signed by the parent) to indicate absence for the specific service.

For most IEPs best practice is not to use an IEP signed by the parent when the IEP is developed as consent of services. Parents should be given a reasonable amount of time to review the IEP as is done in New Jersey where, following the development of the IEP, parents are given a 15-day review period to consider the proposed IEP. To initiate services before the 15 day period has expired, the parent must sign a statement waiving the 15-day period. In Massachusetts parents have 30 days after receiving the IEP to consent, in whole or in part, the IEP.[412] Of course, if the parents are in complete agreement with the IEP, and the services and accommodations clearly and appropriately meet a child's needs, and the parents are fully aware of the services designated in the IEP, consenting to the IEP and services might very well be appropriate. If parents are unclear, undecided, or not sufficiently informed about all elements of the IEP, the parents should not provide consent at the meeting, should school personnel suggest that consent must be immediately provided. In any case, upon receipt of consent those services accepted are implemented as soon as possible.

Massachusetts Department of Education

Parental response to proposed IEP and proposed placement. Immediately following the development of the IEP, and within 45 school working days after receipt of the parent's written consent to an initial evaluation or reevaluation, the district shall provide the parent with two (2) copies of the proposed IEP and proposed placement along with the required notice, except that the proposal of placement may be delayed according to the provisions of 603 CMR 28.06(2)(e) in a limited number of cases.

(a) No later than thirty (30) days after receipt of the proposed IEP and proposed placement, the parent shall:

1. Accept or reject the IEP in whole or in part; request a meeting to discuss the rejected portions of the IEP or the overall adequacy of the IEP; or if mutually agreed upon, accept an amended proposal; and

2. Accept or reject the proposed placement.
(b) Upon parental response to the proposed IEP and proposed placement, the school district shall implement all accepted elements of the IEP without delay.iv

–Education Laws and Regulations, 603 CMR 28.05

Additional Reports

9. Additional Reports and Summaries	
Report	Summary

Rather than combining all the content from supporting documents in the IEP, append these reports to the IEP document. Most reports such as the report for the individual evaluation are independent of the IEP, but sections of this report might be appended to the IEP. However, for most IEPs there is simply no need to replicate the individual evaluation in the IEP unless the information is necessary for providing services or accommodations or for achieving goals. For students exhibiting behavioral problems an analysis of the student's behavior or a Functional Behavioral Analysis might be important supporting documents. For these and other relevant reports, list the name of the report and essential information in the IEP, and then append the report (if necessary) to the IEP.

Because most reports are available in the student's file, information and reports should only be appended to the IEP that provide important information for implementing the IEP. An extensive list of standardized scores, already contained in the individual evaluation, would have questionable value when appended to the IEP. On the other hand, a Functional Behavioral Assessment, and especially a Behavioral Intervention Plan, might be very useful to all service providers for understanding a child's needs, and for using the plan designed to meet these needs.

Service providers at the IEP meeting can provide useful input as to whether a report should be appended to the IEP. If, based on past experience, an attachment or appended report is never used and has no bearing on the implementation of the IEP, the report should not be part of the IEP document or included with the IEP as an attachment.

Virginia has acknowledged the need for appended reports to the IEP by creating a two-part IEP. Section 1 of the Virginia IEP is required as the foundation for all IEPs, while Section 2 provides additional forms and areas of consideration to be used "as needed." For Section 1 additional forms are provided for levels of performance, goals, placement decision, prior notice and refusal for services. For Section 2 additional reports are available for secondary transition services, extended school year services, literacy passport test (for Virginia's State Assessment System), Virginia State Assessment Program (VASP).[414] For example, Virginia has a form for "refusal of services" which includes reasons for the refusal(s), description of each evaluation procedure, test, record, or report used as a basis for the refusal, description of any options considered and the reasons why those options were rejected, and description of any other factors which are relevant to the refusal(s). This information probably should be part of the IEP but not for every IEP, and certainly the form should not be included when not needed.

IEP Checklists

There are several different types of checklists that are useful for IEP Team members but not necessarily for inclusion in the IEP itself. The IDEA and the regulations often specify considerations or processes that the IEP Team must engage but a checklist developed to show these considerations or processes have been followed does little to enhance IEPs. For example, the five factors required for consideration often appear in the IEP as a checklist, but IDEA–2004 does not intend that the IEP Team should expend time checking each of the factors for every student.

The following special factors should be considered and discussed at the IEP meeting:

❏ **In the case of a child whose behavior impedes his or her learning or that of others, consider the use of positive behavioral interventions and supports, and other strategies, to address that behavior.**

❏ **In the case of a child with limited English proficiency, consider the language needs of the child as such needs relate to the child's IEP.**

❏ **In the case of a child who is blind or visually impaired, provide for instruction in Braille and the use of Braille unless the IEP Team determines, after an evaluation of the child's reading and writing skills, needs, and appropriate reading and writing media (including an evaluation of the child's future needs for instruction in Braille or the use of Braille), that instruction in Braille or the use of Braille is not appropriate for the child.**

❏ **Consider the communication needs of the child, and in the case of a child who is deaf or hard of hearing, consider the child's language and communication needs, opportunities for direct communications with peers and professional personnel in the child's language and communication mode, academic level, and full range of needs, including opportunities for direct instruction in the child's language and communication mode.**

❏ **Consider whether the child needs assistive technology devices and services.**[415]

The above checklist often appears in an abbreviated form such as:

The following special factors should be considered and discussed at the IEP meeting:

❏ **Behavior**	❏ **Not Applicable**
❏ **Limited English proficiency**	❏ **Not Applicable**
❏ **Braille needs**	❏ **Not Applicable**
❏ **Communication needs**	❏ **Not Applicable**
❏ **Assistive Technology**	❏ **Not Applicable**

The special factors cited in IDEA–2004 must be considered when appropriate by the IEP Team, and a checklist might be useful for showing that each factor has been considered and discussed, but the task is to consider each factor when appropriate and not show that each factor has been considered. For the vast majority of children with disabilities Braille is not a relevant factor, and the IEP should not be weighed down by this pretextual approach to compliance.

Many IEP checklists attempt to assist the IEP Team in providing useful services and accommodations. There is never more prevalent than IEP checklists for accommodations as shown below:

❑ Alternative materials
❑ Assignment notebooks
❑ Assistive communication
❑ Braille services
❑ Calculator
❑ Enhanced instructions
❑ ESL services
❑ Extended breaks
❑ Extended time
❑ Extra sample items
❑ Highlighted text
❑ Individual testing
❑ Interpreter
❑ Large print
❑ Modified response
❑ Modified tests
❑ More sample items
❑ Morning/afternoon testing
❑ Multi-day testing
❑ Note-taking assistance
❑ Oral tests

❑ Peer tutor
❑ Practice testing
❑ Preferential seating
❑ Reader services
❑ Reading instructions
❑ Reading non-reading items
❑ Reduced paper/pencil tasks
❑ Reduced testing time
❑ Repeated drill/practice
❑ Scribe services
❑ Short-answer tests
❑ Signing instructions
❑ Signing items
❑ Simplifying instructions
❑ Special location
❑ Special norms
❑ Special seating
❑ Taped lectures
❑ Tests exemption
❑ Using a calculator
❑ Using a scribe

The many variations of checklists for listing possible accommodations might be useful for assisting the IEP Team when selecting accommodations in that the Team members might become aware of accommodations not previously known. This is not always a good thing in that there is always the possibility that a list of accommodations might result in the selection of accommodations that fall into the category **might-be-helpful**, **seems-like-a-good-idea**, or **couldn't-hurt accommodations**. If the checked accommodations are not based on data and, more importantly, are not needed, the accommodations might not be helpful, might not be a good idea and indeed might hurt a child by restricting access to the classroom or curriculum. In any case, if a checklist for accommodations is used, include the checklist as part of the IEP guidelines or in an appendix and not the IEP itself.

Developing IEP Guidelines

The use of IEP checklists and related support information is often best included in a set of IEP Guidelines rather than in the IEP form. Every IEP Team should have guidelines for the development and implementation of the IEP. Useful sources of information for IEP Guidelines include elements of P.L. 108–446, especially Section 614 (Evaluations, Eligibility Determinations, Individualized Education Programs, and Educational Placements) or, when IDEA–2004 is codified in the United States Code, section 20 USC 1414. The regulations for IDEA–2004 (34 CFR 300) are developed by the Office of Special Education and Rehabilitative Services (OSERS) and include a Notice of Interpretation which provides excellent guidelines for IEP Teams and the implementation and development of IEPs. For IDEA–1997 these guidelines were included in Appendix A to part 300–Notice of Interpretation. Unfortunately, the regulations for IDEA–197 were not published until 1999.[416]

At the State level IEP Teams should be aware of the various considerations and requirements imposed by State laws, rules or codes. Many states have documentation for developing IEPs as well as documentation for parents and sample IEPs.

IDEA-IEP Resources

Many of the questions that IEP Team members might have will be answered by the law itself (P.L. 108–446), the regulations for IDEA–2004, and State guidelines and documentation. However, there are several additional sources that will be useful for understanding the intent of IDEA in relation to IEPs. The suggestions and guidelines offered in the House (HR 108–77) and Senate reports (SR 108–185) for IDEA–2004 provide a first-hand interpretation of the reasoning for various IDEA sections. The Conference report between the House and Senate for 108–446 also provides insight into IEP processes and how these issues were resolved by the House and Senate conferees.[417] The Appendix in the Code of Federal Regulations is actually a series of questions concerning IDEA (e.g., from IDEA–1997: 8. Do parents have the right to a copy of their child's IEP.) Another useful source of IEP-related information is the analysis of comments appended to the regulations but not codified in the code. Attachment 1–Analysis of Comments and Changes "is an analysis of the significant issues raised by the public comments received on the NPRM published on October 22, 1997 (62 FR 55026), and a description of the changes made in the proposed regulations since publication of the NPRM."

Appendix A

SAMPLE IEP FORM

Individualized Education Program					
1. Student Information					
Name:		**Address:**		**City:**	
Phone:		**DOB:**		**School:**	
Grade:		**Parent**		**IEP Manager:**	
IEP Meeting Date:			**IEP Meeting Purpose:**		
IEP Dates:	**Beginning Date:**		**Ending Date:**		

2. Background, Disability and Concerns	
Student Summary:	(Reason for referral, description of educational and other needs, strengths and weaknesses, the child's disability and disability-related needs)
Parent and Teacher Input:	(Include specific concerns of parents and classroom teachers)
Special Concerns:	(Include specfial concerns, ESL needs, medical alerts, etc.)
Age of Majority:	

3. Present Levels of Academic Achievement and Functional Performance	
Summary of Levels of Academic Performance:	
Curriculum and Functional Performance Needs:	

4. Modifications	
Classroom Accommodations:	(Describe the effective accommodations currently being used in the classroom.)
Assistive Technology and Aids:	(Describe any tiems, piece of equipment, or product system used to increase, maintain, or improve functional capabilities.)
Test Accommodations:	(Describe the reasonable and State and local test accommodations permitted.)
Alternate Assessment Needs:	(If standardized tests are not appropriate, describe the alternate test being used.)

5. Measurable Annual Goals

(Each Measurable Annual Goal must include a **measured beginning level of performance** and a corresponding **measurable annual goal** to meet academic, functional needs and postsecondary needs.)

Describe how progress is reported to parents:

MAG (Include a description of the assessment used to measure each goal)	Measured Beginning Level of Performance	Measured Annual Level of Performance

6. Services			
Beginning date of services:			
Service	**(Describe the specific service provided.)**	**Frequency**	**Duration**
Special Education:			
Related Services:			
Support for School Personnel:			
Nonacademic and Other Services			

7. Location of Services
(Indicate the **frequency**, **location**, and **duration** of each service.)

Statement of Nonparticipation:	(Extent child will not participate with nondisabled children in the regular class.)				
Time	**Monday**	**Tuesday**	**Wednesday**	**Thursday**	**Friday**
1					
2					
3					
4					
5					
6					
7					
8					
9					
10					

8. IEP Team Members		
Member	Name (print or type)	Signature
Parent(s):		
Regular Ed. Teacher:		
Special Ed. Teacher:		
Qualified Special Ed. Supervisor:		
Individual-Special Expertise:		
Student:		
Other:		
Other:		

9. Additional Reports and Summaries	
Report	Summary

Appendix B
Public Law 108-446

SEC. 614. EVALUATIONS, ELIGIBILITY DETERMINATIONS, INDIVIDUALIZED EDUCATION PROGRAMS, AND EDUCATIONAL PLACEMENTS.[418]

(a) **EVALUATIONS, PARENTAL CONSENT, AND REEVALUATIONS.**–

(1) **INITIAL EVALUATIONS.**–

(A) **IN GENERAL.**–A State educational agency, other State agency, or local educational agency shall conduct a full and individual initial evaluation in accordance with this paragraph and subsection (b), before the initial provision of special education and related services to a child with a disability under this part.

(B) **REQUEST FOR INITIAL EVALUATION.**–Consistent with subparagraph (D), either a parent of a child, or a State educational agency, other State agency, or local educational agency may initiate a request for an initial evaluation to determine if the child is a child with a disability.

(C) **PROCEDURES.**–

(i) **IN GENERAL.**–Such initial evaluation shall consist of procedures–

(I) to determine whether a child is a child with a disability (as defined in section 602) within 60 days of receiving parental consent for the evaluation, or, if the State establishes a timeframe within which the evaluation must be conducted, within such timeframe; and

(II) to determine the educational needs of such child.

(ii) **EXCEPTION.**–The relevant timeframe in clause (i)(I) shall not apply to a local educational agency if–

(I) a child enrolls in a school served by the local educational agency after the relevant timeframe in clause (i)(I) has begun and prior to a determination by the child's previous local educational agency as to whether the child is a child with a disability (as defined in section 602), but only if the subsequent local educational agency is making sufficient progress to ensure a prompt completion of the evaluation, and the parent and subsequent local educational agency agree to a specific time when the evaluation will be completed; or

(II) the parent of a child repeatedly fails or refuses to produce the child for the evaluation.

(D) **PARENTAL CONSENT.**–

(i) **IN GENERAL.**–

(I) **CONSENT FOR INITIAL EVALUATION.**–The agency proposing to conduct an initial evaluation to determine if the child qualifies as a child with a disability as defined in section 602 shall obtain informed consent from the parent of such child before conducting the evaluation. Parental consent for evaluation shall not be construed as consent for placement for receipt of special education and related services.

(II) **CONSENT FOR SERVICES.**–An agency that is responsible for making a free appropriate public education available to a child with a disability under this part shall seek to obtain informed consent from the parent of such child before providing special education and related services to the child.

(ii) **ABSENCE OF CONSENT.**–

(I) **FOR INITIAL EVALUATION.**–If the parent of such child does not provide consent for an initial evaluation under clause (i)(I), or the parent fails to respond to a request to provide the consent, the local educational agency may pursue the initial evaluation of the child by utilizing the procedures described in section 615, except to the extent inconsistent with State law relating to such parental consent.

(II) **FOR SERVICES.**–If the parent of such child refuses to consent to services under clause (i)(II), the local educational agency shall not provide special education and related services to the child by utilizing the procedures described in section 615.

(III) **EFFECT ON AGENCY OBLIGATIONS.**–If the parent of such child refuses to consent to the receipt of special education and related services, or the parent fails to respond to a request to provide such consent–

(aa) the local educational agency shall not be considered to be in violation of the requirement to make available a free appropriate public education to the child for the failure to provide such child with the special education and related services for which the local educational agency requests such consent; and

(bb) the local educational agency shall not be required to convene an IEP meeting or develop an IEP under this section for the child for the special education and related services for which the local educational agency requests such consent.

(iii) **CONSENT FOR WARDS OF THE STATE.**–

(I) **IN GENERAL.**–If the child is a ward of the State and is not residing with the child's parent, the agency shall make reasonable efforts to obtain the informed consent from the parent (as defined in section 602) of the child for an initial evaluation to determine whether the child is a child with a disability.

(II) **EXCEPTION.**–The agency shall not be required to obtain informed consent from the parent of a child for an initial evaluation to determine whether the child is a child with a disability if–

(aa) despite reasonable efforts to do so, the agency cannot discover the whereabouts of the parent of the child;

(bb) the rights of the parents of the child have been terminated in accordance with State law; or

(cc) the rights of the parent to make educational decisions have been subrogated by a judge in accordance with State law and consent for an initial evaluation has been given by an individual appointed by the judge to represent the child.

(E) **RULE OF CONSTRUCTION.**–The screening of a student by a teacher or specialist to determine appropriate instructional strategies for curriculum implementation shall not be considered to be an evaluation for eligibility for special education and related services.

(2) **REEVALUATIONS.**–

(A) **IN GENERAL.**–A local educational agency shall ensure that a reevaluation of each child with a disability is conducted in accordance with subsections (b) and (c)–

(i) if the local educational agency determines that the educational or related services needs, including improved academic achievement and functional performance, of the child warrant a reevaluation; or

(ii) if the child's parents or teacher requests a reevaluation.

(B) **LIMITATION**.–A reevaluation conducted under subparagraph (A) shall occur–

(i) not more frequently than once a year, unless the parent and the local educational agency agree otherwise; and

(ii) at least once every 3 years, unless the parent and the local educational agency agree that a reevaluation is unnecessary.

(b) **EVALUATION PROCEDURES**.–

(1) **NOTICE**.–The local educational agency shall provide notice to the parents of a child with a disability, in accordance with subsections (b)(3), (b)(4), and (c) of section 615, that describes any evaluation procedures such agency proposes to conduct.

(2) **CONDUCT OF EVALUATION**.–In conducting the evaluation, the local educational agency shall–

(A) use a variety of assessment tools and strategies to gather relevant functional, developmental, and academic information, including information provided by the parent, that may assist in determining–

(i) whether the child is a child with a disability; and

(ii) the content of the child's individualized education program, including information related to enabling the child to be involved in and progress in the general education curriculum, or, for preschool children, to participate in appropriate activities;

(B) not use any single measure or assessment as the sole criterion for determining whether a child is a child with a disability or determining an appropriate educational program for the child; and

(C) use technically sound instruments that may assess the relative contribution of cognitive and behavioral factors, in addition to physical or developmental factors.

(3) **ADDITIONAL REQUIREMENTS**.–Each local educational agency shall ensure that–

(A) assessments and other evaluation materials used to assess a child under this section–

(i) are selected and administered so as not to be discriminatory on a racial or cultural basis;

(ii) are provided and administered in the language and form most likely to yield accurate information on what the child knows and can do academically, developmentally, and functionally, unless it is not feasible to so provide or administer;

(iii) are used for purposes for which the assessments or measures are valid and reliable;

(iv) are administered by trained and knowledgeable personnel; and

(v) are administered in accordance with any instructions provided by the producer of such assessments;

(B) the child is assessed in all areas of suspected disability;

(C) assessment tools and strategies that provide relevant information that directly assists persons in determining the educational needs of the child are provided; and

(D) assessments of children with disabilities who transfer from 1 school district to another school district in the same academic year are coordinated with such children's prior and subsequent schools, as necessary and as expeditiously as possible, to ensure prompt completion of full evaluations.

(4) **DETERMINATION OF ELIGIBILITY AND EDUCATIONAL NEED.**– Upon completion of the administration of assessments and other evaluation measures—

(A) the determination of whether the child is a child with a disability as defined in section 602(3) and the educational needs of the child shall be made by a team of qualified professionals and the parent of the child in accordance with paragraph (5); and

(B) a copy of the evaluation report and the documentation of determination of eligibility shall be given to the parent.

(5) **SPECIAL RULE FOR ELIGIBILITY DETERMINATION.**–In making a determination of eligibility under paragraph (4)(A), a child shall not be determined to be a child with a disability if the determinant factor for such determination is—

(A) lack of appropriate instruction in reading, including in the essential components of reading instruction (as defined in section 1208(3) of the Elementary and Secondary Education Act of 1965);

(B) lack of instruction in math; or

(C) limited English proficiency.

(6) **SPECIFIC LEARNING DISABILITIES.**–

(A) **IN GENERAL.**–Notwithstanding section 607(b), when determining whether a child has a specific learning disability as defined in section 602, a local educational agency shall not be required to take into consideration whether a child has a severe discrepancy between achievement and intellectual ability in oral expression, listening comprehension, written expression, basic reading skill, reading comprehension, mathematical calculation, or mathematical reasoning.

(B) **ADDITIONAL AUTHORITY.**–In determining whether a child has a specific learning disability, a local educational agency may use a process that determines if the child responds to scientific, research-based intervention as a part of the evaluation procedures described in paragraphs (2) and (3).

(c) **ADDITIONAL REQUIREMENTS FOR EVALUATION AND REEVALUATIONS.**–

(1) **REVIEW OF EXISTING EVALUATION DATA.**–As part of an initial evaluation (if appropriate) and as part of any reevaluation under this section, the IEP Team and other qualified professionals, as appropriate, shall–

(A) review existing evaluation data on the child, including–

(i) evaluations and information provided by the parents of the child;

(ii) current classroom-based, local, or State assessments, and classroom-based observations; and

(iii) observations by teachers and related services providers; and

(B) on the basis of that review, and input from the child's parents, identify what additional data, if any, are needed to determine–

(i) whether the child is a child with a disability as defined in section 602(3), and the educational needs of the child, or, in case of a reevaluation of a child, whether the child continues to have such a disability and such educational needs;

(ii) the present levels of academic achievement and related developmental needs of the child;

(iii) whether the child needs special education and related services, or in the case of a reevaluation of a child, whether the child continues to need special education and related services; and

(iv) whether any additions or modifications to the special education and related services are needed to enable the child to meet the measurable annual goals set out in the individualized education program of the child and to participate, as appropriate, in the general education curriculum.

(2) **SOURCE OF DATA**.–The local educational agency shall administer such assessments and other evaluation measures as may be needed to produce the data identified by the IEP Team under paragraph (1)(B).

(3) **PARENTAL CONSENT**.–Each local educational agency shall obtain informed parental consent, in accordance with subsection (a)(1)(D), prior to conducting any reevaluation of a child with a disability, except that such informed parental consent need not be obtained if the local educational agency can demonstrate that it had taken reasonable measures to obtain such consent and the child's parent has failed to respond.

(4) **REQUIREMENTS IF ADDITIONAL DATA ARE NOT NEEDED**.–If the IEP Team and other qualified professionals, as appropriate, determine that no additional data are needed to determine whether the child continues to be a child with a disability and to determine the child's educational needs, the local educational agency–

(A) shall notify the child's parents of–

(i) that determination and the reasons for the determination; and

(ii) the right of such parents to request an assessment to determine whether the child continues to be a child with a disability and to determine the child's educational needs; and

(B) shall not be required to conduct such an assessment unless requested to by the child's parents.

(5) **EVALUATIONS BEFORE CHANGE IN ELIGIBILITY**.–

(A) **IN GENERAL**.–Except as provided in subparagraph (B), a local educational agency shall evaluate a child with a disability in accordance with this section before determining that the child is no longer a child with a disability.

(B) **EXCEPTION.**–

(i) **IN GENERAL.**–The evaluation described in subparagraph (A) shall not be required before the termination of a child's eligibility under this part due to graduation from secondary school with a regular diploma, or due to exceeding the age eligibility for a free appropriate public education under State law.

(ii) **SUMMARY OF PERFORMANCE.**–For a child whose eligibility under this part terminates under circumstances described in clause (i), a local educational agency shall provide the child with a summary of the child's academic achievement and functional performance, which shall include recommendations on how to assist the child in meeting the child's postsecondary goals.

(d) **INDIVIDUALIZED EDUCATION PROGRAMS.**–

(1) **DEFINITIONS.**–In this title:

(A) **INDIVIDUALIZED EDUCATION PROGRAM.**–

(i) **IN GENERAL.**–The term 'individualized education program' or 'IEP' means a written statement for each child with a disability that is developed, reviewed, and revised in accordance with this section and that includes–

(I) a statement of the child's present levels of academic achievement and functional performance, including–

(aa) how the child's disability affects the child's involvement and progress in the general education curriculum;

(bb) for preschool children, as appropriate, how the disability affects the child's participation in appropriate activities; and

(cc) for children with disabilities who take alternate assessments aligned to alternate achievement standards, a description of benchmarks or short-term objectives;

(II) a statement of measurable annual goals, including academic and functional goals, designed to–

(aa) meet the child's needs that result from the child's disability to enable the child to be involved in and make progress in the general education curriculum; and (bb) meet each of the child's other educational needs that result from the child's disability;

(III) a description of how the child's progress toward meeting the annual goals described in subclause (II) will be measured and when periodic reports on the progress the child is making toward meeting the annual goals (such as through the use of quarterly or other periodic reports, concurrent with the issuance of report cards) will be provided;

(IV) a statement of the special education and related services and supplementary aids and services, based on peer-reviewed research to the extent practicable, to be provided to the child, or on behalf of the child, and a statement of the program modifications or supports for school personnel that will be provided for the child—

(aa) to advance appropriately toward attaining the annual goals;

(bb) to be involved in and make progress in the general education curriculum in accordance with subclause (I) and to participate in extracurricular and other nonacademic activities; and

(cc) to be educated and participate with other children with disabilities and nondisabled children in the activities described in this subparagraph;

(V) an explanation of the extent, if any, to which the child will not participate with nondisabled children in the regular class and in the activities described in subclause (IV)(cc);

(VI)

(aa) a statement of any individual appropriate accommodations that are necessary to measure the academic achievement and functional performance of the child on State and districtwide assessments consistent with section 612(a)(16)(A); and

(bb) if the IEP Team determines that the child shall take an alternate assessment on a particular State or districtwide assessment of student achievement, a statement of why—

(AA) the child cannot participate in the regular assessment; and

(BB) the particular alternate assessment selected is appropriate for the child;

(VII) the projected date for the beginning of the services and modifications described in subclause (IV), and the anticipated frequency, location, and duration of those services and modifications; and

(VIII) beginning not later than the first IEP to be in effect when the child is 16, and updated annually thereafter–

(aa) appropriate measurable postsecondary goals based upon age appropriate transition assessments related to training, education, employment, and, where appropriate, independent living skills;

(bb) the transition services (including courses of study) needed to assist the child in reaching those goals; and

(cc) beginning not later than 1 year before the child reaches the age of majority under State law, a statement that the child has been informed of the child's rights under this title, if any, that will transfer to the child on reaching the age of majority under section 615(m).

(ii) **RULE OF CONSTRUCTION**.–Nothing in this section shall be construed to require–

(I) that additional information be included in a child's IEP beyond what is explicitly required in this section; and

(II) the IEP Team to include information under 1 component of a child's IEP that is already contained under another component of such IEP.

(B) **INDIVIDUALIZED EDUCATION PROGRAM TEAM**.–The term 'individualized education program team' or 'IEP Team' means a group of individuals composed of–

(i) the parents of a child with a disability;

(ii) not less than 1 regular education teacher of such child (if the child is, or may be, participating in the regular education environment);

(iii) not less than 1 special education teacher, or where appropriate, not less than 1 special education provider of such child;

(iv) a representative of the local educational agency who–

(I) is qualified to provide, or supervise the provision of, specially designed instruction to meet the unique needs of children with disabilities;

(II) is knowledgeable about the general education curriculum; and

(III) is knowledgeable about the availability of resources of the local educational agency;

(v) an individual who can interpret the instructional implications of evaluation results, who may be a member of the team described in clauses (ii) through (vi);

(vi) at the discretion of the parent or the agency, other individuals who have knowledge or special expertise regarding the child, including related services personnel as appropriate; and

(vii) whenever appropriate, the child with a disability.

(C) **IEP TEAM ATTENDANCE.**–

(i) **ATTENDANCE NOT NECESSARY.**–A member of the IEP Team shall not be required to attend an IEP meeting, in whole or in part, if the parent of a child with a disability and the local educational agency agree that the attendance of such member is not necessary because the member's area of the curriculum or related services is not being modified or discussed in the meeting.

(ii) **EXCUSAL.**–A member of the IEP Team may be excused from attending an IEP meeting, in whole or in part, when the meeting involves a modification to or discussion of the member's area of the curriculum or related services, if–

(I) the parent and the local educational agency consent to the excusal; and

(II) the member submits, in writing to the parent and the IEP Team, input into the development of the IEP prior to the meeting.

(iii) **WRITTEN AGREEMENT AND CONSENT REQUIRED.**–A parent's agreement under clause (i) and consent under clause (ii) shall be in writing.

(D) **IEP TEAM TRANSITION.**–In the case of a child who was previously served under part C, an invitation to the initial IEP meeting shall, at the request of the parent, be sent to the part C service coordinator or other representatives of the part C system to assist with the smooth transition of services.

(2) **REQUIREMENT THAT PROGRAM BE IN EFFECT**.–

(A) **IN GENERAL**.–At the beginning of each school year, each local educational agency,
State educational agency, or other State agency, as the case may be, shall have in effect, for each child with a disability in the agency's jurisdiction, an individualized education program, as defined in paragraph (1)(A).

(B) **PROGRAM FOR CHILD AGED 3 THROUGH 5**.–In the case of a child with a disability aged 3 through 5 (or, at the discretion of the State educational agency, a 2-year-old child with a disability who will turn age 3 during the school year), the IEP Team shall consider the individualized family service plan that contains the material described in section 636, and that is developed in accordance with this section, and the individualized family service plan may serve as the IEP of the child if using that plan as the IEP is–

   (i) consistent with State policy; and

   (ii) agreed to by the agency and the child's parents.

(C) **PROGRAM FOR CHILDREN WHO TRANSFER SCHOOL DISTRICTS**.–

   (i) **IN GENERAL**.–

      (I) **TRANSFER WITHIN THE SAME STATE**.–In the case of a child with a disability who transfers school districts within the same academic year, who enrolls in a new school, and who had an IEP that was in effect in the same State, the local educational agency shall provide such child with a free appropriate public education, including services comparable to those described in the previously held IEP, in consultation with the parents until such time as the local educational agency adopts the previously held IEP or develops, adopts, and implements a new IEP that is consistent with Federal and State law.

      (II) **TRANSFER OUTSIDE STATE**.–In the case of a child with a disability who transfers school districts within the same academic year, who enrolls in a new school, and who had an IEP that was in effect in another State, the local educational agency shall provide such child with a free appropriate public education, including services comparable to those described in the previously held IEP, in consultation with the parents until such time as the local educational agency conducts an evaluation pursuant to subsection (a)(1), if determined to be necessary by such agency, and develops a new IEP, if appropriate, that is consistent with Federal and State law.

(ii) **TRANSMITTAL OF RECORDS**.–To facilitate the transition for a child described in clause (i)–

(I) the new school in which the child enrolls shall take reasonable steps to promptly obtain the child's records, including the IEP and supporting documents and any other records relating to the provision of special education or related services to the child, from the previous school in which the child was enrolled, pursuant to section 99.31(a)(2) of title 34, Code of Federal Regulations; and

(II) the previous school in which the child was enrolled shall take reasonable steps to promptly respond to such request from the new school.

(3) **DEVELOPMENT OF IEP**.–

(A) **IN GENERAL**.–In developing each child's IEP, the IEP Team, subject to subparagraph (C), shall consider–

(i) the strengths of the child;

(ii) the concerns of the parents for enhancing the education of their child;

(iii) the results of the initial evaluation or most recent evaluation of the child; and

(iv) the academic, developmental, and functional needs of the child.

(B) **CONSIDERATION OF SPECIAL FACTORS**.–The IEP Team shall–

(i) in the case of a child whose behavior impedes the child's learning or that of others, consider the use of positive behavioral interventions and supports, and other strategies, to address that behavior;

(ii) in the case of a child with limited English proficiency, consider the language needs of the child as such needs relate to the child's IEP;

(iii) in the case of a child who is blind or visually impaired, provide for instruction in Braille and the use of Braille unless the IEP Team determines, after an evaluation of the child's reading and writing skills, needs, and appropriate reading and writing media (including an evaluation of the child's future needs for instruction in Braille or the use of Braille), that instruction in Braille or the use of Braille is not appropriate for the child;

(iv) consider the communication needs of the child, and in the case of a child who is deaf or hard of hearing, consider the child's language and communication needs, opportunities for direct communications with peers and professional personnel in the child's language and communication mode, academic level, and full range of needs, including opportunities for direct instruction in the child's language and communication mode; and

(v) consider whether the child needs assistive technology devices and services.

(C) **REQUIREMENT WITH RESPECT TO REGULAR EDUCATION TEACHER**.–A regular education teacher of the child, as a member of the IEP Team, shall, to the extent appropriate, participate in the development of the IEP of the child, including the determination of appropriate positive behavioral interventions and supports, and other strategies, and the determination of supplementary aids and services, program modifications, and support for school personnel consistent with paragraph (1)(A)(i)(IV).

(D) **AGREEMENT**.–In making changes to a child's IEP after the annual IEP meeting for a school year, the parent of a child with a disability and the local educational agency may agree not to convene an IEP meeting for the purposes of making such changes, and instead may develop a written document to amend or modify the child's current IEP.

(E) **CONSOLIDATION OF IEP TEAM MEETINGS**.–To the extent possible, the local educational agency shall encourage the consolidation of reevaluation meetings for the child and other IEP Team meetings for the child.

(F) **AMENDMENTS**.–Changes to the IEP may be made either by the entire IEP Team or, as provided in subparagraph (D), by amending the IEP rather than by redrafting the entire IEP. Upon request, a parent shall be provided with a revised copy of the IEP with the amendments incorporated.

(4) **REVIEW AND REVISION OF IEP**.–

(A) **IN GENERAL**.–The local educational agency shall ensure that, subject to subparagraph (B), the IEP Team–

(i) reviews the child's IEP periodically, but not less frequently than annually, to determine whether the annual goals for the child are being achieved; and

(ii) revises the IEP as appropriate to address–

(I) any lack of expected progress toward the annual goals and in the general education curriculum, where appropriate;

(II) the results of any reevaluation conducted under this section;

(III) information about the child provided to, or by, the parents, as described in subsection (c)(1)(B);

(IV) the child's anticipated needs; or

(V) other matters.

(B) **REQUIREMENT WITH RESPECT TO REGULAR EDUCATION TEACHER.**–A regular education teacher of the child, as a member of the IEP Team, shall, consistent with paragraph (1)(C), participate in the review and revision of the IEP of the child.

(5) **MULTI-YEAR IEP DEMONSTRATION.**–

(A) **PILOT PROGRAM.**–

(i) **PURPOSE.**–The purpose of this paragraph is to provide an opportunity for States to allow parents and local educational agencies the opportunity for long-term planning by offering the option of developing a comprehensive multi-year IEP, not to exceed 3 years, that is designed to coincide with the natural transition points for the child.

(ii) **AUTHORIZATION.**–In order to carry out the purpose of this paragraph, the Secretary is authorized to approve not more than 15 proposals from States to carry out the activity described in clause (i).

(iii) **PROPOSAL.**–

(I) **IN GENERAL.**–A State desiring to participate in the program under this paragraph shall submit a proposal to the Secretary at such time and in such manner as the Secretary may reasonably require.

(II) **CONTENT.**–The proposal shall include–

(aa) assurances that the development of a multi-year IEP under this paragraph is optional for parents;

(bb) assurances that the parent is required to provide informed consent before a comprehensive multi-year IEP is developed;

(cc) a list of required elements for each multi-year IEP, including–

(AA) measurable goals pursuant to paragraph (1)(A)(i)(II), coinciding with natural transition points for the child, that will enable the child to be involved in and make progress in the general education curriculum and that will meet the child's other needs that result from the child's disability; and

(BB) measurable annual goals for determining progress toward meeting the goals described in subitem (AA); and

(dd) a description of the process for the review and revision of each multi-year IEP, including–

(AA) a review by the IEP Team of the child's multi-year IEP at each of the child's natural transition points;

(BB) in years other than a child's natural transition points, an annual review of the child's IEP to determine the child's current levels of progress and whether the annual goals for the child are being achieved, and a requirement to amend the IEP, as appropriate, to enable the child to continue to meet the measurable goals set out in the IEP;

(CC) if the IEP Team determines on the basis of a review that the child is not making sufficient progress toward the goals described in the multi-year IEP, a requirement that the local educational agency shall ensure that the IEP Team carries out a more thorough review of the IEP in accordance with paragraph (4) within 30 calendar days; and

(DD) at the request of the parent, a requirement that the IEP Team shall conduct a review of the child's multi-year IEP rather than or subsequent to an annual review.

(B) **REPORT**.–Beginning 2 years after the date of enactment of the Individuals with Disabilities Education Improvement Act of 2004, the Secretary shall submit an annual report to the Committee on Education and the Workforce of the House of Representatives and the Committee on Health, Education, Labor, and Pensions of the Senate regarding the effectiveness of the program under this paragraph and any specific recommendations for broader implementation of such program, including–

(i) reducing–

(I) the paperwork burden on teachers, principals, administrators, and related service providers; and

(II) noninstructional time spent by teachers in complying with this part;

(ii) enhancing longer-term educational planning;

(iii) improving positive outcomes for children with disabilities;

(iv) promoting collaboration between IEP Team members; and

(v) ensuring satisfaction of family members.

(C) **DEFINITION**.–In this paragraph, the term 'natural transition points' means those periods that are close in time to the transition of a child with a disability from preschool to elementary grades, from elementary grades to middle or junior high school grades, from middle or junior high school grades to secondary school grades, and from secondary school grades to post-secondary activities, but in no case a period longer than 3 years.

(6) **FAILURE TO MEET TRANSITION OBJECTIVES**.–If a participating agency, other than the local educational agency, fails to provide the transition services described in the IEP in accordance with paragraph (1)(A)(i)(VIII), the local educational agency shall reconvene the IEP Team to identify alternative strategies to meet the transition objectives for the child set out in the IEP.

(7) **CHILDREN WITH DISABILITIES IN ADULT PRISONS**.–

(A) **IN GENERAL**.–The following requirements shall not apply to children with disabilities who are convicted as adults under State law and incarcerated in adult prisons:

(i) The requirements contained in section 612(a)(16) and paragraph (1)(A)(i)(VI) (relating to participation of children with disabilities in general assessments).

(ii) The requirements of items (aa) and (bb) of paragraph (1)(A)(i)(VIII) (relating to transition planning and transition services), do not apply with respect to such children whose eligibility under this part will end, because of such children's age, before such children will be released from prison.

(B) **ADDITIONAL REQUIREMENT**.–If a child with a disability is convicted as an adult under State law and incarcerated in an adult prison, the child's IEP Team may modify the child's IEP or placement notwithstanding the requirements of sections 612(a)(5)(A) and paragraph (1)(A) if the State has demonstrated a bona fide security or compelling penological interest that cannot otherwise be accommodated.

(e) **EDUCATIONAL PLACEMENTS.**–Each local educational agency or State educational agency shall ensure that the parents of each child with a disability are members of any group that makes decisions on the educational placement of their child.

(f) **ALTERNATIVE MEANS OF MEETING PARTICIPATION.**–When conducting IEP team meetings and placement meetings pursuant to this section, section 615(e), and section 615(f)(1)(B), and carrying out administrative matters under section 615 (such as scheduling, exchange of witness lists, and status conferences), the parent of a child with a disability and a local educational agency may agree to use alternative means of meeting participation, such as video conferences and conference calls.

NOTES

1. 614(d)(3)(iv)
2. 614(d)(1)(A)(i)(VI)(aa)
3. 614(d)(3)(F)
4. 615(b)(6)
5. 614(a)(1)(D)
6. 614(d)(3)(E)
7. 614(b)(5)(A)
8. The exception for benchmarks is actually listed under present levels of academic achievement in H.B 1350 614(d)(1)(A)(i)(I)(cc)
9. 614(d)(1)(C)
10. 617(g)
11. 614(d)(5) (A) DEVELOPMENT OF 3-YEAR IEP
12. 614(d)(1)(A)(i)(I)
13. 614(a)(2)
14. 614(d)(3)(C)
15. 614(d)(1)(A)(i)(IV)
16. 14(d)(1)(A)(ii) (I)&(II)
17. 614(a)(1)(C)(i)
18. IDEA–1997, 34 CFR 300.343(b)(1)&(2)
19. 614(d)(1)(A)(i)(VIII)
20. Senate report 105–17
21. *Honig v. Doe,* 484 US 305 (1988) and 98 L Ed 2d 686 (1988), p. 699
22. 614(d)(1)(A)(i)(II)(aa)
23. House of Representatives report 94–332 that accompanied bill H.R. 7217 (and then P.L. 94–142 in 1975)
24. House report 94–332, p. 13
25. Senate report 94–168, p. 1435
26. 20 USC 1414(d)
27. Parents, of course, are members of the IEP but the phrase "IEP Team members and the parents" emphasizes the partnership between school and parents in the development and implementation of the IEP.
28. IDEA–1997, 20 U.S.C. 1414(e)
29. 614(d)(A)(1)(ii)
30. HR 108–77, p. 110
31. from the Committee on Health, Education, Labor, and Pensions to accompany Senate bill 1248.
32. 614(b)(5)

33. 614(b)(5)
34. 601(c) Congressional findings
35. HR 108–77
36. 614(d)(1)(A)(ii)
37. 614(d)(1)(C)
38. Senate report 108–77 (HR 108–77), p. 110, 108TH CONGRESS REPORT, HOUSE OF REPRESENTATIVES *1st Session* 108–77, IMPROVING EDUCATION RESULTS FOR CHILDREN WITH DISABILITIES ACT OF 2003, APRIL 20, 2003.–Committed to the Committee of the Whole House on the State of the Union and ordered to be printed, Mr. BOEHNER, from the Committee on Education and the Workforce, submitted the following R E P O R T together with MINORITY VIEWS [To accompany H.R. 1350]
39. HR 108–77.
40. HR 108–77.
41. HR 108–77, pp. 115–116, (Senate report 108–77), 108TH CONGRESS REPORT, HOUSE OF REPRESENTATIVES *1st Session* 108–77 IMPROVING EDUCATION RESULTS FOR CHILDREN WITH DISABILITIES ACT OF 2003 APRIL 29, 2003.–Committed to the Committee of the Whole House on the State of the Union and ordered to be printed Mr. BOEHNER, from the Committee on Education and the Workforce, submitted the following R E P O R T together with MINORITY VIEWS [To accompany H.R. 1350] [Including cost estimate of the Congressional Budget Office] The Committee on Education and the Workforce, to whom was referred the bill (H.R. 1350) to reauthorize the Individuals with Disabilities Education Act, and for other purposes, having considered the same, report favorably thereon with an amendment and recommend that the bill as amended do pass.
42. IDEA–1977, 34 CFR 300.350(a)
43. .S. Supreme Court, *HENDRICK HUDSON DIST. BD. OF ED. v. ROWLEY,* 458 U.S. 176 (1982) 458 U.S. 176 *BOARD OF EDUCATION OF THE HENDRICK HUDSON CENTRAL SCHOOL DISTRICT, WESTCHESTER COUNTY, ET AL. v. ROWLEY,* BY HER PARENTS, ROWLEY ET UX. CERTIOARI TO THE UNITED STATES COURT OF APPEALS FOR THE SECOND CIRCUIT No. 80–1002. Argued March 23, 1982. Decided June 28, 1982
44. HR 108–77, p. 115
45. 615(b)(6)
46. 614(d)(1)(A)(i)
47. The concept of achieving maximum potential was subsequently modified by *Hudson v. Rowley,* 458 U.S. 176 (1982) so that the standard is satisfactory educational performance.
48. House report 94–332 (which accompanied bill HR 7217 which became PL 94–142), p. 13.
49. Public Law 94–142 in 1975 (S.R. 6)
50. P.L. 94–142 (H.R. 7217)
51. 602(14)
52. *Hudson v. Rowley,* 458 U.S. 176 (1982)
53. Education of the Handicapped Special Supplement, September, 1977, p. 5. See also Federal register, Volume 42, Number 163, Tuesday, August 23, 1977.
54. 602(9)
55. 20 USC 1412(5)(B)
56. 614(d)(1)(A)(i)(II)(aa)
57. Section 2(a)(6)

58. 636(d) CONTENT OF PLAN–

59. 614(d)(2)(B)

60. 29 USC 722(b)(1)) Options for developing an individualized plan for employment. See http://www4.law.cornell.edu/uscode/29/722.html

61. 29 USC 722(b)(2)(B)

62. See also 29 USC 722

63. 29 USC 794(a)

64. Council for Administrators of Special Education. Student access: a resource guide for educators. Albuquerque, N.M., Author, 1992 (ERIC No. 349 769).

65. IDEA–1997, 34 CFR 300.7(b)

66. 34 CFR 104(j)(1), also see 29 USC 705(9)

67. 34 CFR 104(j)(2)(iii)

68. 34 CFR 104(j)(2)

69. 601(c)(3)

70. 614(d)(1)(A)

71. PL 94–142, Section 602(a)(19)

72. IDEA–1990, 34 CFR 300.18

73. P. L. 105–17, 20 U.S.C. 1414(d)(1)((A)(i)

74. P. L. 105–17, 20 U.S.C. 1414(d)(1)((A)(ii)

75. P. L. 105–17, 20 U.S.C. 1414(d)(1)((A)(iii)

76. *Ibid.*

77. P. L. 105–17, 20 U.S.C. 1414(d)(1)((A)(iv)

78. P. L. 105–17, 20 U.S.C. 1414(d)(1)((A)(v)

79. P. L. 105–17, 20 U.S.C. 1414(d)(1)((A)(vi)

80. P. L. 105–17, 20 U.S.C. 1414(d)(1)((A)(vii)

81. P. L. 105–17, 20 U.S.C. 1414(d)(1)((A)(viii)

82. 614(d)(1)(A)(i)(I)

83. 614(d)(A)`(VI)(aa)

84. 614(d)(1)(A)(VIII)

85. Sec. 302 Effective Dates.

86. *Hudson v. Rowley,* 458 U.S. 176 (1982)

87. *Hudson v. Rowley,* 458 U.S. 176 (1982), pp. 187–204

88. 601(c)(5)(F)

89. *Brown v. Board of Education,* 347 U.S. 483 (1954)

90. 20 U.S.C. 1414(a)(3)

91. Title I - Improving The Academic Achievement Of The Disadvantaged, Office of Elementary and Secondary Education, Office of Innovation and Improvement

92. 614(d)(3)(C)

93. 615(b)(3)

94. 615(c)

95. IDEA–1997, 34 CFR 300.504

96. 615(d)(1)

97. IDEA–1997, 20 U.S.C. 1515(d)(1)(B)

98. 615(d)(2)

99. HR 108–77

100. IDEA–1997, 1414(A)(1)(C)

101. 614(a)(1)(D)(ii)(I)&(II)

102. 614(a)(1)(D)(ii)(III)

103. Senate report 108–185

104. IDEA–1990 34 CFR 300.342(b)(2)

105. IDEA–1990, 34 CFR 300.343(c) Time. And IDEA–1997, 34 CFR 300.343(b)

106. New York State Education Department (1998). Regulations of the Commissioner of Education, Part 200.4(d). For New York the 60 day period is from consent to a recommendation to the Board of Education for services.

107. Idaho Special Education Manual (2001). Bureau of Special Education, Idaho Department of Education, p. 16.

108. Education Laws and Regulations, 603 CMR 28.00: Special Education, In effect January, 2001, 28.04(2): Referral and Evaluation, http://www.doe.mass.edu/lawsregs/603cmr 28b.html#28.04

109. Ibid., 28.05: The Team Process and Development of the IEP, (1) Convening the Team.

110. Guidelines for Individual Evaluation of California Students with Disabilities, Birth Through Age Twenty-One, October, 1998.

111. Vermont Department of Education Special Education Regulations 2362.2.3 Time Frame and Consent

112. Ibid., 2363.2 Timelines

113. New York State Education Department, Regulations of the Commissioner of Education, Part 200.4(d), (January, 1998).

114. NEW HAMPSHIRE RULES FOR THE EDUCATION OF CHILDREN WITH DISABILITIES Page 32 July 1, 2002, Ed 1107.04(d) QUALIFIED EXAMINERS

115. 23 ILLINOIS ADMINISTRATIVE CODE CH. I, S.226.110 SUBTITLE A SUB-CHAPTER f

116. House bill 1350, Sense of Congress (b)(1)

117. HR 1350, April 30, 2003, Sec. 104 GAO Report (b)(1)&(2)

118. 20 U.S.C. 1414(a)(24)

119. Improving America's Schools Act (Public Law 103–282, Section 1114) when appropriate (viz., enabling disadvantaged and at-risk students meet high standards).

120. *Lee v. Macon County Bd. of Education,* 267 F. Supp (M.D. Ala. 1967) which was first filed in 1963

121. The District Court of the United States for the Middle District of Alabama, Eastern Division, *Lee v. Phenix City Board of Education* civil Action No. 70–T–854, Order Approving Consent Decree on State-Wide Special Education Issue; see http://www.usdoj.gov/crt/edo/documents/leeor.htm

122. 609(b)(4)

123. Idaho State Education Manual (September, 2001). Bureau of Special Education, Idaho State Department of Education, Section 5, p. 11.

124. Special Education in North Dakota, Guidelines: Evaluation Process (1999). North Dakota Department of Public Instruction.

125. Rules of the Alabama State Board of Education, State Department of Education, Chapter 290–8–9, Special Education Services, 290–8–9–.01(2).

126. Idaho Special Education Manual (2001). Bureau of Special Education, Idaho State Department of Education, p. 11.

127. New York State Education Department (1998). Regulations of the Commissioner of Education, Part 200.4(a)(2).

128. IDEA–1990, 34 CFR 300.532(e)

129. 614(b)(4)(A)

130. Illinois Administrative Code, Chapter I, (A)(f)(B), S. 226.120

131. North Dakota Department of Public Instruction (1999), Office of Special Education, Guidelines: evaluation process

132. Arizona Department of Education, Title 7. Education, R7–2–401(E), http://www.sosaz/public_services/title_07/7-02.htm

133. Ohio Department of Education (2000), Model Policies and Procedures for the Education of Children with Disabilities, Columbus, Ohio.

134. 10–206 6/30/00. ADMINISTRATIVE RULES OF MONTANA, 10.16.3321, SUPER-INTENDENT OF PUBLIC INSTRUCTION, CHAPTER 16, SPECIAL EDUCA-TION, Sub-Chapter 1, Responsibilities of the Superintendent of Public Instruction

135. DEPARTMENT OF PUBLIC INSTRUCTION, MODEL SPECIAL EDUCATION POLICY DOCUMENT, John T. Benson, State Superintendent, 3/1995

136. New York State Education Department (1998). Regulations of the Commissioner of Education, Part 200.3 and 200.4(c).

137. 615(b)(1)

138. 614(b)(4)

139. 614(b)(4)(B)

140. IDEA–1997, 34 CFR 300, Appendix A, Question #19

141. New Jersey Administrative Code, 6A:14–3.1

142. 6A: 14–3.2 Case manager. Chapter 14, Special Education, New Jersey Administrative Code, Title 6A, Education. See http://www.state.nj.us/njded/code/title6a/chap14/

143. IDEA–1990, 34 CFR 300.532(e)

144. IDEA–1997, 34 CFR 300.534(a)(1)

145. 614 636(a)(3)

146. See Wisconsin PDI, Model Special Education Policy Document, 1995, (IV).

147. 614(b)(4)(A)

148. 614(b)(4)(B)

149. 614(b)(2)(A)(i)&(ii)

150. 34 CFR 300.532(c)(2)

151. 34 CFR 300.543(a)

152. 34 CFR 300.543(b)

153. 64(d)(1)(B)

154. 614(f)

155. 615(c)

156. IDEA–1997, 34 CFR 300.345(c)

157. IDEA–1997, 34 CFR 300.24(b)(7)

158. IDEA–1997, 34 CFR, 300.345(e)

159. 614(d)(3)(C)

160. 614(d)(1)(C) IEP TEAM ATTENDANCE

161. 614(d)(3)(C)

162. 614(d)(1)(C)

163. 614(d)(3)(E)

164. see 614(d)(5)

165. HR 108–77

166. IDEA–1997, 34 CFR 300.454(c)

167. see IDEA–1977, Appendix A, #9

168. 614(a)(D)(ii)

169. http://www.nde.state.ne.us/SPED/iepproj/prepare/meet.html, IEP: Preparing for the IEP: The IEP Meeting

170. https://www.edinfo.state.ia.us/tcdiscussion/faq_displayAnswer.asp?question=415

171. Vermont Department of Education–State Board of Education Manual of Rules and Practices, Special Education, Page 45, SPECIAL EDUCATION 2360 8/29/2003

172. IDEA–1997, 34 CFR 300, Appendix A, Question #9

173. 614(d)(3)(D)

174. 614(d)(3)(D)&(F0

175. IDEA–2004, Senate report for

176. 104 CFR 33(b)(2), 45 FR 30936, May 9, 1980; 45 FR37426, June 3

177. 2362.2.6 (p. 54). State Board of Education Manual of Rules and Practices (2002). Vermont Department of Education, Special Education Regulations, and Other Pertinent Regulations, Vermont State Board of Education, Manual of Rules and Practices: see http://www.state.vt.us/educ/new/html/board/rules_fulltoc.html and http://www.state.vt.us/educ/new/pdfdoc/board/rules/2360.pdf

178. 614(b)(2)

179. 614(b)(2)

180. No Child Left Behind (NCLB) act (P.L. 107–10, Title I – Improving The Academic Achievement of The Disadvantaged, Section 1111(b)(1)(D) STANDARDS

181. 614(d)(1)(A)(i)(I)

182. P.L. 10–10, Title I – Improving the Academic Achievement of the Disadvantaged, Section 1114(b)(1)(B)

183. 614(c)(1)(A)

184. 614(c)(1)(B)(iv)

185. 614(c)(1)(B)(i)-(iii)

186. 614(d)(2)

187. IDEA–1997, 34 CFR 3000.7(b)(9)

188. Twenty-fourth Annual Report to Congress, Number of Children Ages 6–21 Served Under IDEA, Part B by Disability, During the 2000–01 School Year, AA3

189. HR 1350, April 30, 2003, Sec. 104 GAO Reports (b)(1)&(2)

190. 602(30)

191. 614(b)(6)

192. http://www.connsensebulletin.com/up042503.html

193. IDEA–1997, 34 CFR 300.543

194. 614(b)(5)

195. IDEA–1997, 34 CFR 300.7(c)(9)

196. IDEA–1997, 34 CFR 300.532(f)

197. 614(b)(1)(B)

198. R43–243.1(C) Mental Disability, see http://www.myschools.com/offices/ec/regulatory/getpage.cfm?ID-155

199. Vermont Department of Education, Special Education Regulations, and Other Pertinent Regulations, The Vermont State Board of Education, Manual of Rules and Practices, Effective August 16, 2001, 2362.1 Categories of Disability (p. 36)

200. IDEA–1997, 34 CFR 300.7(c)(4)

201. 601(c)12(C)

202. Data based on 24th Report to Congress on the Implementation of the Individuals with Disabilities Education Act, U.S. Department of Education 2002. Table AB8, Number of Children Ages 6–21 Served in Different Educational Environments Under IDEA, part B by Disability, During School Years 1990–91 Through 1999–2000

203. IDEA–1997, 34 CFR 300.7(c)(9)

204. IDEA–1997, 34 CFR 300.307(b)(9)

205. See IDEA–1997, 34 CFR 300.532

206. NYS Part 200, 204(b) *Individual evaluation*

207. Part 200(b)

208. 614(b)(2)(C)

209. 614(b)(3)(B)

210. 614(b)(3)(C)

211. 614(b)(3)(A)(i)&(ii)

212. The varying grade levels needed at different grade levels is based on the increasing standard deviation of grade equivalents at different grades. The standard deviation of grade levels can be estimated by (GradeLevel+5). 15 so that for a child at a grade level of 3.0, the estimated standard deviation would be (3.0+5).15=1.2; the estimated standard deviation for a child in grade 6.0 would be (6.0+5).15=1.65.

213. H 1350, January 20, 2004

214. IDEA–1997, 34 CFR 300, Appendix A

215. 614(b)(ii)

216. 614(b)(3)(A)(iv)&(v)

217. HR 108–77

218. P.O. 107–10, Title I – Improving The Academic Achievement Of The Disadvantaged, Section 1111(b)(3)(C)(I)&(II)

219. 612(a)(16) PARTICIPATION IN ASSESSMENT–`(A) IN GENERAL-(i)

220. 612(a)(16)(C)(ii)

221. 614(d)(1)(A)(VI)(bb)

222. 612(a)(5)(B)

223. Joint Explanatory Statement of the Committee of Conference, Page 9940

224. 898 F.2d 1186 (6th Cir. 1990)

225. Senate report for IDEA–2004

226. 34 CFR 300, Appendix A, Question #1

227. 601(b)(1)

228. Pyecha, J.N. and others (1980) A national survey of Individualized Education Programs (IEPs) for handicapped children. Volume I: Executive Summary. Final report. Research Triangle Institute, Durham, N.C. (ERIC #199 970)

229. Bateman, B.D. Writing Individualized Education Programs (IEPs) For Success, Secondary Education and Beyond, Learning Disabilities Association, 1995. Retrieved September 22, 2000 from the World Wide Web: http://www.ldonline.org/ld_indepth/iep/success_ieps.html

230. Schipper, W., and Wilson, W. (1978). *Implementation of individualized education programming: Some observations and recommendations.* National Association of State Directors of Special Education, Washington, D.C. ERIC #ED 155 881.

231. Pyecha, J. N. (1980). A national survey of Individualize Education Programs (IEPs) for handicapped children. Volume I: Executive Summary. Final report. Research Triangle Institute, Durham, N.C., ERIC #199 970, p. 154.

232. 898 F.2d 1186 (6th Cir, 1990), p. 1190

233. 617(e)

234. 617(e)

235. HR 108–77, p. 122

236. HR 108–77

237. 611(e)(2)(c)(ii)

238. 614(d)(1)(A)(ii) RULE OF CONSTRUCTION–

239. 108TH CONGRESS, REPORT, HOUSE OF REPRESENTATIVES *1st Session* 108-77, IMPROVING EDUCATION RESULTS FOR CHILDREN WITH DISABILITIES ACT OF 2003, April 23, 2003.–Committed to the Committee of the Whole House on the State of the Union and ordered to be printed, Mr. BOEHNER, from the

Committee on Education and the Workforce, p. 110.

240. 614(d)(5) MULTI-YEAR IEP DEMONSTRATION, (A) PILOT PROGRAM.

241. 614(d)(5)(A)(iii)

242. 614(d)(5)(A)(iii)(II)(dd)(BB)

243. 601(c)(5)(G)

244. 601(c)(9)

245. IDEA–1997, 34 CFR 300, Appendix A

246. Minority views, p. 381, 108TH CONGRESS REPORT "HR 108–77

247. 614(d)(3)(A)

248. 614(d)(3)(C)

249. 614(d)(3)(C)(i)

250. 602(34)(B)

251. 636(a)(1)

252. CONFERENCE REPORT ON H.R. 1350 – (House of Representatives - November 17, 2004), Page: H9946

253. Pyecha, J. N. and others (1980) A national survey of Individualized Education Program (IEPs) for handicapped children. Volume I: Executive Summary. Final report. Research Triangle Institute, Durham, N.C. (ERIC #199 970), p. 66.

254. IDEA–1997, 34 CFR 300, Appendix A, Question #24

255. 614(d)(1)(A)(i)(I)

256. 614(d)(3)(B)

257. Attachment 1 - Analysis of Comments and Changes, Federal register, Vol. 64, No. 48, March 12, 1999, 12591.

258. 2363.7(b). State Board of Education Manual of Rules and Practices (2002). Vermont Department of Education, Special Education Regulations, and Other Pertinent Regulations, Vermont State Board of Education, Manual of Rules and Practices: see http://state.vt.us/educ/new/html/board/rules_fulltoc.html and http://www.state.vt.us/educ/new/pdfdoc/board/rules/2360.pdf

259. New Hampshire rules for the education of children with disabilities. http://www.ed.state.nh.us/SpecialEd/2002%20RULES.PDF, NEW HAMPSHIRE RULES FOR THE EDUCATION OF CHILDREN WITH DISABILITIES (2002), RSA 186–C:7–b Braille Instruction for Functionally Blind Pupils.

260. 614(d)(3)(B)(iv)

261. 614(d)(A)(1)(i)(VI)(aa)

262. see the Senate report for IDEA–2004

263. P.L. 107–10, Title I - Improving The Academic Achievement Of The Disadvantaged

264. P.L. 107–10, Section 1111(b)(20(G)(iv)

265. 614(d)(1)(A)(i)(II)

266. 614(d)(1)(A)(i)(III)

267. House bill 1350, 614(d)(1)(A)(i)(VIII)

268. *Oberti v. Board of Education,* 789 F.Supp. 1322 (D.N.J. 1992), 1328

269. 614(d)(1)(A)(i)(VIII)

270. http://www.ld.org/advocacy/IDEA04FedReg.cfm

271. see http://www.state.nj.us/njded/students/ieptoc.htm

272. IDEA–1997, 34 CFR 300.500(b)(3)(iv)

273. see Massachusetts IEP, DOE

274. see North Dakota IEP, North Dakota of Public Instruction

275. http://www.doe.mass.edu/sped/iep/forms/IEP1-8.pdf

276. 602(14)

277. IDEA–1997, 34 CFR 300.532(d)

278. SR 105–17

279. See http://marriage.about.com/cs/teenmarriage/a/majority.htm

280. 23 ILLINOIS ADMINISTRATIVE CODE CH. I8, S.226.690 SUBTITLE A SUB-CHAPTER f Section 226.690 Transfer of Parental Rights, see http://www.isbe.net/rules/archive/pdfs/226ark.pdf

281. http://www.pen.k12.va.us/VDOE/Instruction/Sped/transfer_rights.pdf, Transfer Of Rights For Students with Disabilities Upon Reaching The Age of Majority In Virginia (2000), Virginia Department of Education Office of Special Education and Student Services

282. Guidance on Implementation of the Reauthorization of the Individuals with Disabilities Education Act, January, 19989, Policy 97–09, From Rita D. Levay, To District Superintendents http://www.vesid.nysed.gov/specialed/publications/idea/jan98.htm

283. SR 108–185 (Senate bill 1248), p. 28

284. IDEA–1997, 34 CFR 300, Appendix A, #1

285. Senate report 1248, November 3, 2003

286. 614(d)(1)(A)(i)(I)

287. IDEA–1990, 34 CFR 300, Appendix Question #36(b)

288. IDEA–1997, 34 CFR 300, Appendix A

289. 614(b)(2)(C)

290. 602(2)(A)

291. 614(b)(2)(A)

292. 602(34)(C)

293. 615(k)(1)(D)(ii)

294. Functional Assessment for Special Education, SD Office of Special Education, February 5, 2002

295. 614(b)(2)(A)(ii)

296. IDEA–1997, 34 CFR 300.533(a)(1)

297. IDEA–1997, 34 CFR 300.542

298. 614(d)(1)(A)(i)(VI)(bb)

299. No Child Left Behind (NCLB) act (P.L. 107–10, Title I - Improving The Academic Achievement of The Disadvantaged

300. 34 CFR 200, 68698 Federal Register / Vol. 68, No. 236 / Tuesday, December 9, 2003 / Rules and Regulations

301. *Ibid.*, p. 68698

302. Kentucky Alternate Portfolio see http://www.ihdi.uky.edu/kap/faq.asp and http://www.ihdi.uky.edu/kap/faq.asp

303. *Ibid.*

304. Mississippi Statewise Assessment System, Guidelines for Testing Special Populations: Students with Disabilities English Language Learners, Section 3, Planning, Conducting, and Reporting the Results of Alternate Assessments, Mississippi Department of Education, April 2004, Procedures for implementing low stakes and high stakes Alternate Assessments for Students with Disabilities under IDEA

305. Georgia Department of Education, Georgia Alternate Assessment (GAA), Administrator's Manual 2004–2005, Kathy Cox, Office of Curriculum and Instruction, Testing Division, http://www.doe.k12.ga.us/_documents/curriculum/testing/gaa_manual.pdf

306. Kentucky Alternate Portfolio, http://www.ihdi.uky.edu/kap/faq.asp

307. This is based on the number (1%) that will be counted toward the NCLB annual yearly

progress.

308. See IDEA–1997, 34 CFR 300, Appendix A, #1, Present Levels of Educational Performance

309. 614(d)(1)(A)(i)(I)

310. April 30, 2003, HR 1350 EH, 108th CONGRESS, 1st Session

311. 615(d)(1)(A)(I)(cc)

312. Massachusetts DOE/Individualized Education Program, http://www.doe.mass.edu/sped/iep/forms/word/IEP1-8.doc

313. 614(3)(1)(A)(i)(VI)

314. IEP Accommodations Checklist Revised May 2003, Alabama State Department of Education.

315. Alabama Student Assessment Program Policies and Procedures for Students of Special Populations, Bulletin 2003, No. 11, Ed Richardson, Alabama State Department of Education, Montgomery, Alabama, p. 7

316. 614(d)(3)(C)

317. 614(b)(3)(A)(v)

318. 614(d)(3)(B)(iv)

319. 602(1)&(2)

320. http://sun1.sph.org/products/stanford.htm

321. http://sun1.sph.org/product/brig_green.html

322. http://sun1.sph.org/products/keymath.html

323. Tennessee Comprehensive Assessment Program (TCAP) http://www.state.tn.us/education/tsallowaccin.pdf

324. Texas Education Agency, Technical Digest, 2002–2003, http://www.tea.state.tx.us/student.assessment/resources/techdig/chap7.pdf

325. NCLB, Section 1111(b)(3)(ix)

326. 614(d)(A)(1)(i)(V)

327. North Dakota, Appendix D, Use of Standards in the IEP Process, pp. 2–3, http://dpi.state.nd.us/speced/guide/iep/index.shtm, and http://state.nd.us/speced/guide/iep/app_d.pdf

328. Guidelines for Selecting Test Accommodations for Students with Disabilities, http://www.doe.state.la.us/lde/ssa/786.html

329. *Ibid.*

330. http://www.dpi.state.wi.us/dpi/oea/accomdis.html

331. 614(d)(3)(A)(iii)-(v)

332. UNITED STATES DEPARTMENT OF EDUCATION, Washington, D.C. 20202, January 12, 2001, Memorandum, Chief State School Officers, From Michael Cohen, Assistant Secretary for Elementary and Secondary Education and Judith E. Neumann, Assistant Secretary for Special Education and Rehabilitative Services, Clarification of the Rile of the IEP Team in Selecting Individual Accommodations . . . , http://www.dssc.org/frc/fed/JointAssessmentMemo.final.pdf

333. http://education.umn.edu/NCEO/TopicAreas/OutOfLevel/outoflevel.htm

334. Virginia Department of Education's Sample IEP Form

335. *Evans v. Rhinebeck,* 930 F.Supp. 83 (S.D.N.Y. 1996)

336. IDEA–1997, Appendix A, Question #1

337. 614(d)(1)(A)(i)

338. IDEA–1997, 34 CFR 300, Appendix A, Question #2

339. PL 94–142, Section 602(a)(19)

340. 614(d)(1)(A)(i)(II) a statement of measurable annual goals, including academic and func-

tional goals, designed to—

~(aa) meet the child's needs that result from the child's disability to enable the child to be involved in and make progress in the general curriculum; and

~(bb) meet each of the child's other educational needs that result from the child's disability;

341. 614(d)(1)(A)(i)(III)

342. Senate report 108–185 (Senate bill 1248), p. 25

343. SR 108–77, p. 84.

344. SR 108–185 (Senate bill 1248), p. 28

345. Illinois Learning Standards (1997). See http://www.isbe.state.il.us/ils/science/scg11.html http://www.isbe.state.il.us/ils/

346. HR 1350, April 30, 2003, (d)(1)(A)(i)(cc)

347. http://dpi.state.nd.us/speced/guide/iep/sample.pdf

348. 614(d)(3)(C)

349. Sec. 1111(b)(2)(G)

350. Senate report 108–185 (Senate bill 1248), p. 29

351. Thompson, S., Thurlow, M., Quenemoen, R., Esler, A. Addressing Standards and Assessments on State IEP forms (Synthesis Report 38). Minneapolis, MN: University of Minnesota, National Center on Educational Outcomes. Retrieved April 19, 2004, from the World Wide Web: http://education.umn.edu/NCEO/OnlinePubs/Synthesis38.html

352. George D. Nelson, benchmarks and Standards as Tools for Science Education Reform, 5/6/98, http://www.negp.gov/Reports/20nelson.htm

353. 34 CFR 300.552(e)

354. Alaska Comprehensive System of Student Assessments (CSSA), Alternate Assessment, Guide to Collecting Materials for the Student Portfolio, August, 2001, p. 4.

355. Content Standards for California Public Schools, California Department of Education, 1999. See http://www.cde.ca.gov/cdepress/standards-pdfs/mathematics.pdf

356. *77 v. Board of Education,* 89 F.Supp. 1322 (D.N.J. 1992)

357. 614(d)(1)(A)(i)(IV)

358. 614(d)(1)(A)(i)(VII)

359. see IDEA–1997, 34 CFR 300.552

360. 612(a)(5)(A)

361. 602(33)

362. 601(d)(1)(A)

363. 874 F.2d 1036(5th Cir. 1989)

364. *Greer v. Rome City School District,* 950 F.2d 688 (11th Ctr. 1991), pages 698 and 696.

365. *Daniel v. State Board of Education,* 874 F2.d 1036 (5th Cir. 1989), p. 1048.

366. *Oberti v. Board of Education,* 789 F.Supp. 1322 (D.N.J. 1992)

367. *Daniel v. State Board of Education,* 874 F2d 1036 (5th Cir. 1989), p. 1048.

368. 602(29)

369. IDEA–1997, 300.26(b)(3)

370. 612(a)(5)(A)

371. IDEA–1997, 34 CFR 300.551(b)(1)

372. 602(34)

373. 614(d)(1)(A)(i)(VIII)

374. Also part of this section is the age of majority requirement: cc) beginning not later than 1 year before the child reaches the age of majority under State law, a statement that the child has been informed of the child's rights under this title, if any, that will transfer to the child on reaching the age of majority under section 615(m).

375. See IDEA–1997 34 CFR 300.309 and *Armstrong v. Kline* 476 F.Supp. 583(1979)

376. HR 108–77, p. 109

377. 108TH CONGRESS, REPORT, HOUSE OF REPRESENTATIVES, *1st Session,* HR 108–77, p. 109–110

378. See IDEA–1997, 34 CFR 300.24(b)(15)

379. 612(a)(14)(B) ~ ~ (i)

380. Tennessee IEP form (03/16/01), along with the instructions, can be found at http://www.state.tn.us/education/msped.htm.

381. Florida Department of Education, 2000, http://www.firn.edu/doe/bin00014/pub-home.htm\Developing, Quality Individual Education Plans

382. *Oberti v. Board of Education,* 789 F.Supp. 1322 (D.N.J. 1992), 1332

383. IDEA–1997, 34 CFR 300.553 Nonacademic settings

384. 614(d)(1)(A)(i)(IV)(bb)

385. See IDEA–1997, 34 CFR 300.305

386. *Daniel v. State Bd. of Education,* 874 F2d 1036 (5th Cir. 1989), http://www.kidstogether.org/ct-danl.htm

387. *Daniel v. State Bd. of Education,* 874 F2d 1036 (5th Cir. 1989), http://kidstogether.org/ct-danl.htm

388. Senate report 105–17

389. IDEA–1997, 34 CFR 300.552(b),(c),(d)

390. *Harmann v. Loudoun* (4th Cir., 1997) see http://caselaw.lp.findlaw.com/scripts/getcase.pl?navby=search&case=/uscircs/4th/962809p.html

391. see IDEA–1997, 34 CFR 300.552

392. 614(d)(1)(A)(i)(II)(aa)

393. See IDEA–1997, 34 CFR 300, Attachment 1 – Analysis of Comments and Changes, Federal Register, Vol. 64, No. 48, Friday, March 12, 1999/Rules and Regulations, p. 12593.

394. *Ibid.*

395. 2363.8(e). State Board of Education Manual of Rules and Practices (2002). Vermont Department of Education, Special Education Regulations, and Other Pertinent Regulations, Vermont State Board of Education, Manual of Rules and Practices: see http://www.state.vt.us/educ/new/html/board/rules_fulltoc.html and http://www.state.vt.us/educ/newpdfdoc/board/rules/2360.pdf, p. 65–65.

396. *Daniel, R.R. v. State Board of Education,* 874 f.2d 1036 (5th Cir. 1989), 1048

397. *Oberti,* 789 F.Supp. 1322 (D.N.J. 1992)

398. *Daniel v. State Board of Education,* 874 F2d 1036 (5th Cir. 1989), http://www.kidstogether.org/ct-danl.htm

399. See 118 F3d 998 (4th Cir. 1997), United States Court of Appeals, Eastern District of Virginia

400. 612(5)

401. 612(a)(5)(A)

402. IDEA–1997, 34 CFR 300.551(b)(1)

403. 34 CFR 300.351

404. see 602(10)(F), page h9936

405. 613(a)(4)(A)(i)

406. IDEA–1997. 34 CFR 300, Appendix, Question #35

407. *Ibid.*

408. IDEA–1997, 34 CFR 300.551(b)(2)

409. IDEA–1997, 34 CFR 300.552

410. IDEA–1990, 34 CFR 300, Appendix C. see Questions #29 and #30.
411. IDEA–1997, 34 CFR 300.500(b)(1)
412. Massachusetts Department of Education, Education Laws and Regulations, 603 CMR 28.05(7)
413. Massachusetts Department of Education, Education Laws and Regulations, 603 CMR 28.05(7)
414. Virginia Department of Education – Sample IEP Form – May 2001, http://www.pen. k12.va.us/VDOE/Instruction/Sped/iep_form.pdf
415. 614(d)(3)(B)
416. Federal Register, Vol. 64, No. 48, March 12, 1999, Rules and Regulations
417. From the Committee on Education and the Workforce, for consideration of the House bill and the Senate amendment and modifications committed to conference.
418. Source: Senate report, Calendar No. 362, 108TH CONGRESS, Report, SENATE 1st Session, 108–185

REFERENCES

American Psychiatric Association. (1994). *Diagnostic and statistical manual of mental disorders (DSM-IV)*. Washington, D.C.: Author.

Burns, E. (1979). *The development, use and abuse of educational tests*. Springfield, IL: Charles C Thomas, Publisher, Ltd.

Burns, E. (1998). *Test Accommodations for Students with Disabilities*. Springfield, IL: Charles C Thomas, Publisher, Ltd.

Burns, E. (2001). *Developing and Implementing IDEA-IEPs: An Individualized Education Program (IEP) Handbook for Meeting Individuals with Disabilities Education Act (IDEA) Requirements*. Springfield, IL: Charles C Thomas, Publisher, Ltd.

Burns, E. (2003). *A Handbook for Supplementary Aids and Services: A Best practice and IDEA Guide "to Enable Children with Disabilities to be Educated with Nondisabled Children to the maximum Extent Appropriate*. Springfield, IL: Charles C Thomas, Publisher, Ltd.

Burns, E. (2004). *The Special Education Consultant Teacher*. Springfield, IL: Charles C Thomas, Publisher, Ltd.

National Council on Disability (2000), *Back to school on civil rights: Advancing the Federal commitment to leave no children behind*. 1331 F Street, NW, Suite 1050, Washington, D.C.

Rothstein, L. F. (1995). *Special education law* (2nd ed). New York: Longman.

283

INDEX